American Dietetic Association

Infant Feedings

Guidelines for Preparation of Human Milk and Formula in Health Care Facilities

Second Edition

Pediatric Nutrition Practice Group

Sandra T. Robbins, RD, CSP, and Robin Meyers, MPH, RD, Editors

D0557702

Diana Faulhaber, Publisher
Elizabeth Nishiura, ProductionManager
Krisan Matthews, Assistant Development Editor

Copyright 2011, American Dietetic Association. All rights reserved. No part of this publication may be reproduced, stored in a retrieval system, or transmitted in any form or by any means without the prior written consent of the publisher. Printed in the United States of America.

The views expressed in this publication are those of the authors and do not necessarily reflect policies and/or official positions of the American Dietetic Association. Mention of product names in this publication does not constitute endorsement by the authors or the American Dietetic Association. The American Dietetic Association disclaims responsibility for the application of the information contained herein.

10 9 8 7 6 5 4 3 2

Library of Congress Cataloging-in-Publication Data

Infant feedings: guidelines for preparation of human milk and formula in health care facilities / Pediatric Nutrition Practice Group; Sandra T. Robbins and Robin Meyers, editors. — 2nd ed.
     p. ; cm.
Includes bibliographical references and index.
ISBN 978-0-88091-444-4
1. Infant formulas—Standards. 2. Breast milk—Collection and preservation—Standards. 3. Infants—Nutrition—Standards. 4. Hospitals—Food service—Standards. I. Robbins, Sandra T. II. Meyers, Robin. III. American Dietetic Association. Pediatric Nutrition Practice Group.
[DNLM: 1. Food Service, Hospital—standards—Guideline. 2. Food Handling—standards—Guideline. 3. Infant Formula—standards—Guideline. 4. Milk, Human—Guideline. WX 168]

RJ216.I4985 2011
613.2'69—dc22

2011004217

Contents

SECTION I

Guidelines for Preparation of Human Milk and Formula in Health Care Facilities

SECTION II

Contributors

This book is the second revision in a series of publications on the subject by the Pediatric Nutrition Practice Group of the American Dietetic Association (ADA) and published by ADA. The most recent was the 2004 publication *Infant Feedings: Guidelines for Preparation of Formula and Breastmilk in Health Care Facilities*. The original publication in this series, *Preparation of Formula for Infants: Guidelines for Health Care Facilities*, was published in 1991. The current contributors gratefully recognize the contributions of the original authors, advisers, and reviewers of both previous editions.

Infant Feedings: Guidelines for Preparation of Human Milk and Formula in Health Care Facilities (2011)

Contributors

Sandra Robbins, RD, CSP (Coeditor)
Inova Fairfax Hospital for Children, Falls Church, VA

Robin Meyers, MPH, RD (Coeditor)
The Children's Hospital of Philadelphia, Philadelphia, PA

Deborah Hutsler, MS, RD
Children's Hospital Medical Center, Akron, OH

Susan Kinzler, RD
ARAMARK Healthcare at Children's Hospital of Philadelphia, Philadelphia, PA

Rachelle Lessen, MS, RD, IBCLC
The Children's Hospital of Philadelphia, Philadelphia, PA

Amy Sapsford, RD, CSP, CLE
Cincinnati Children's Hospital Medical Center, Cincinnati, OH

Suzanne Smith, MS, RD
Levine Children's Hospital, Charlotte, NC

Caroline Steele, MS, RD, CSP, IBCLC
CHOC Children's Hospital, Orange, CA

Laura Benson Szekely, MS RD
Akron Children's Hospital, Akron, OH

Susan C. Teske, MS, RD, CNSD
Children's Health System, Birmingham, AL

Terry Whaley, MPH, RD
Texas Children's Hospital, Houston, TX

Advisers/Liaisons
Diane Anderson, PhD, RD
Baylor College of Medicine, Houston, TX

Dan March
Mead Johnson Nutrition Company, Evansville, IN

Georgia Morrow, RN, IBCLC
Mothers' Milk Bank of Ohio, Grant Medical Center, Columbus, OH

Melody Thompson, MS, RD
Abbott Nutrition and Nationwide Children's Hospital, Columbus, OH

Rachel Buchanan-Adams, MS, RD
Nestle Infant Nutrition, Decatur, TX

Infant Feedings: Guidelines for Preparation of Formula and Breastmilk in Health Care Facilities (2004)

Contributors
Sandra Robbins, RD, CSP (Editor)
Leila Beker, PhD, RD (Coeditor)
Deb Hustler, MS, RD
Rachelle Lessen, MS, RD, IBCLC
Amy Sapsford, RD, CLE
Sue Teske, MS, RD, CNSD
Terry Whaley, MPH, RD

Advisers
Diane Anderson, PhD, RD
Sheila Campbell, PhD, RD
Beth Leonberg, MS, MA, RD, CSP, FADA, CNSD
Dan March, BS
Mardi Mountford, MPH
Nancy L. Nevin-Folino, RD, CSP, FADA
Melody Thompson, MS, RD

This project was supported in part by grants from Health Resources Services Administration, Maternal and Child Health Branch, Grant # 5 T79 MC 00023-03 and Cincinnati Children's Hospital.

Preparation of Formula for Infants: Guidelines for Health Care Facilities (1991)

Planning Committee

Diane M. Anderson, MS, RD (Codirector)

Linda J. Boyne, MS, RD (Codirector)

M. Elizabeth Brannon, MS, RD

Mariel Caldwell, MPH, MS, RD

Harry S. Dweck, MD

Barbara Harness

Lyllis Ling, MS, RD

Mardi K. Mountford, MPH

JoAnne Tresley Nathan

Alice Smith, MS, RD

Editorial Consultant

Jo Anne Cassell, MS, RD

Project Administrator

Lorraine Partlow Smalley, RD

Cooperating Organizations (1991)

The project was supported in part by project MCJ 176020 from the Maternal and Child Health program (Title V, Social Security Act), Health Resources and Services Administration, Department of Health and Human Resources. The Guidelines were originally developed in cooperation with the following organizations:

American Dietetic Association Pediatric Nutrition Practice Group

American Academy of Pediatrics

American Hospital Association

American Nurses Association

American Society for Hospital Food Service Administrators

American Society of Hospital Pharmacists

Association for Practitioners in Infection Control

Association of State and Territorial Health Officials

Association of State and Territorial Public Health Nutrition Directors

Association of State and Territorial Public Health Laboratory Directors

Food and Drug Administration

Infant Formula Council

Society of Hospital Epidemiologists of America

Acknowledgments

Expert reviews by the following individuals contributed greatly to this publication:

Diane M. Anderson, PhD, RD
Baylor College of Medicine, Houston, TX

Amy Brandes, RD, IBCLC
Seton Family of Hospitals, Austin, TX

Linda Heller, MS, RD, CSP, CLE
Children's Hospital Los Angeles, Los Angeles, CA

Susan Konek, MA, RD, CSP
The Children's Hospital of Philadelphia, Philadelphia, PA

Beth L. Leonberg, MS, MA, RD, CSP, FADA
Drexel University, Philadelphia, PA

Paula Charuhas Macris, MS, RD, CSO, CD, FADA
Seattle Cancer Care Alliance, Seattle, WA

Joan Younger Meek, MD, MS, RD, FABM, FAAP, IBCLC
Florida State University College of Medicine, Orlando, FL

Mardi Mountford, MPH
International Formula Council, Atlanta, GA

Foreword

Like many quality assurance issues, safe feeding for a hospitalized infant is considered a "given." Until a problem arises, persists, and is linked to infant feeding in a facility, procedures for handling human milk and formula are often not given the same attention as medication safety. A simple Internet search on "safety of infant feeding in hospitals" yields general descriptions of recommendations for infant feeding; hospitals' Web sites touting their perinatal policies to encourage breastfeeding (eg, by rooming in, following "baby friendly" practices); and other such indirect references to infant feeding. In contrast, a search on medication safety in hospitals immediately brings up references to national reports about the frequency of medication errors; focus on procedures to improve and monitor medication safety; and promotion of a culture of safety. The contrast is striking. However, any Nutrition Quality Improvement Committee in a large pediatric hospital is likely aware of instances of expressed human milk being fed to the wrong infant; errors in formula preparation; errors in feeding orders; contaminated equipment or supplies; and/or bedside liberties taken for administration of enteral feedings (eg, additives to human milk or formula at the bedside; failure to follow policy for cleaning bottles, tubes and bags).

This updated volume provides remarkably detailed guidelines that any hospital or facility providing care for infants and young children should follow to ensure safe preparation, handling, and administration of human milk and formulas. As more women are successfully pumping and able to provide their infants with human milk through prolonged hospital stays, it is essential that facilities have strict procedures in place for infection control and to avoid errors in administration. The rapid proliferation in the number of new formula products dictates that policies be in place to ensure appropriate use, aseptic techniques for preparation, standard procedures for responding to a product recall, and so on. These updated guidelines are critically important, especially given the complexity and severity of the conditions that afflict many of the patients on in-patient units now. All of these topics, and more, are detailed in this new edition.

Procedures and policies are only as good as their implementation. This book is a rich resource to guide potential quality improvement surveillance. Registered dietitians and other providers who routinely determine and implement hospital policies for infant feedings could provide invaluable data to the field by using the guidelines in this book to conduct baseline assessments; follow the assessment with surveillance of implementation; and document outcomes associated with changes in policy. Such proactive quality initiatives may perpetuate the continued underrecognition of the complexity of infant feeding safety in health care facilities. However, if we are successful in averting bad outcomes and prolonged stays due to feeding errors, that will be a good thing.

Nancy F. Krebs, MD, MS
Professor of Pediatrics
Head, Section of Nutrition
Dept of Pediatrics, University of Colorado Denver
Medical Director, Clinical Nutrition Department
The Children's Hospital, Denver

Introduction

Sandra Robbins, RD, CSP

The goal of this publication is to contribute to patient safety. Use of human milk is encouraged in most circumstances. Serious foodborne illnesses have been traced to infant feedings or colonized infant feeding systems.

Organization of This Publication

Section 1 presents a summary of the infant feedings guidelines and may be used alone. Chapters 1 through 8 contain more detail and technical support as well as documentation of the sources used to derive the guidelines. Appendixes at the end of many chapters provide resources and sample implementation tools. It is hoped that these sections will facilitate establishment of facility-specific policies and procedures for preparation of infant feedings.

What's New in This Edition?

This edition updates all topics and expands and highlights the information on handling of human milk in health care facilities. Since the publication of the last edition in 2004, many facilities have developed and/or upgraded their infant feeding preparation rooms. However, there are still many nurseries and neonatal intensive care units (NICUs) where no feeding preparation room exists. This edition highlights procedures for handling infant feedings when there is no feeding preparation room. The chapters on physical facilities (Chapter 1), equipment (Chapter 2), and personnel (Chapter 3) are updated to current standards and provide new information about development and management of infant feeding preparations.

In the 7 years since our last publication, there have been more publications supporting the use of human milk in NICUs. In addition, there are more resources for donor milk when mother's own milk is not available. This literature and guidance on safe handling mother's own and donor human milk are described in Chapter 4. Despite great interest in getting human milk to the sickest of NICU infants, literature about optimal milk handling practices is in these immunocompromised patients is sparse. After literature review and much discussion by experienced NICU and lactation professionals, the guidelines for handling human milk in this edition were created. As greater experience generates more literature, guidelines may be revised.

Since we issued recommendations in the first edition of the *Infant Feedings* guidelines (2004), the infant formula industry has made more sterile liquid feedings options available to health care facilities. The new guidelines in this second edition again recommend that the use of sterile liquid formula in health care facilities is preferred over the use of powdered formula when formula is needed and a nutritionally appropriated sterile liquid is available. Chapter 5 discusses how to accomplish this objective. Recipes for preparation of powdered formulas were not included in this edition. Due to the pace of changes in formulas marketed, recipe tables become obsolete quickly. Instead, readers are referred to sources of current information for preparation of dilutions that do not come ready-to-feed or as concentrated liquid formula. Recipes for use of both 40 kcal/oz and 30 kcal/oz concentrated liquids are included.

At home, different practices for handling powdered formula may be acceptable compared with what is needed for the sickest of hospitalized patients. Discharge education has been added to Chapter 6. Also, industry recommendations for handling of formulas that contain probiotics are included in this chapter.

The literature review of microbiology and infection control has been greatly updated in Chapter 7. Disaster planning for the handling of infant feedings has been added to Chapter 8.

Development of the Guidelines

This edition was prepared in 2009 and 2010 through a cooperative review by pediatric clinical nutrition, lactation and clinical nutrition management professionals from the Pediatric Nutrition Practice Group of the American Dietetic Association. Lactation consultants, representatives from other disciplines, and representatives from the infant formula industry provided review and have contributed.

Application of the Guidelines

The guidelines in this edition should not be considered regulations. They are based on research and scientific evidence currently available. In the absence of pediatric studies, findings described in adults literature and the consensus of experienced practitioners in the field were used. Redundancy in the guidelines and supporting documents was incorporated to emphasize important points.

The desired outcomes for these guidelines are to help ensure that (*a*) infants within a health care facility receive optimal nutritional care; (*b*) health care facility personnel have state-of-the art guidelines for the preparation of human milk or formula for infants under their care; and (*c*) the public is assured that infants in health care facilities will receive proper nourishment prepared in a safe manner. If these goals can be achieved, the desire of each and every participant will be fulfilled—that all infants thrive to their maximum potential without developing foodborne illness.

Glossary

Aseptic technique: A procedure aimed at protecting patients from infection by minimizing the presence of pathogenic microorganisms. In handling of feedings and feeding systems, this means adherence to good hand-hygiene practices, use of "no touch" technique in preparation and administration of human milk or formula, and meticulous attention to details that minimize microbial exposure and proliferation in selection, storage, transporting and administering feedings.

Dry blending: A process in which dry ingredients are mixed together in a blender to make a premix or complete formula.

Liquid-to-dry production: A process whereby all the ingredients are combined in a liquid state and then dried in a spray dryer to produce a complete formula. This can also be a combined process whereby some of the ingredients are mixed in a liquid state and then dried in a spray dryer to make a base powder. The remaining ingredients are then dry blended with the base powder to produce a complete formula.

Spray drying: Liquid ingredients (milk or whey and oils) and/or water suspensions of dry ingredients are mixed together and then sprayed under high pressure into a hot chamber of air to form a powder.

Frequently Used Abbreviations

ABM	Academy of Breastfeeding Medicine
ADA	American Dietetic Association
CDC	Centers for Disease Control and Prevention
CFU	Colony forming units
CMV	Cytomegalovirus
ELBW	Extremely low birth weight
FDA	Food and Drug Administration
FTE	Full-time equivalent
GI	Gastrointestinal
GRAS	Generally recognized as safe
HACCP	Hazard Analysis and Critical Control Points
HIV	Human immunodeficiency virus
HMBANA	Human Milk Banking Association of North America
HTLV-1	Human T-cell lymphotropic virus 1
HTLV-2	Human T-cell lymphotropic virus 2
MCT	Medium chain triglyceride
MRSA	methicillin-resistant Staphylococcus aureus
NEC	Necrotizing enterocolitis
NICU	Neonatal Intensive Care Unit
NSF	National Safety Foundation
OSHA	Occupational Safety and Health Administration
PNPG	Pediatric Nutrition Practice Group
VLBW	Very low birth weight
VRE	Vancomycin-resistant Enterococci
WHO	World Health Organization
WIC	Special Supplemental Nutrition Program for Women, Infants, and Children

Guidelines for Preparation of Human Milk and Formula in Health Care Facilities

Chapter 1. Physical Facilities

1. If infant feedings are prepared on-site, it is strongly recommended that there be a separate room that

    a. has the appropriate physical separation from direct patient care areas;
    b. has the preparation area divided from the storage and anteroom areas;
    c. is used solely for the purpose of preparing human milk, infant formula, and enteral feedings by aseptic (clean, no-touch) technique.

2. The design of the infant feeding preparation room must facilitate workflow that supports aseptic technique in feeding preparation.
3. A separate handwashing sink with controls for water that do not require the use of hands must be available within the infant feeding preparation area.
4. Feeding preparation and storage areas should be securable to prevent adulteration of formula, human milk, and supplies, and to control the traffic of unauthorized individuals through the room(s).
5. Office space sufficient to support the function of the infant feeding preparation room, including receipt of orders, label preparation, and record keeping, must be available.
6. A clean air supply with appropriate pressure gradient is required for the infant feeding preparation room.
7. The surfaces of the floors, walls, and ceiling of the infant feeding preparation room must be made of material that can be maintained in a sanitary condition.
8. The closet for cleaning supplies should be in close proximity to, but should not open directly into, the infant feeding preparation room.
9. Lighting within the infant feeding preparation room should be easily cleanable, enclosed, and adequate for accurate preparation of formula and maintenance of a sanitary environment.
10. A sufficient number of electrical outlets should be available in the infant feeding room.
11. When there is no feeding preparation room, feeding preparation should not be done at the bedside. A separate infant feeding preparation area should be designated that complies with all construction

considerations for facilities needed to support aseptic technique for preparation of human milk and formula feedings, as described in this chapter.

Chapter 2. Equipment, Utensils, and Supplies

1. The equipment and utensils in the infant feeding preparation room should be in compliance with applicable health regulations and sanitation codes.
2. There should be written guidelines for regularly scheduled preventive and corrective maintenance of equipment in the infant feeding preparation room. The preventive and corrective maintenance must be documented and monitored.
3. Refrigeration must be adequate in capacity to chill ingredient water and to cool prepared formula to 4°C (40°F) within 1 hour of preparation. The refrigerator for infant feedings must be securable to prevent tampering.
4. Freezers used to store expressed human milk should hold milk at −20°C (−4°F) or less.
5. All small equipment and utensils in the infant feeding preparation room must be constructed so that they can be sanitized. This can be accomplished with an autoclave or with a dishwasher that reaches a final temperature of 82°C (180°F).
6. Supplies (eg, gowns, bottles, nipples, sanitizing solutions, utensils, and equipment) must be adequate to implement aseptic technique in the preparation of human milk and infant formula.
7. Single-use bottles and nipples are recommended whenever feasible; they should not be reused. Only specialty products not available as single-use items should be reused.
8. Each mother's expressed human milk must be labeled and stored in a separate bin to discourage misadministration and cross-contamination of feedings.
9. Microwave ovens, upright blenders, and garbage disposals are not recommended for use in infant feeding preparation rooms. Immersion blenders with sticks or whisks that can be sanitized are acceptable.
10. Cleaning supplies must be stored separately from infant formula products and ingredients.
11. Cleaning supplies should be used exclusively for the infant feeding preparation area; cleaning equipment, such as mops, should not be shared with other areas of the facility.
12. Only chilled, sterile ingredient water is recommended for infant feeding preparation.
13. Equipment that ensures that feedings remain chilled to 4°C (40°F) and prevents contamination to the feedings should be available to safely transport infant feedings to the patient care unit.
14. Trash containers in the infant feeding preparation room must be covered and must have a foot-operated lid.

Chapter 3. Personnel

1. Administrative responsibility for the infant feeding preparation room must be assigned to a qualified individual—eg, a registered dietitian, a registered pharmacist, or a registered nurse.
2. The supervisor of the infant feeding preparation room should be experienced in infant formula and human milk handling techniques and preparation operations.
3. Minimum qualifications for infant feeding room technicians should include an ability to read, write, and use mathematic skills at the high school level or above.
4. A dress code that is in keeping with aseptic technique should be defined for feeding preparation room personnel.
5. A written training policy must be developed and implemented that requires an orientation of sufficient duration and substance, training, in-service experiences, and evaluation of competency at appropriate intervals for each staff member responsible for preparation of human milk and infant formulas.

6. A sufficient number of trained staff must be available to ensure the continuity and quality of preparation and distribution of infant feedings.
7. The infant feeding room technician must be in good health, as defined by the employee health policies of the health care facility and appropriate regulatory agencies.
8. Staff working in the infant feeding preparation room must practice good personal hygiene.

Chapter 4. Expressed Human Milk

1. Mechanical expression needs to begin as soon as possible after giving birth, with the use of a hospital-grade electric breast pump.
2. Personal collection kits should be sterilized daily.
3. Human milk expression in the hospital can take place at the infant's bedside or in designated private pump rooms.
4. Mothers must be instructed in writing and/or verbally regarding appropriate pumping, labeling, storage, and transport technique.
5. Human milk must be stored in "food-grade" plastic or glass bottles. Plastic bags designed for this purpose at home are not recommended for inpatient use because of risk of leaking.
6. To discourage errors in human milk delivery, human milk supplied to the facility by the patient's mother must be labeled with complete and accurate information, including infant's name, medical record number, and date and time of pumping.
7. Human milk transported to and from the hospital should be maintained at proper temperatures (2° to 6°C, 35°F to 42°F or frozen), to prevent loss of nutrients and to minimize bacterial growth.
8. Dedicated freezers and refrigerators should be provided for storing human milk. Unless state regulations prohibit, human milk may be stored in the same refrigerator as infant formula. Whenever possible, food should be in a separate refrigerator. If human milk is stored with food, it must be in a labeled, closed bin.
9. Human milk bottles from a single mother should be stored in separate labeled bins or zippered bags to prevent misadministration of human milk and to prevent cross-contamination of that milk with other feedings.
10. For proper human milk storage, refrigerator temperatures should be maintained at 2°C to 4°C (35°F to 40°F) and freezer temperatures at –20°C (–4°F) or less.
11. To prevent unnecessary thawing and loss of frozen milk, freezers should be tilted backward during installation, units should be plugged into the emergency power supply, and an alarm should be installed to alert hospital staff if temperatures go above acceptable levels.
12. A written policy on access to human milk freezers and refrigerators should be established.
13. Fresh human milk can be safely stored at 2°C to 4°C (35°F to 40°F) in the refrigerator for 48 hours.
14. Fortified human milk should be stored in the refrigerator at 2°C to 4°C (35°F to 40°F) and should be used within 24 hours.
15. Frozen milk can be safely stored in a home freezer for 3 months and in a –20°C (–4°F) or lower temperature freezer for 12 months.
16. Unless a NICU has a specific protocol for freezing or pasteurizing the milk of very-low-birth weight (VLBW) infants in an effort to reduce potential pathogens such as cytomegalovirus load, infants should receive fresh milk whenever possible because of the enhanced activity of cellular components.
17. Frozen milk should be used in the order in which it was expressed (oldest milk first).
18. Frozen milk may be placed in the refrigerator to thaw gradually, thawed under running water that does not submerge the lid of the bottle or thawed in a commercial devices designed to thaw human milk. The container must be labeled with the expiration date.
19. Thawed milk must be used within 24 hours.

20. Containers of milk may be warmed under running water or in commercial warmers designed for that purpose. There should be a policy for sanitation of bottle warmers. Microwaves or hot water should *never* be used to warm or thaw human milk. Only milk for bolus feedings should be warmed. Milk used for continuous feedings should not be warmed.
21. Aseptic technique must be used in milk preparation and handling.
22. Fortifiers must be measured accurately, using aseptic technique. If using fortifiers other than commercially available human milk fortifier that is individually packaged, the fortifiers should be premeasured and packaged in the formula room or pharmacy, using techniques described in this chapter. Powdered products must be measured by weight.
23. Bolus tube feeding of human milk is preferred to minimize fat loss and time for bacterial growth.
24. Hang time for feeding human milk should not exceed 4 hours. Syringe and tubing must be changed every 4 hours for continuous feedings.
25. Human milk remaining in a bottle after feeding an infant should be discarded.
26. Health care facilities should have a plan for handling misadministration of human milk (ie, a baby receives human milk other than his or her own mother's milk). The attending physician must be notified, and an incident report may need to be filed. Risk management staff may also be notified, depending on facility protocol for management and follow-up.
27. Any donor milk used for infants *must* be pasteurized. Fresh or thawed pasteurized milk may be stored refrigerated for 48 hours. Acquisition and handling of donor milk should follow current Human Milk Banking Association of North America (HMBANA) guidelines and/or state regulations licensing human milk banks.
28. Hospitals that obtain donor human milk should develop policies related to the ordering, receiving, storage, labeling, and feeding of donor human milk.

Chapter 5. Formula Preparation and Handling

1. There must be written guidelines for safe receiving and storage of infant formula products and ingredients to maintain product integrity.
2. Expired or damaged infant formula products must be discarded in such a way as to prevent human consumption.
3. Care should be taken to avoid freezing temperatures (0°C, 32°F) or excessive heat (35°C, 95°F) in stock storage areas.
4. All cleaning supplies must be stored separately from infant formula products and ingredients.
5. The health care facility should establish a process for identifying suspected problems with a product's integrity or physical appearance (ie, check with the manufacturer).
6. There must be written guidelines for ordering infant feedings, transmitting orders to the feeding preparation room, and maintaining feeding order records for individual patients.
7. The infant feeding order should include the following:
   a. Patient's name
   b. Patient's medical record ID number
   c. Patient's location
   d. Human milk or formula name plus additives
   e. Caloric density/volume/feeding frequency
   f. Name of authorizing physician
   g. Date of order

8. During infant feeding preparation, no other activities (such as heavy cleaning) should take place. Doors to the infant feeding preparation room should be kept closed and secured during feeding preparation. Only authorized personnel should be allowed access to the infant feeding preparation room.

9. In facilities where there is no feeding preparation room, a dedicated clean space with facilities for aseptic technique must be used for formula preparation.

10. Aseptic technique must be practiced for *all* infant feeding preparation. Preparation procedures should be appropriate to the conditions in the specific facility.

11. There must be written guidelines for aseptic technique used in the infant feeding preparation room, including hand hygiene and care of work area, equipment, and supplies. These policies and procedures should address hand soaps and gels.

12. Autoclaving or a thermal process such as a dedicated dishwasher with the capacity to achieve 180°F final temperature is recommended for cleaning equipment used in infant feeding preparation.

13. Single-use containers are recommended for dispensing prepared human milk and formula.

14. Written formulations should be maintained in the infant feeding preparation room for all human milk/infant formulas prepared. Formulations must be verified by two health care professionals for accuracy and appropriateness, preferably by a registered dietitian trained in infant feeding preparation.

15. Commercially sterile ready-to-feed and liquid-concentrate formulas should be used when available and nutritionally appropriate. The powdered form of infant formula should be used *only* when alternative commercially sterile liquid products are not available.

16. Only chilled, commercially sterile ingredient water is suggested for preparation of infant formula. Distilled, deionized, or bottled waters that are not commercially sterile must be sterilized.

17. A new or sanitized container should be used to prepare each formula type, to prevent possible exposure of the patient to allergens.

18. Powdered formula must be measured by weight. The scoop inside the can should be aseptically removed and discarded.

19. Opened cans of formula must be covered and labeled with expiration date. These cans should be stored in a clean, secured location.

20. Written guidelines governing acceptable ingredients that may be added to infant feedings should be available.

21. Medications including electrolytes should *not* be added in the feeding preparation room.

22. Colorants should *not* be added to infant feedings.

23. Prepared infant feedings must *not* be frozen.

24. Terminal heating of infant feedings is not recommended.

25. Generation of labels should occur away from the feeding preparation area (such as in the anteroom), to avoid a break in aseptic technique.

26. Each unit of prepared human milk or formula must have a label that includes the following items:

    a. Patient's name
    b. Patient's medical record/ID number
    c. Patient's location
    d. Human milk or formula name plus additives
    e. Caloric density/volume
    f. Volume in container
    g. Expiration date and time
    h. "For enteral use only"
    i. "Refrigerate until use"

27. Unit of use packaging (single feeding or the appropriate amount for one hang time) of prepared feeding is recommended.
28. In health care facilities, opened, ready-to-feed-formula and house-prepared human milk or formula may be stored in bulk containers and refrigerated for up to 24 hours. All opened human milk or formula products, including liquid concentrate, powders, and additives, should be labeled with an expiration date and time.
29. Dedicated refrigerators with adequate chill capacity (4°C, 40°F) for infant feedings in the preparation room and on the patient care units are recommended. Unless state regulations prohibit, human milk and formula may be stored in the same refrigerator.
30. Labels of human milk and formulas should be verified against the individual patient's feeding order before dispensing the human milk/formula to the patient unit.
31. There must be written guidelines for the safe transport of infant feedings that ensure maintenance of the appropriate temperature (4°C, 40°F) until it reaches the patient care unit refrigerator.
32. There should be written guidelines, developed by the department responsible for preparation of infant feedings and the department of nursing, that prescribe proper clean handling and storage of infant feedings on patient care units.
33. There should be written guidelines for reporting and follow-up of infant feedings that are flawed in any way (eg, defective, adulterated, contaminated, or preparation error).
34. There should be written guidelines for reporting and follow-up of recalled formula products in the health care facility. Formula products recalled by the manufacturer or a regulatory agency should be handled in accordance with their instructions.

Chapter 6. Delivery and Bedside Management of Infant Feedings

1. All expressed human milk, formulas, feeding additives, and supplies should be stored on the patient unit in a secured or limited-access area and under the proper storage conditions.
2. Human milk and formula should not be stored in the same refrigerator as food. If human milk or formula is stored with food, the infant feeding must be in a labeled, closed bin.
3. In the event that feedings are not dispensed in unit-of-use containers, individual feedings poured from a bulk container should be handled on a clean, dry, disinfected surface. The container should be removed from the refrigerator immediately before pouring and returned promptly. Patient information on the container should be verified for current formula order.
4. Any items taken into an individual patient room should not be returned to the storage area or used for other patients.
5. Bottles, nipples, and graduated feeders should be for single use. The exception would be specialized items that can be sanitized between uses.
6. Warming is not recommended for continuous feedings. Warming time for oral or bolus feedings should be limited to no more than 15 minutes. Acceptable methods for warming include electric warming units and warm running water. Water level should not reach the level of the nipple ring or submerge the lid.
7. Microwaves should *never* be used to warm infant feedings.
8. A designated person must verify the formula label before feeding an individual patient.
9. For infants being nipple fed, any feeding remaining in the bottle after 1 hour should be discarded.
10. Medications should be added to feedings only by properly trained personnel and with appropriate checks for compatibility.
11. When available, closed system administration sets should be used. When no closed system is available,

tube-feeding administration systems should be assembled on a clean, dry, disinfected surface, avoiding touch contamination of any portion of the feeding system that will come into contact with the feeding.

12. Aseptic technique should be used when filling, refilling, or changing feeding containers. It is recommended that tube-feeding reservoirs (syringe, bag, or bottles) not be reused in health care facilities.

13. Tubing should be flushed with sterile water or air after intermittent feeds and any medication additions.

14. A policy for hang time for human milk and infant formulas and feeding sets must be established in each facility. Hang times for human milk and formula in the NICU or for other immune-suppressed patients should be 4 hours or less. Ready-to-feed sterile formulas for other patients and closed systems may tolerate longer hang times. Check manufacturer's recommendations for closed systems.

15. Formulas containing probiotics should be fed by bolus administration; it is recommended that they not be fed by continuous infusion.

16. When enteral feeding pumps are used, they should be selected to meet the special feeding needs of infants and neonates.

17. Whenever possible, feeding connections should be distinct from connections used for intravenous or other medical administration systems.

18. The feeding-pump housing should be disinfected before initial use by each patient and on a regular basis during use for a single patient.

19. Modular formula additives should be added to the human milk or formula in the infant feeding preparation room, using aseptic technique whenever possible.

20. If formula additives must be added outside the infant feeding preparation room, premeasured amounts of these additives should be provided. When additives are measured, sterilized measuring devices should be used.

21. Vitamin, mineral, electrolyte, or medication additives are to be added by the appropriate nursing or pharmacy personnel, in compliance with facility and Joint Commission standards for medication administration.

22. Colorants should *not* be added to feedings.

23. A policy should be developed to establish guidelines for parent education for mixing and administering feedings after discharge.

24. Any measuring devices, mixing equipment, or other utensils used at home should be should be clean and dry before coming into contact with human milk, formula, or additives.

Chapter 7. Microbiology and Infection Control

1. Human milk is preferred.

2. Sterile liquid formula products are preferred compared to other formulas; those prepared from nonsterile powdered formula should be used only when a nutritionally appropriate sterile liquid formula is not available.

3. When available, closed enteral feeding systems should be used.

4. Infection control procedures must be in place throughout the enteral feeding process, from procurement to administration.

5. A multidisciplinary committee including nutrition services, nursing, and medicine should approve the infant feeding preparation policies and participate in quality monitoring.

6. The Hazard Analysis and Critical Control Point (HACCP) plan for human milk, infant formula, and enteral feeding should address all aspects of the feeding process, including infection control elements. The key elements of such a plan include the following:

    a. Prevention of exogenous contamination of infant feeding products during receiving, preparation, storage, delivery, and administration

    b. Prevention of growth of organisms present in the prepared feedings during receiving, preparation, delivery, storage, and administration

    c. Detection, as soon as possible, of any infection or toxin that may be due to feeding contamination

7. The infant formula container or ingredient container must be inspected before use. The product must not be used if the expiration date has passed or if the container is damaged, leaking, or swollen.

8. The product contents must be inspected after opening the container. The product must not be used if it appears adulterated, contaminated, or otherwise abnormal (eg, lumpy, grainy liquid or clumped powder).

9. Aseptic technique must be practiced for *all* expressed human milk and formula preparation. Preparation procedures should be appropriate to the conditions in the specific facility.

10. The use of chilled sterile ingredient water is recommended to facilitate achieving formula temperature of 4°C (40°F) quickly.

11. All feedings in the NICU and facility-prepared infant feedings for other patient care units should be packaged in quantities required for a feeding or per 4-hour period.

12. Outside the NICU, commercially sterile feedings that have not been manipulated (no water, modules, or medications added) may extend hang time to 8 hours when fed to immune-competent children.

13. Formulas containing probiotics should not be fed by continuous infusion.

14. The manufacturer should be consulted for questions involving the microbiological quality of the infant formula product or ingredients.

15. Surveillance cultures of infant feedings are not recommended routinely by the Centers for Disease Control and Prevention. State regulations may differ.

16. When patients have symptoms of foodborne illness, consideration of contaminated enteral feedings should be a part of the diagnostic evaluation.

17. Probiotics should be used with caution in high-risk populations.

Chapter 8. Quality Assurance

1. The department responsible for preparation of infant feedings must establish an HACCP plan that includes continuous quality improvement functions as well as corrective action and follow-up, when deemed necessary. A separate HACCP plan may be needed for expressed human milk.

2. The HACCP plan must include measurable indicators for use in monitoring the most important aspects of infant feeding preparation, storage, delivery, and feeding administration.

3. The infant feeding preparation HACCP plan should be integrated into the facility's overall performance improvement program, as described in Chapter 7. The seven steps that must be considered when formulating an interdisciplinary HACCP plan are as follows:

    a. Assess potential hazards.

    b. Identify critical control points (CCPs).

    c. Establish policies and procedures for CCPs.

    d. Monitor CCPs.

    e. Plan for procedure failure, and take corrective action when needed.

    f. Verify that the system is working.

    g. Set up a record-keeping system.

4. Results of continuous monitoring of quality improvement should be routinely reviewed in accordance with the facility's performance improvement plan.

5. Maintenance of safe infant feeding availability should be included in the facility's disaster plan.

Chapter 1

Physical Facilities

Terry Whaley, MPH, RD

Health care organizations face many challenges when setting up a new infant feeding preparation room or when remodeling existing facilities. This chapter presents practical applications of basic layout and design principles to assist health care facilities in planning safe, effective, and efficient infant feeding preparation rooms.

Since the previous guidelines addressing the layout and design of infant formula preparation rooms were published in 2004, functions within the formula room have been altered by advances in nutrition, formula technology, emerging pathogens, and health care economics (1,2). A more extensive selection of ready-to-feed formulas and use of human milk, donor milk, and manipulated human milk for infants is available today; however, individually prepared formulas continue to be important as knowledge of the nutrition needs of infants increases. Additionally, technology has enhanced the ability of health care professionals to provide more flexible modalities of nutrition support. In contrast with these advances, many health care facilities are experiencing staff reductions, which potentially limit available personnel for infant formula preparation.

Practices among institutions continue to vary greatly around the United States, despite the guidelines published previously (2). A fatal infectious outbreak that was tracked to contaminated formula has focused attention on formula preparation and handling (3,4).

Designating Space

Recommendations included in this publication are best accomplished by providing a separate room for the preparation and handling of infant feedings. Most references will be made to the infant feeding preparation room (1,2,5,6). Not all health care facilities have the space available or the need for a separate room to be used exclusively for preparing feedings for infants. This decision will be based on space available, feeding volume,

9

and demand. However, a specific location away from the bedside, with adequate space and equipment, as outlined in this document, must be provided for any infant feeding preparation needs (5).

The area for preparation of infant feedings must ensure the preparation and delivery of safe infant formula products, using aseptic technique (2,7,8). A room that is routinely used for another purpose, with similar requirements for cleanliness and equipment, may provide an acceptable work area.

The management of human milk is discussed in Chapter 4. If permitted by state regulation, the infant feeding preparation room may also be used for handling human milk, provided the preparations are separate from infant formula preparations. Similar guidelines apply for the handling, preparation, and storage of expressed human milk.

During the time for human milk or infant formula preparation, there must be no other activity in the room or designated area. Formulas used for children and adults should be stored and prepared separately from infant formula. Preparation of formula for different age groups should be scheduled so that mistakes are minimized. At no time should this area be used for the storage or preparation of anti-neoplastic agents, chemicals, cleaning supplies, or equipment (other than those used in the preparation of feedings).

Location of the Infant Feeding Preparation Room

The overall efficiency of an infant feeding preparation room depends on its location in the health care facility, the provision of ample space, the layout of work areas, and the selection of appropriate equipment. Feeding room locations will vary with the type and size of the health care facility, available space, and other physical constraints. In some cases, the infant feeding preparation room will be connected with the nutrition services department. In other facilities, it will be located in or near a patient care area but not where there is direct patient care—eg, in the pharmacy or in central supply. Determination of the location of a dedicated infant feeding preparation room should be made based on the following factors:

1. Appropriate physical separation from patient care and other "soiled" areas within the facility (eg, toilets or waste disposal)
2. Away from the traffic flow of personnel, patients, and visitors
3. An area that facilitates aseptic (clean, no-touch) technique to prepare the feedings
4. Maximum protection from airborne contamination, including open windows, drafts, and vents
5. Consideration of cost of construction or renovation
6. Consideration of cost of staffing and other operational costs
7. Compliance with licensing and regulatory agencies (local, state, and federal)
8. Proximity to the point of use (ie, patient care areas)

Functional Programming

The first step in designing any facility is the development of a functional program. In brief, functional programming is a process by which an identified service (in this case, preparation of expressed human milk or formula for infants) is evaluated to determine the most desirable method of achieving the programming mission. The people involved with this process should include, but are not limited to, the staff who will be responsible for supervising feeding preparation, an architect, staff with budget responsibility for the development and operation of the feeding preparation, and staff who are knowledgeable about regulations that apply to the functions of the area. The end result of the process is a document that describes the objectives and operational systems for the service, staffing levels, and necessary equipment. It includes a narrative or graphic representation of the interrelationships between departments and functional areas within the affected departments. The information required to develop a functional program for the infant formula preparation room is presented in Chapter 5.

One outcome of the preparation of a functional program is a document that outlines detailed space requirements for that facility. These individual space requirements are translated into subsequent schematic drawings that describe the anticipated workflow of the area. Consultation with an architect experienced in hospital and medical facilities is strongly recommended (5).

The allocation of space for the infant feeding preparation room and for the various functional areas within the formula room is determined by several variables:

- The total number of dispensing units (bottles, cans, feeding containers) in inventory
- Types and number of feedings to be prepared
- Type of equipment selected
- Frequency of product deliveries
- Staffing levels
- Division of labor

In many health care facilities, one technician staffs the infant feeding preparation room. Hence, a multi-room formula preparation unit would be counterproductive because a large percentage of time would be spent walking between areas. For this reason, proposed staffing patterns must be included in the functional programming phase of the planning process. It is not imperative that each functional area be allocated a separate room. Division of functional areas within the formula room can be accomplished with the use of partitions, full-height walls, or with a well-planned workflow, including clearly delineated flow patterns.

Table 1.1 presents programs for space requirements in health care facilities with two levels of service demands. Option A outlines a program with 464 "net," or usable, square feet, which can meet the needs of most health care facilities. The total gross square feet includes net square feet plus unusable space, such as that occupied by walls, columns, and utility chases. Option B presents minimum space requirements for an infant formula preparation room with 229 total net square feet. This option is more appropriate for health care facilities that do not prepare large amounts of formula for infants daily. Some local fire codes and regulations require the addition of an emergency exit. (See Figure 1.1, later in this chapter, for suggested layouts.)

Layout and Design

Work area and equipment layout should follow the logical flow of materials through the storage, preparation, and cleanup process. It should also foster the efficiency of each activity performed (5,9).

To minimize the potential of cross-contamination, access from a corridor should allow any soiled wares to get to the cleanup area without passing through the clean-preparation area. The preparation area should only be accessible by way of the anteroom to ensure that all individuals entering the infant feeding preparation room from the outside are properly dressed and scrubbed. Facility-prepared formulas for infants should exit the feeding room without passing through the cleanup area.

TABLE 1.1 *Space Allocation for Infant Formula Preparation Room*

Function	Option A[a] (sq ft)	Option B[b] (sq ft)
Ante area	37	35
Storage, product, and supplies	107	32
Preparation	93	72
Cleanup area	60	50
Janitorial closet	19	0
Office space	49	40
Circulation	99	0
Total net (usable) sq ft	464	229
Total gross sq ft	506	255

[a]Space allocation (in square feet) that will meet the needs of most health care facilities for the production of infant formula. (See Figure 1.1, Option A.)

[b]Suggested minimum space allocation for health care facilities that prepare relatively few units of infant formula in a separate formula room. (See Figure 1.1, Option B.)

The infant feeding preparation room should consist of (*a*) storage, (*b*) preparation, (*c*) cleanup, and (*d*) anteroom areas. The preparation area and all product storage areas, cabinets, and refrigerators should be lockable or securable. The anteroom can accommodate both hand hygiene and office procedures (10). It is not necessary that each of these functions occupy a separate room; however, when combined, judicious care must be taken to ensure the use of aseptic technique and to maintain a sanitary environment (8,11). Preparing formula for infants in an open but designated area increases the potential for microbiological contamination and tampering.

Use of a laminar flow hood to prepare formulas is a decision that each facility should make based on working conditions, staffing, and air quality. Pharmacies are not required to use laminar flow hoods to prepare oral medications. Powdered formulas are not sterile, and preparing them under a laminar flow hood does not improve the sterility of the product.

Storage   Adequate space for receiving and storing supplies should be near, but not in, the infant feeding preparation room itself. The prototype design depicted in Figure 1.1 suggests that storage be located in a separate area within the anteroom. This design permits cases of product to be delivered and opened, and boxes to be discarded, without passing through a "clean" area. It also allows product to be readily accessible to the preparation area. A small supply of product and ingredient inventory may be maintained in the formula preparation area, as long as it is not stored above the work area. Formula storage areas must be securable to prevent loss or adulteration of formula and supplies. Storage of human milk requires designated refrigeration and a freezer that hold at −20°C if long-term storage is needed or donor milk is used.

Even if only ready-to-feed formulas for infants are to be used, attention should be given to providing adequate space for storage. Many commercially available formulas for infants require space for final preparation, and such space should be used for no other purpose.

Anteroom   The purpose of the anteroom is to serve as a buffer zone between the infant feeding preparation room and the rest of the health care facility. It can also serve as a workroom for the feeding room supervisor/

FIGURE 1.1 *Suggested Layouts for Infant Feeding Preparation Rooms*

technician to do calculations and other paperwork, as well as a space for a data communication/computer system. Ideally, the anteroom should have an unobstructed view of the preparation area. Specifically, the anteroom provides an area where personnel can practice appropriate hand hygiene before entering the preparation area (10). Cabinetry should allow for an adequate supply of clean gowns, bonnets, etc. Toilet facilities should be in a separate room.

A sink used exclusively for hand hygiene is imperative in the anteroom or near the preparation area (6,10,12). The sink should have controls for water that do not require the use of hands (6,12,13). There should be a shelf for hand-hygiene supplies and a towel dispenser for single-use paper towels (10).

Preparation Area   The preparation area consists of a stainless steel work surface with a utility sink, utensil storage, and refrigerator for holding facility-prepared infant feedings (2). Depending on procedures required by the individual health care facility, optional equipment used in the preparation process might include a horizontal laminar flow hood, a sterilizer/autoclave, a blast chiller, and a freezer (see Chapter 2 and Chapter 5). Tools and utensils should be stored at the workstation where they are used.

Adequate electrical outlets with sufficient power supply should be provided for equipment used in the preparation of infant formula. All wiring should be grounded, and all electrical materials and equipment should be installed in compliance with local codes and standards (consult your facility's engineering services department) (14). Electrical outlets for refrigerators and freezers should be backed up by emergency generators in case of power outages.

All water supplied for feeding preparation must meet federal standards for drinking water and be commercially sterile. Chemically softened water is not appropriate for use in the preparation of infant formula (see Chapter 5). Because neonates and chronically ill children have immature or compromised immune systems and are more susceptible to infections, the water source may be a source of potential contamination if sterile water is not used. Chilled sterile water should be used in the preparation of formula in health care facilities, or formula prepared with room-temperature water should be placed in a blast chiller to minimize the time required to bring the formula to 4°C (40°F).

To maximize the use of space, wall cabinetry can be used for storing supplies, utensils, and minor equipment. To avoid dust collection above the feeding preparation area, there should be no exposed horizontal surfaces above the wall cabinet. Enclosed soffit areas are acceptable. To minimize the potential for product contamination, cabinetry should not be installed directly over the work area where infant formulas are prepared.

Once prepared, labeled, and dated, human milk and infant formula must be promptly placed in a refrigerator, where it is held at a safe temperature (4°C [40°F]) until delivered to patient care units.

Cleanup   Because many infant feeding preparation rooms do not reuse bottles or other storage containers, a separate cleanup room is not mandatory. When a separate cleanup room is not provided, alternative provisions must be made by cleaning equipment and utensils in another area in the facility (eg, foodservice dishwashing) or in a designated area within the infant feeding preparation room. The latter is preferred because strict sanitation controls would be difficult to monitor in another area of the health care facility.

If cleanup is done within the infant feeding preparation room, the processes of preparation and cleanup should be separated by both time and space (6). Once the preparation process has been completed for one service period, the room and all utensils should be thoroughly cleaned. The layout of the preparation area should ensure that the "clean" end of the sanitation area is adjacent to the preparation space and that the "soiled" portion of the cleanup area is away from the preparation area.

Small equipment can be sterilized in an autoclave or dishwasher. When a dishwasher with an 82°C (180°F) or greater final rinse cycle is used, a single-compartment sink for pre-rinsing will suffice in the infant feeding preparation room. To minimize potential for contamination, as well as labor costs, only single-use containers or infant bottles are recommended. If bottles are reused, a two- or three-compartment sink with bottle-washing brushes and a rinse nozzle is suggested. Even then, bottles must be sanitized with heat or appropriate chemicals. Appropriate chemicals are those that are acceptable for food contact surfaces and approved by the facility's infection control committee. Bottle brushes must be removable for cleaning and preferably capable of withstanding the autoclaving process. In the event that neither a dishwasher nor a sterilizer/autoclave is accessible, a three-compartment sink is mandatory.

A stainless steel sink with double drain boards or counter space on both sides is recommended in the infant feeding preparation room for washing equipment and utensils. A three-compartment sink (wash, rinse, and sanitize) is acceptable for sanitizing equipment in the event that the dishwasher malfunctions. The three-compartment sink could also be used for cleanup when small amounts of human milk or formula are prepared. Utility sinks should not be located directly next to the preparation area, because dirty water could splash from the sink to the preparation area. Dedicated cleaning supplies should be stored separately from formula products and equipment.

Office   Office space should be accessible to corridor traffic, but not to the "clean" environment of the preparation area. In addition to files, cabinets, and bookshelves, space should be allocated for a work station with computer, printer, and fax.

Construction Features

The cleanliness of the floor surface should be apparent and easily maintained (5,6,12). Floor drains are not recommended unless required by local code. Smooth, hard surface walls and ceilings are desirable (eg, ceramic tile or fiberglass-reinforced plastic panels) to minimize the harboring of microorganisms (6,12,13). If fiberglass-reinforced plastic panels are used, many building codes require that the product meet local fire standards. Sheet rock (dry wall) should be painted with light-colored, epoxy-based paints.

Ceilings should be a hard surface painted with epoxy-based paint or covered with nonporous acoustic tile. To minimize dust, suspended ceiling panels should be sealed at their edges to the framing with a silicone sealant.

The proper amount and type of lighting in the infant feeding preparation room is important for cleanliness, safety, and efficiency. Lighting fixtures that are recessed and flush against the wall or ceiling are preferred. Lighting fixtures should be easily cleaned, enclosed, and adequate for accurate preparation of formula and maintenance of a sanitary environment (15). The Illuminating Engineering Society of North America (IES) has developed recommended lighting budget figures for foot-candle levels and watts per square foot for health care facilities. The IES recommends 50-foot candles of general lighting at a surface where an employee is working on food preparation. Twenty-foot candles is the recommendation for inside equipment such as reach-in and under-counter refrigerators and at a distance of 30 inches above the floor in areas used for hand washing, equipment washing, and storage (14,15). Fixtures should be located so that workers do not have to work in their own shadow or the shadow of equipment (12).

Ventilation requirements are intended to maintain a clean air supply in the infant feeding preparation room and environmentally acceptable conditions for the staff. To minimize contamination, the ventilation system should be either separate from the rest of the health care facility (minimum filtration 90% as determined by the American Society of Heating, Refrigerating, and Air Conditioning Engineers) or a high-efficiency particulate air (HEPA) forced-air filtration system (9). The exhaust system should extract air at a lower capacity than the incoming air to create an appropriate positive pressure gradient in the preparation area.

If a separate ventilation system or a HEPA–type forced-air filtration system is not available, it is acceptable to prepare infant formula according to established operating procedures under a laminar flow hood (16,17).

Guidelines for Facilities Without Separate Feeding Rooms

In hospitals with small volumes of human milk or formula or minimal space available for feeding preparation, a separate infant feeding preparation room may not be practical. Refer to Box 1.1 for points to consider in such facilities. Table 1.2 provides more information on single-room and shared formula-preparation areas.

BOX 1.1 *Physical Facility Option When There Is No Feeding Preparation Room*

A section of the food production area, a galley on a patient care floor, or dedicated space in the nursery can be designated as the feeding preparation area. All the construction considerations of standard food preparation areas must be followed when choosing or designing an area. To minimize cleanup area requirements in operations of this scale, only single-use containers and bottles should be used. Preparation equipment should be sanitized in standard dishwashing equipment approved by local food ordinance or, ideally, autoclaved by the hospital's sterilization department. (See Table 1.2 for more information on single-room and shared formula-preparation areas and Chapter 2 for small equipment needs.)

TABLE 1.2 *Single-Room Feeding Preparation Area (Option C) and Shared Feeding Preparation Area (Option D)*[a]

Function	Option C (sq ft)	Option D (sq ft)
Ante area	0	0
Storage (products and supplies)	80	18
Preparation	27	18
Cleanup area	27	18
Janitorial closet	0	0
Office space	0	0
Circulation	50	0
Total net (usable) sq ft	**184**	**54**

[a]Space allocation for facilities with limited space for feeding preparation. Option C is for a single, separate feeding preparation room. Option D indicates the minimum space required when using a shared preparation area.

When a preparation area is shared, all other activities should cease in the area before feeding preparation begins. Food supplies or other items used in patient care should be removed from an area large enough to provide sufficient work room for the feeding preparation. Personnel not involved in feeding preparation should be excluded from the area. Work surfaces should be thoroughly washed, rinsed, and sanitized using hospital-approved chemicals. The mixing equipment used only for formula preparation and the supplies should be removed from sanitary storage and brought to the area.

Personnel involved should wash hands thoroughly and put on disposable protective equipment, which may include gowns, bonnets, gloves, and shoe covers, depending on hospital requirements for infection control. Human milk and formulas should be prepared using aseptic technique. Disposable equipment should be used for preparing human milk feedings, or the equipment should be sterilized between each source of milk. When mixing formula, disposable equipment can also be used, or equipment should be sanitized between different types of formula (eg, cow milk–based vs hydrolysate).

Ideally, the prepared feedings should be placed immediately in a designated refrigerator separate from other food supplies. If separate refrigeration facilities are not available, an area of a shared space should be designated for human milk and formula storage. Small quantities of feedings could be stored in covered plastic food storage boxes to further isolate the feedings from other food supplies. Human milk and formula can be stored in the same refrigerator as long as there are no state regulations to the contrary, and as long as provisions are made so that human milk never mixes with another infant's feedings.

Conclusion

The planning team has the opportunity to assess, evaluate, and choose the system and facility most suitable to meet the anticipated needs of the patient population. A systems approach to the planning of a feeding preparation facility will assist in a more efficient utilization of resources and in the provision of quality and medically appropriate nutrition support.

REFERENCES

1. American Hospital Association. *Procedures and Layout for the Infant Formula Room.* Chicago, IL: American Hospital Association; 1965.
2. Robbins S, Beker L, eds. I*nfant Feedings: Guidelines for Preparation of Formula and Breastmilk in Health Care Facilities.* Chicago, IL: American Dietetic Association; 2003.
3. Food and Drug Administration. Health professional's letter on *Enterobacter sakazakii* infections associated with use of powdered (dry) infant formulas in neonatal intensive care units revised October 10, 2002. http://www.fda.gov/Food/FoodSafety/Product-SpecificInformation/InfantFormula/AlertsSafetyInformation/ucm111299.htm. Accessed October 4, 2010.
4. Centers for Disease Control and Prevention. *Enterobacter sakazakii* infections associated with the use of powdered infant formula—Tennessee 2001. *MMWR Morb Mortal Wkly Rep.* 2002;51:297–300.
5. American Institute of Architects Academy of Architecture for Health, the Facilities Guidelines Institute. *Guidelines for Design and Construction of Hospital and Health Care Facilities.* Washington, DC: American Institute of Architects; 2006.
6. Food and Drug Administration. FDA Food Code. http://www.fda.gov/Food/FoodSafety/RetailFoodProtection/FoodCode/FoodCode2009/default.htm. Accessed December 7, 2009.
7. Larson E. APIC guidelines for handwashing and hand antisepsis in healthcare setting. *Am J Infect Control.* 1995;23:251–269.
8. Bennett B. Principles of aseptic technique: Adapted from: Essentials for animal research: a primer for research personnel. http://www.miami.edu/acuc/Aspetic.html. Accessed December 2, 2009.
9. American Society of Heating, Refrigerating, and Air Conditioning Engineers. *ASHRAE Handbook: Fundamentals.* Vol 23. I-P ed. Atlanta, GA: American Society of Heating, Refrigerating, and Air Conditioning Engineers, Inc; 2009.
10. Boyce J, Pittet D. Guidelines for hand hygiene in health-care settings: recommendations of the healthcare infection control practices advisory committee and the HICPAD/SHEA/APIC/IDSA hand hygiene task force. *MMWR Morb Mortal Wkly Rep.* 2002;51(RR-16):1–58.
11. Ayliffe G, Path M, Collins B, Davies J. Contamination of infant feeds in hospitals. *Midwife Health Visit Community Nurse.* 1976;12:18–20.
12. Food and Drug Administration. *Food Service Sanitation Manual.* Washington, DC: US Department of Health, Education, and Welfare;197826,33,36,37. US Department of Health, Education and Welfare Publication 78–2081.
13. American Institute of Architects. *Guidelines for Construction and Equipment of Hospitals and Medical Facilities. 1993 Edition.* Washington, DC: Institute of Architects Press; 1993.
14. Illuminating Engineering Society of North America. *Lighting Handbook.* 9th ed. NY: IESNA Publications Dept; 2000.
15. Food and Drug Administration. FDA Food Code 2009: Chapter 6—Physical Facilities Lighting 6–303.11 Intensity. http://www.fda.gov/Food/FoodSafety/RetailFoodProtection/FoodCode/FoodCode2009/ucm188092.htm. Accessed September 8, 2010.
16. Avis K, Levchuk J. Special considerations in the use of vertical laminar flow workbenches. *Am J Hosp Pharm.* 1984;41:81–86.
17. Hendrickson R, ed. *Remington: The Science and Practice of Pharmacy.* 21st ed. Baltimore, MD: Lippincott Williams and Wilkins; 2006.

Chapter 2

Equipment, Utensils, and Supplies

Terry Whaley, MPH, RD

Equipment in the infant feeding preparation room should be made of stainless steel or other corrosion-resistant, durable, nonabsorbent material. This equipment must comply with local, state, and federal health regulations and sanitation codes that apply to equipment for food production. Equipment must be constructed so that all parts may be easily cleaned and sanitized (1). All equipment should be checked routinely for equipment integrity; defective items should be replaced. There should be written guidelines for regularly scheduled preventive and corrective maintenance of equipment in the infant feeding preparation room. This preventive and corrective maintenance must be documented and monitored.

When selecting equipment for the infant feeding preparation room, it is important to consider the following factors:
- Number and variety of feedings to be prepared
- Accessibility to needed equipment that may be located outside the room (such as dishwasher or autoclave)
- Applicable health regulations and sanitation codes, including codes for plumbing and air quality
- Budget
- Serviceability and dependability of equipment
- Preventive and corrective maintenance of equipment for preparation of infant feedings
- Provision of adequate supplies and equipment to implement aseptic technique in the preparation of feedings for infants.

Large Equipment

Refrigerator   Refrigerators in feeding preparation areas and on patient units should be placed in secure areas with limited access to prevent adulteration or tampering. The refrigerator in the infant feeding preparation room must have an adequate capacity to cool all facility-prepared feedings for infants to 2°C to 4°C (35°F to 40°F) within 1 hour of preparation (1). When a new refrigerator is purchased, one with an external thermometer and alarm system is recommended. Use of chilled ingredients will facilitate good temperature control (see Chapter 5).

However, many factors other than the cooling capacity of the refrigerator unit will determine the length of time actually required to cool any specific batch of feedings for infants. These factors include:

- The temperature of water used in preparation
- The temperature of human milk or formula ingredients used in preparation
- The heat exchange properties of the material used in the storage container
- The volume in the container
- How containers are spaced in the refrigerator
- The size of the refrigerator and its other contents
- Frequency and duration of door openings

All factors should be considered when determining the type and size of refrigerator needed in the infant feeding preparation room. To promote consistent achievement of safe feeding storage temperature as quickly as possible, commercial refrigerators are recommended in the feeding preparation room and on patient care units. The costs and specifications of domestic and commercial refrigerators must be considered, as well as the specific needs of the health care facility. Best practice is to have refrigerators and freezers with an alarm system to notify staff when the temperature is outside of the safe food storage range, and with a compressor designed to recover the temperature quickly. The alarm should be audible to staff 24 hours per day; this may require a system that allows temperature monitoring from a remote location. Commercial refrigerators have a BTU capacity that allows for cooling a larger volume than the average domestic unit. The inside finish of such a refrigerator is more resistant to corrosion and is better able to withstand daily cleaning. Because domestic refrigerators do not usually have approval from the National Sanitation Foundation (NSF), the facility intending to use one must check with its local health department to see whether NSF approval is required. Whatever model is chosen, shelving should be adequate for good air circulation.

Freezer   If human milk is stored and fortified in the feeding preparation room, a freezer that will hold milk at –20°C (–4°F) or lower is needed for long-term storage of the milk (see Chapter 4). A commercial grade freezer with external thermometer reading and alarm system is recommended.

Dishwasher   In a self-contained infant feeding preparation room, a commercial dishwasher that can reach a wash temperature of 66°C to 74°C (150°F to 165°F) and a rinse temperature of 82°C to 91°C (180°F to 195°F) is needed to meet most local sanitation codes and NSF standards (1). An under-the-counter, commercial dishwasher washes one 20″ × 20″ rack in approximately 3 minutes. Usually, two racks are provided with the purchase of the machine. A vent is not needed for an under-the-counter machine. Use of the facility's foodservice dishwasher is not recommended. If it is necessary to use the foodservice dishwasher, controlled practices to prevent cross-contamination and ensure sanitization are required. Equipment may be hand-washed and autoclaved as an alternative to commercial dishwashing.

Sinks   A separate sink for hand washing is required. The sink should have controls for water and soap that can be operated without the use of hands. Hand-washing supplies should meet the guidelines of the health care facility's infection control committee.

A single-compartment sink is adequate if used only to rinse equipment before washing in the dishwasher. A three-compartment sink is acceptable for sanitizing equipment in the event the dishwasher or autoclave malfunctions.

Carts   Carts are needed to transport infant feedings from the preparation room to the patient units. Carts must provide cover for infant feeds during transport to ensure cleanliness and temperature control (1). This may be accomplished either with a covered cart or with the use of a covered container in which the feedings can be placed in a thermal container with ice packs. The temperature of facility-prepared feedings must be maintained between 2°C and 4°C (35°F and 40°F) during transport (1). An insulated container may be adequate for keeping the feedings in this temperature range. For delivery of large quantities of infant feedings over long distances, a refrigerated cart may be necessary to ensure proper temperature control.

Optional Large Equipment

Laminar Flow Hood   The use of a laminar airflow hood may provide an additional barrier to potential contaminants. Each facility should determine whether an airflow hood is desired; use of this kind of equipment is optional. Use of a laminar flow hood is *not* meant to replace aseptic technique. If used, it must be according to the established operating procedures (eg, adequate lighting, positioning of product in the air field, positioning of the operator's hands in relation to the filter). Infant feeding room personnel must be carefully trained and must maintain competency on hood operating procedures (see Chapter 5). If powdered formula, which by definition is not sterile, becomes airborne in a laminar flow hood, the sterile environment is disrupted until the hood is terminally cleaned.

Laminar flow hoods come in various sizes and with a vertical, horizontal, or curvilinear airflow. The appropriate size of the hood can be determined by the volume of infant feedings prepared. The laminar flow hood should be inspected and certified according to testing standards established by the American Society of Heating, Refrigerating, and Air Conditioning Engineers, or the manufacturer's instructions.

Blast Chiller   A blast chiller is a specially designed refrigerator that cools foods to less than 4°C (40°F) in fewer than 90 minutes. Rapid chilling minimizes the time the feedings are in the danger for microbial growth. Even high-quality commercial refrigerators are not designed to cool foods as quickly as blast chillers. In large-volume facilities or facilities that use room-temperature water, a blast chiller should be considered. Many manufacturers offer small, under-counter blast chillers that minimize the need for additional space.

Autoclave   An autoclave is considered optional equipment for the infant feeding preparation room. It may be used to sterilize equipment or ingredient water. Ingredient water is any water used to reconstitute or dilute formulas. When there is no commercially sterile water for oral use available, an autoclave can be used to prepare sterilized water for feeding preparation. If necessary, an autoclave located in another part of the hospital can be used.

Small Equipment

Hand Gel Dispensers

Hand gel consistent with facility standards should be available near feeding preparation area and clean up areas (See Chapter 5).

Measuring and Mixing Devices

Equipment for mixing liquids and powders in the infant feeding preparation room includes handheld whisks; a portable, handheld mixer with removable beater or whisk that can be easily sanitized; mixing containers; mixing spoons; covered pitchers; graduated cylinders; beakers; funnels; and flasks. Equipment used with mechanical mixing devices should be made of stainless steel in order to properly sanitize and avoid glass shards. Handheld utensils with hollow handles should be avoided because of the risk of microbial contamination inside the handle. Food-grade plastic cylinders are acceptable for measuring liquids. Single-use devices are convenient for the handling of human milk. When devices are used for human milk from more than one woman, they must be sterilized between uses.

Can Opener   A punch-type can opener used in the infant feeding preparation room must be one that is dishwasher safe, can be sanitized with an alcohol pad, or autoclaved for proper sanitation.

Electric can openers cannot be adequately sanitized and are not recommended. A manual, seam-gripping can opener can shave tiny metal shards into the products and is not recommended.

Scales   The scale used in the infant feeding preparation room should register in gram units and be accurate to one decimal place. Gram scales that are sensitive to the 0.1 gram may be necessary to accurately measure modular ingredients added to formulas for the smallest infants. The scale should be calibrated at intervals recommended by the manufacturer to maintain accuracy.

Trays   Trays or other containers may be used to move feedings for infants from the infant feeding preparation area to the refrigerator, to the transport cart, and to assemble supplies. Trays should be of such size, material, finish, and design that they can be appropriately sanitized (1).

Thermometers   A refrigerator thermometer is necessary to confirm and monitor the temperature of the refrigerator and freezer. A food thermometer should be available to monitor feeding temperature.

Bins/Plastic Bags   If expressed human milk is stored in a community refrigerator or freezer, each individual infant's milk must be isolated from other feedings. Bins or resealable plastic bags are acceptable for this purpose.

Trash Container   The infant feeding preparation room must contain a covered trash container with a foot-operated lid.

Telephone   If there is a telephone in the feeding preparation area, sanitize the entire phone with alcohol on a daily basis and when soiled.

Paper Towel Dispenser   The paper towel dispenser should provide single-use paper towels for hand washing and cleanup.

Clock/Calendar   A wall-mounted clock and calendar are recommended.

Janitorial Equipment   Storage of janitorial equipment should be outside the feeding preparation room (2).

Calculator   A calculator that can be cleaned with an alcohol pad daily or one that is enclosed by a washable plastic cover should be available in the infant feeding preparation room.

Covered Laundry Hamper   A covered laundry hamper, placed in the infant feeding anteroom or office area, can be used for depositing reusable gowns after wearing.

Office Equipment   Office equipment that may be helpful in the anteroom of the infant feeding preparation room includes a desk, a filing cabinet, a chair or work stool, a bookcase, a bulletin board, and equipment for order transmission, recording information on feeding requests and changes, and label generation. Methods of transmitting feeding orders may vary but can include the use of a pneumatic tube system, a fax machine, or a clinical information system used for online order entry. A printer for electronic order requisitions, reports, and labels is required for those facilities that use an electronic medical record. Because computers are a known source of touch contamination, they should ideally be located in the anteroom. Hand hygiene should be practiced immediately before feeding preparation. An optional copier and fax machine could minimize traffic in and out of the feeding preparation area. Chairs and stools should be covered with material that is easily sanitized.

Bar Coding Equipment   Bar coding systems designed for labeling human milk are available. A scanning device and label printer may be needed to support use of these systems.

Utensils and Supplies

Ingredient Water   Water that meets the criteria outlined in Chapter 5 should be available in the infant feeding preparation room for use as ingredient water. Chilled sterilized water should be used for infant formula preparation unless a blast chiller is available. Sterilized water for oral use is available and is preferred over sterilized water labeled for other uses.

Formula   All necessary formula products should be available in the infant feeding preparation room. Boxes should be unpacked in the storage area or anteroom, and supplies brought into the preparation area on a clean cart.

Modular Components and Additives   An inventory of commonly used modular components and additives should be maintained in the infant feeding preparation area. Adequate space for storage of opened packages must be available.

Measuring Devices   Liquids should be measured in graduated cylinders, beakers, liquid measuring cups, syringes, or pitchers. If used, liquid measuring cups should be high-quality, laboratory grade with accurate graduations. Polypropylene plastic measuring cups are acceptable. They have easily read graduations and are autoclavable. Disposable oral syringes for measuring small quantities of liquid additives should be available in the infant feeding preparation room and discarded after single use. As mentioned previously, dry ingredients should be measured by gram weight.

Storage Containers, Bottles, and Nipples for Infant Feedings   Unit-of-use or bulk glass or food-grade plastic containers with lids are recommended for storage of prepared infant feedings. Single-use glass bottles distributed by infant formula companies must *not* be reused because heating may weaken the structure of the bottle. Sterile water bottles may be used for storage of prepared feedings for one-time-only use and then discarded. The original label of the bottle must be covered with a new one reflecting the new contents. Plastic bottles and graduated feeders used for formula that contain a medium-chain triglyceride (MCT) oil additive must be approved by the manufacturer for use. MCT oil dissolves some plastics. Any non-glass reusable containers (eg, plastic) should be sanitized according to manufacturer's instructions. Disposable nipples, rings, and nipple covers are recommended. These disposable items should never be reused in the hospital. Reusable bottles and nipples should be sanitized regularly. Storage containers designed for human milk are available. For health care facilities, single-use containers are recommended. Some breast pumps come with collection bottles. If these bottles are reused, they should be sanitized (preferably sterilized) between uses for hospitalized infants.

Safety Tabs   Safety tabs or safety strips may be used for facility-prepared bottles containing infant feedings. Tabs or strips are used to ensure that the bottle has not been opened before the feeding period.

Labels   All units of facility-prepared feedings for infants must carry an identifying label (1). (For a complete discussion of feedings labels, see Chapter 5.)

Apparel   Disposable or reusable gowns may be used in the infant feeding preparation room. Reusable gowns should be labeled with the employee's name and include the date when last laundered (at least weekly or whenever soiled). Personnel in the room may also need disposable bonnets, face masks, beard covers, and gloves. For the preparation of formula, gloves are not required as long as effective hand sanitation techniques are used. Gloves are recommended when handling human milk.

Office Supplies   Appropriate office supplies should be provided to ensure the proper conduct of business in the infant feeding preparation room.

Cleaning Supplies   Dishwasher detergent, bleach, sanitizing solution, and other cleaning supplies used in the infant feeding preparation room must be approved for foodservice use by the health care facility's infection control committee. All cleaning supplies should be used exclusively in the infant feeding preparation room. Cleaning supplies must be stored separately from infant feeding products and ingredients (3).

Equipment *Not* To Be Used

Scoops   Each powdered formula has a scoop sized to the unique properties of the individual formula. Because of variability in packing up to 25%, scoops and household measuring devices should *never* be used to portion powdered products in health care facilities. Instead, powdered formulas should be weighed on a gram scale.

Microwave Oven   Microwave ovens must *never* be used for infant feeding preparation because of the danger of overheating and the formation of hot spots in the solution (2,4). During the microwave process the bottle may remain cool while the feeding inside is overheated unintentionally (5). Overheating liquids can also cause nutrient losses (6), and potentially burn infants when the feeding is administered (see Chapter 5).

Upright Blenders   Upright blenders are not recommended for formula preparation because of their inherent risks (7,8), including the following:

- Potential for microbial contamination due to inability to adequately sanitize the bearing mechanism
- Inability to adequately sanitize the rubber gaskets should they become cracked or damaged
- Cross-contamination of allergens, such as cow's milk protein and soy protein

Stick/immersion blenders with whisks capable of being sanitized after each use are acceptable for formula preparation. A new whisk should be used with each different type of formula.

Garbage Disposal   A garbage disposal is not recommended for use in the infant feeding preparation room because of the potential for contamination from garbage that has been aerosolized and from standing water.

Equipment for Facilities Lacking a Feeding Preparation Room

Some facilities will determine that a feeding preparation room is not feasible. In this case, a dedicated space for feeding preparation is needed. (See Box 2.1 for equipment needed in a dedicated space for feeding preparation.) If there is no such space, it is recommended that only commercial ready-to-feed formulas or unfortified human milk be used.

BOX 2.1   *Equipment for Human Milk or Formula Preparation When There Is No Feeding Preparation Room*

If a dedicated space for feeding preparation is used, the following equipment should be available:

- Hospital-approved sanitizing solution or sanitizing cloth for work area
- Hand gel approved by the infection control committee of the facility
- Gram scale sensitive to 0.1 g for weighing powder
- Disposable measuring device for liquids
- Sterilized water
- Individually wrapped spoon for stirring
- Container with lid to mix feeding
- Bottles/syringes for unit dosing
- Labels for individual feeding units
- Covered trash can
- Refrigeration for feedings not intended for immediate use

REFERENCES

1. Food and Drug Administration. FDA Food Code 2009. http://www.fda.gov/Food/FoodSafety/RetailFoodProtection/FoodCode/FoodCode2009/default.htm. Accessed December 7, 2009.

2. Dixon JJ, Burd DA, Roberts DG. Severe burns resulting from an exploding teat on a bottle of infant formula milk heated in a microwave oven. *Burns.* 1997;23:268–269.

3. American Institute of Architects Academy of Architecture for Health, The Facilities Guidelines Institute. *Guidelines for Design and Construction of Hospital and Health Care Facilities.* Washington, DC: American Institute of Architects; 2006.

4. Puczynski M, Rademaker D, Gatson RL. Burn injury related to the improper use of a microwave oven. *Pediatrics.* 1983;72:714–715.

5. Hibbard RA, Blevins R. Palatal burn due to bottle warming in microwave oven. *Pediatrics.* 1988;82:382–384.

6. De la Fuente M, Olano A, Juarez M. Mineral balance in milk heated using microwave energy. *J Agric Food Chem.* 2002;10:2274–2277.

7. Kiddy K, Josse E, Griffin N. An outbreak of serious Klebsiella infections related to food blenders. *J Hosp Infect.* 1987;9:191–193.

8. Oliviera MH, Bonelli R, Aido KE, Batista CR. Microbiological quality of reconstituted enteral formulations used in hospitals. *Nutrition.* 2000;16:729–733.

Chapter 3

Personnel

Susan Teske, MS, RD, CNSD

The production of safe, reliable infant feedings requires personnel in administrative, supervisory, and technical capacities. They must be trained and skilled in their respective duties, and conscientious in their performance. The success of operations in the infant feeding preparation room depends largely on the skill and vigilance of the personnel assigned to it. Diligent workers can provide safe infant feedings despite limitations of facilities and equipment, whereas careless personnel using the best of facilities cannot (1). Standard operating procedures and standard sanitation procedures are basic to food safety programs at any health care facility (2).

Administration

Administrative oversight for the infant feeding preparation room must be assigned to a qualified professional (eg, registered dietitian, registered pharmacist, or registered nurse) at an appropriate supervisory level. This individual must be experienced in feeding room techniques and operations. In some facilities, a supervisor and a technician may be present; in smaller facilities, there may be only a technician. The administrative duties, therefore, depend on the size of the facility, administrative structure, and volume of feeding preparation. Responsibilities include the following:

- Organizational responsibilities
    - Designing, developing, and implementing policies and procedures for the operation of the infant feeding preparation room that comply with state and local regulatory agencies and guidelines of professional organizations (2,3)
    - Budgeting for the operations of the infant feeding preparation room and purchasing of supplies and equipment
    - Developing standardized formulations or recipes for human milk and formula preparation
    - Communicating and collaborating with other departments

- Following procedures for reporting product recalls and suspected equipment malfunctions
- Developing an emergency preparedness plan and maintaining a state of readiness for emergencies and disasters (4,5)

- Human resources
  - Overseeing the infant feeding preparation room supervisor and/or technician who is directly responsible for day-to-day operations
  - Hiring, training, and scheduling of feeding preparation room personnel
  - Evaluating performance, skills, and competencies of staff and providing appropriate educational opportunities (6)

- Quality control
  - Making periodic inspections of the infant feeding preparation room
  - Checking time and temperature records on heating and refrigeration equipment
  - Checking feeding orders for compliance with policies and procedures and essential elements for patient orders
  - Developing and implementing a Hazard Analysis and Critical Control Point (HACCP) system to prevent and minimize potential risk factors that may contribute to bacterial contamination of feedings and enteral feeding systems (2,3,7–16)
  - Maintaining inspection schedules for evaluation of feeding preparation room equipment (which may include, but not be limited to, gram scales and the laminar airflow hood used in the feeding preparation room)

A sample position description may be found in Appendix 3-A.

Infant Feeding Preparation Room Staff

The infant feeding room staff in some facilities may be only one technician who is responsible for the preparation and delivery of all feedings for infants. (Note: This book refers to this position as the infant feeding room technician; however, precise titles vary among individual health care facilities.) Duties of the infant feeding room technician may include the following:

- Receiving orders and maintaining records of current orders; communicating with patient care unit secretaries and medical personnel to clarify unclear orders
- Preparing infant feedings using aseptic techniques and all policies and procedures developed for the operation of the infant feeding preparation room
- Labeling prepared feedings per facility policy
- Delivering prepared feedings to designated areas
- Ordering and maintaining adequate supplies to meet patient needs
- Checking and disposing of all outdated product per facility policy, rotating supply inventory
- Operating all equipment needed to prepare feedings for infants
- Maintaining sanitation in the preparation area
- Communicating with the registered dietitians regarding individualized or nonstandard recipes or orders
- Filing and maintaining temperature records and other records as required for audit

- Securing the infant feeding preparation room
- Assisting with the training of ancillary or support personnel as necessary

A sample position description may be found in Appendix 3-B.

Minimum Qualifications for Feeding Room Technician Position   The infant feeding room technician must be in good health (as defined by the employee health policies of the health care facility and appropriate regulating agencies) and able to read, write, and perform necessary mathematical tasks at the high school level or above. A math competency test, including basic algebra, may be useful in screening potential candidates.

The infant feeding room technician ideally should not be assigned to duties outside the infant feeding preparation room, except in small facilities in which full-time service is not required. If the infant feeding room technician has other responsibilities, preparation of feedings for infants should always be completed during designated time periods and without interruption. Other assigned duties should not include those that would increase the risk of contamination, such as preparation of raw foods, processing used food trays (either from patient rooms or from the cafeteria), or heavy cleaning.

Number of Employees   The number of employees assigned to the infant feeding preparation room will depend on the volume of work and the type of personnel available in the health care facility. Feedings prepared in the infant feeding preparation room are mixed for a 24-hour period. Ideally, feedings will be unit–dosed, but bulk supply for 24 hours may be dispensed to the patient care unit. At this time, infant feeding preparation rooms are not staffed to prepare and deliver individual feedings 24 hours a day. In all facilities, it is essential that, for relief or emergency duty, at least one alternate technician be thoroughly trained in the duties of the infant feeding preparation room technician. In a large facility, three or more individuals should be trained to accommodate schedule changes, time off, and illness or leave of absence. Staffing levels should be proportional to the volume of prepared feedings required.

Productivity   Productivity is a measure of output vs input. It is defined as output/labor + capital + supplies (17,18). Productivity measures for feeding preparation room staff have not been published to date.

In the absence of accepted definitions, evaluative approaches have been used to measure productivity, such as cost per patient-day or ratio of employee full-time equivalents (FTEs) per patient. These do not measure the level of activity or the efficiency of resource utilization. A systematic process to evaluate productivity, including qualitative and quantitative measures, is needed.

It is important to consider time required for staff to complete specific tasks, the resources or supplies used, and how often the tasks are done. Time studies are a valuable tool to quantify productivity. They use direct observations, self-reported time logs, or a combination of the two (19). Each task must be broken down into its components. For example, preparation of a formula from powder would include each of the following tasks:

- Recipe preparation
- Hand washing before formula preparation
- Cleaning non–food contact surfaces
- Collecting utensils and ingredients
- Weighing the powder on a gram scale

- Measuring the water
- Mixing the ingredient
- Creating the label
- Labeling the bottle
- Delivering the bottle to the patient unit

If feeding preparation room staff is responsible for delivering formula to the patient units, the distance and time required to complete deliveries should be evaluated. Qualitative measures may include the number of feeding deliveries missed, the number of feedings prepared incorrectly, cost containment, satisfaction of nursing staff, and infection control surveillance outcomes (microbiological cultures of non–food-contact surfaces). Box 3.1 provides findings from an informal 2009 survey conducted by this chapter's author of productivity in infant feeding preparation rooms.

BOX 3.1   *Informal Data on Infant Feeding Preparation Room Productivity*

In 2009 the author of this chapter conducted an informal survey by e-mailing a single survey tool to all members of the Medical Management Planning (MMP) benchmarking group, the American Dietetic Association Clinical Nutrition Management Listserv, and the Child Health Corporation of America (CHCA) food/nutrition services Listserv. CHCA represents 44 noncompeting children's hospitals or pediatric health care delivery systems throughout the United States. Members of the CHCA food/nutrition services Listserv include foodservice directors and clinical nutrition directors/managers. MMP represents a network of 19 children's hospitals across the United States. The survey was sent to the clinical nutrition directors/managers of the MMP benchmarking group. The survey tool consisted of the following series of 12 open-ended questions:

1. Do you have a formula preparation room?

2. How many patient care units are served by formula room?

   a. Number of beds per patient care unit?

3. What is the estimated average distance (for the delivery of feedings) from the formula room to the patient care units served by the formula room?

4. How many deliveries are made each day from the formula room?

   a. Batch deliveries

   b. Single order deliveries (e.g.: new, prn or stat)

5. Who delivers the formula?

   a. Formula room staff

   b. Central transportation staff

   c. Other (please specify): _____

6. What are the hours of operation of the formula room?

7. How many FTEs are dedicated to the formula room?

   a. Formula techs

(continued)

BOX 3.1   *(continued)*

    b. Direct supervision

    c. Other (please specify): _____

8. How many units of formula are produced per day (average)?

    a. Bulk supply (24h volume in bulk containers)

    b. Unit dose

9. How many units of ready-to-use formula (closed systems or rtf formula bottles) are dispensed per day (average) from the formula room?

10. What other duties are assigned (e.g.: cleaning of formula refrigeration/freezers, inventory control/ordering supplies, monitor refrigerator temperatures, etc.) to the employees who staff the formula room?

11. Do you have a separate breastmilk bank or area for dispensing/preparation of breastmilk?

    a. If yes, who staffs that area?

    b. How many FTEs are dedicated to the breastmilk bank/preparation room?

    c. How many units of breastmilk are dispensed per day?

    d. How many units of breastmilk are prepared with the addition of a fortifier or other additive?

        i. Bulk supply (24h volume in bulk containers)

        ii. Unit dose

12. How do you measure the productivity of your formula room staff?

Twenty-five facilities responded to the survey. There was substantial variability in the responses and the types of facilities responding. The most frequently reported hours of operation for the feeding preparation room were 8.5 hours per day (with the survey responses ranging from 8.5 to 17.5 hours per day). The average number of hours of operation was 12 hours per day. Two facilities reported having different, shorter hours on the weekends compared with weekdays. Four facilities reported having an after-hours process for nursing staff to either access the feeding preparation room or an after-hours cart with commonly needed formulas/ingredients in unit doses. The average and most frequently reported number of full-time equivalents (FTEs) for feeding preparation room staff was 2.7 FTEs (ranging from 1.1 to 7 FTEs). The amount of FTEs required for supervision ranged from 0.02 to 1 FTE, with an average of 0.4 FTE.

Variables affecting staffing levels included the number of feedings prepared, the number of patient units served by the feeding preparation room, the handling of human milk in addition to formula, and how feedings were delivered each day. Four of the 25 facilities reported that their feeding preparation room staff was involved with the handling of human milk. Two facilities reported preparing and delivering feedings to other hospitals or satellite facilities.

On average, there were 9 patient units served per facility with 30 patients per unit. The average number of feedings prepared each day was 60. Many facilities reported preparing unit doses of nutrient additives for nursing to add to human milk on the patient unit.

(continued)

BOX 3.1   *(continued)*

Typically, feedings were delivered in one batch delivery per day, with an average of 10 deliveries during the hours of operation for single orders needed before the batch delivery was made. Generally, the feeding preparation room staff delivered the feeding to the patient units. However, some facilities reported that other departments were involved in the delivery process. Ready-to-feed and closed-system formulas were often stored on patient units as floor stock.

The use of nonproductive time—the expected amount of time dedicated to required duties other than feeding preparation—must be factored into an employee's productivity. Duties assigned to the feeding preparation room staff seemed to vary with the organizational structure of the department and facility. Among the duties of feeding preparation room staff were the following:

- Monitoring temperatures of feeding preparation room equipment: refrigerators, freezers, dish machine
- Cleaning of the feeding preparation room and its equipment
- Inventory control in the feeding preparation room: rotate inventory, maintain par levels
- Ordering supplies for the feeding preparation room
- Inventory of "after-hours night kits" on each unit
- Refilling floor stock (ready-to-feed formulas and nipples)
- Preparing feeding labels
- Managing human milk: storing, thawing, dispensing
- Ordering donor human milk
- Conducting physical inventory (daily, weekly)
- Recording human milk and feeding refrigerator temperatures on each unit
- Cleaning human milk and feeding refrigerators on units
- Documenting delivery of feedings to units
- Monitoring dates on fresh, frozen, and thawed human milk
- Delivering snacks/nourishments
- Projects

The following factors were reported as considerations when evaluating productivity:

- Total number of feedings prepared
- Total number of patient orders
- Number of ready-to-feed formulas dispensed
- Number of unit doses prepared
- Number of patient orders per employee
- Number of missed deliveries
- Revenue

Hazards of the Position   The infant feeding preparation room technician is responsible for lifting cases of formula that may weigh as much as 25 pounds. Most or all work time is spent standing. Burns and cuts/lacerations are a possibility if equipment is not handled appropriately.

Personal Hygiene and Dress Code   Infant feeding preparation room staff must meet the guidelines of the facility and of the CDC to maintain appropriate personal hygiene, including personal cleanliness, particularly of hair, nails, and skin (2,20).

While on duty, the infant feeding preparation room technician should remove all hand jewelry to prevent possible contamination of the product being prepared (21). This includes rings, bracelets, and watches (2).

Fingernails should be short and unpolished. Artificial nails or nail tips are not allowed and should be removed (22–27). If artificial nails cannot be immediately removed, latex-free surgical gloves may be worn and changed between periods of formula preparation (28–31). If tears in gloves occur, the gloves should be replaced. Gloves are not recommended for extended use because they do not prevent transmission of all organisms.

A laundered, short-sleeved scrub suit or uniform should be worn when preparing infant feedings. The scrubs must be covered by a fully buttoned, clean lab coat when employees leave the formula room to enter other areas of the health care facility. The lab coat should be removed before entering the infant feeding preparation room. Clothes should be changed in a gowning room, if possible; otherwise, a locker room will suffice. Lab coats should be labeled with the employee's name and date last laundered. Lab coats should be laundered at least weekly or when soiled. Alternatively, an employee may wear a disposable lab coat with cuffs while preparing feedings in the feeding preparation room; this disposable coat should be removed before leaving the room.

Hair must be completely covered with a disposable bonnet during feeding preparation and must be put on before hand-washing. Facial hair must be covered appropriately. Bonnets and facial hair covers should be worn and replaced each time the employee reenters the infant feeding preparation room.

Shoes worn in the infant feeding preparation room must be closed in both the toe and heel. Shoes should have nonskid soles and be comfortable for extended periods of standing as well as for walking. Stockings or socks should be worn at all times. Shoes should not be visibly soiled.

Training   A written training policy must be developed and implemented (32,33). It should require an orientation of sufficient duration and substance, training through mentorship, in-service experiences, and evaluation of proficiency at the appropriate intervals for each staff member responsible for the preparation of infant feedings (3). The desired outcome of training staff in competency areas such as HACCP is the accurate preparation of feedings and the prevention of bacterial contamination.

A sample competency test is provided in Appendix 3-C. Evaluation of competency should include both an assessment of knowledge (cognitive ability) and an assessment of practice through direct observation of skills (12,34,35). The training period for the infant feeding room technician will depend on the employee's previous experience in a health care facility. Successful completion of the training program must be documented.

The training should include the following components:

- Thorough understanding of the operation of an infant feeding preparation room (see Chapter 5)
- Hand hygiene techniques (16,36–38) and standard precautions (39)
- Principles and importance of aseptic technique (36)
- Dress code
- Care and use of equipment
- Techniques to use for sanitizing equipment and utensils
- Proper storage and cleanup techniques
- Proper use of a laminar flow hood, if one will be used

- Order format that is used by the health care facility
- Use of the clinical information system for order communication, for printing labels and production lists, and for generating patient charges as applicable to the institution
- Use of standardized recipes
- Sample calculations for infant feeding preparation
- Formula and product information, including forms available, standard dilutions/concentrations, product indications, and general nutrition composition information
- Preparation, packaging, and delivery of feedings for infants
- Importance of documentation
- Continuous quality-improvement activities
- Age-specific competencies (eg, product indications and volume and dilution standards)
- Disaster preparedness program

Contaminated feedings can cause foodborne illness such as diarrhea, necrotizing enterocolitis, pneumonia, and meningitis in enterally fed patients. Training of staff who prepare feedings is designed to minimize risk of colonization in preparation of enteral feedings. Bacterial contamination of enteral feedings is often attributed to faulty handling. Training should include staff who mix feeds as well as nursing staff, and should cover the safe handling and administration of enteral feedings (7,16,40,41). Box 3.2 describes training for personnel in facilities that do not have a feeding preparation room.

BOX 3.2   *Training Requirements for Personnel in Facilities Without a Feeding Preparation Room*

In the event that there is no feeding preparation room, all employees, including nursing staff, who prepare formula and handle human milk, should have documentation of an annual competency in feeding preparation. Topics should include:

- Use of standardized recipes
- Hand hygiene before feeding preparation
- Feeding preparation using aseptic technique
- Labeling requirements for the human milk and formula
- Cleaning techniques
- Inventory control, including removal of expired products
- Proper storage of human milk

Personnel Health Rules   Regulations from the Centers for Disease Control and Prevention (CDC) 1998 guidelines for infection control in health care personnel (20) and the Food and Drug Administration's (FDA) 2009 Food Code (21) should be observed, as should any state and local regulations. All personnel assigned to the infant feeding preparation room should be in good physical health (2). Whether assigned permanently or as relief duty, personnel should be impressed with the extreme susceptibility of infants to certain infections. Staff who have been diagnosed with an illness due to, or as a carrier of, *Salmonella typhi*, *Shigella* species (spp), *E coli O157:H7*, methicillin-resistant *Staphylococcus aureus* (MRSA), vancomycin-resistant *Enterococci* (VRE), or hepatitis A virus should be excluded from working in the infant feeding preparation room and from food handling (2,20,21).

Annual Physical Examinations   Before being assigned to the infant feeding preparation room, the employee should have an annual skin test for tuberculosis and/or a physical examination, according to the health care facility's employee health policies (20).

Routine Illness   Infant feeding preparation room staff should receive instructions to immediately report any illness they experience, however slight, including malaise, fever, gastrointestinal disturbance (particularly vomiting or diarrhea), upper respiratory infection, soreness or inflammation of the mouth or throat, or pustular skin lesions, such as boils or infected, draining wounds. Reporting mechanisms should follow the health care facility's guidelines for food handlers (21). Institution policies should encourage employees to report illness without penalization.

Face masks may be considered during mild respiratory illnesses, in periods of persistent coughing or sneezing, or with a runny nose. Depending on the recommendations of the facility's infection control committee, however, face masks should be changed every 15 to 20 minutes (or more frequently with coughing or sneezing if masks become saturated with moisture) (42,43). Latex-free gloves should be used when handling human milk and when preparing any formula if the technician has open, nondraining wounds on the hands or if the staff member is not able to remove rings. In these cases, latex-free gloves should be changed between batches of human milk, when damaged or visibly soiled, and any time the staff member leaves and reenters the feeding preparation room. Refer to the FDA Food Code for management and personnel specifics (21).

Nonessential Personnel in the Feeding Preparation Room

There should be no casual visitors to the infant feeding preparation room. Distractions should be minimized. During feeding preparation, there should be no admittance of support or allied staff to the infant feeding preparation room. After feeding preparation periods, all personnel entering the room must follow the same cleanliness standards and same dress code as the infant feeding preparation room staff. Eating and drinking should not be allowed in the feeding preparation area.

REFERENCES

1. American Hospital Association. *Procedures and Layout for the Infant Formula Room.* Chicago, IL: American Hospital Association; 1965.
2. Cody MM, Kunkel ME. *Food Safety for Professionals.* 2nd ed. Chicago, IL: American Dietetic Association; 2002.
3. Bankhead R, Boullata J, Brantley S, et al. Enteral nutrition practice recommendations. *JPEN J Parenter Enteral Nutr.* 2009;33:122–167.
4. American Dietetic Association. Emergency Preparedness Task Force. April 2008. Emergency Preparedness—What RDs and DTRs Should Know. http://www.eatright.org/Members/content.aspx?id=2187. Accessed September 28, 2010.
5. Schultz R, Pouletsos C, Combs A. Considerations for emergencies & disasters in the neonatal intensive care unit. *MCN Am J Matern Child Nurs.* 2008;33:204–210; quiz 211–212.
6. Smith SL. Guidelines for safety and quality assurance when preparing infant feedings. *Newborn and Infant Nurs Rev.* 2008;8:101–107.
7. Almeida RCC, Matos CO, Almeida PF. Implementation of a HACCP system for on-site hospital preparation of infant formula. *Food Control.* 1999;10:181–187.

8. American Dietetic Association. Position of the American Dietetic Association: food and water safety. *J Am Diet Assoc.* 2009;109:1449–1460.

9. Roy S, Rigal M, Doit C, et al. Bacterial contamination of enteral nutrition in a paediatric hospital. *J Hosp Infect.* 2005;59:311–316.

10. Barrett JS, Shepherd SJ, Gibson PR. Strategies to manage gastrointestinal symptoms complicating enteral feeding. *JPEN J Parenter Enteral Nutr.* 2009;33:21–26.

11. Forsythe SJ. Enterobacter sakazakii and other bacteria in powdered infant milk formula. *Matern Child Nutr.* 2005;1:44–50.

12. Arias ML, Monge R, Chavéz C. Microbiological contamination of enteral feeding solutions used in Costa Rican hospitals. *Arch Latinoam Nutr.* 2003;53:277–281.

13. Missouri Department of Health and Senior Services. Disaster/emergency preparedness plan draft 4/19/07, ER# 3.00500. http://www.dhss.mo.gov/WIC/WICupdates/Attachments/DisasterPreparednessPlanLWPs.doc. Accessed December 21, 2010.

14. McCabe-Sellers BJ, Beattie SE. Food safety: emerging trends in foodborne illness surveillance and prevention. *J Am Diet Assoc.* 2004;104:1708–1717.

15. McClusky KW. Implementing hazard analysis critical control points. *J Am Diet Assoc.* 2004;104:1699–1700.

16. Best C. Enteral tube feeding and infection control: how safe is our practice? *Br J Nurs.* 2008;17:1036, 1038–1041.

17. Ruchlin HS, Leveson I. Measuring hospital productivity. *Health Serv Res.* 1974;9:308–323.

18. Puckett RR, Connell BC, Dahl MK, Jackson R, McClusky KW, American Dietetic Association. Practice paper of the American Dietetic Association: a systems approach to measuring productivity in health care food service operations. *J Am Diet Assoc.* 2005;105:122–130.

19. *Measuring Employee Productivity: Data Collection and Analysis Methods for Productivity Studies at Intel.* Santa Clara, CA: Intel Information Technology; 2004.

20. Boyard E, Tablan O, Williams W, et al. Guideline for infection control in health care personnel, 1998. *Am J Infect Control.* 1998;26:291–354.

21. US Food and Drug Administration. FDA Food Code 2009. http://www.fda.gov/Food/FoodSafety/RetailFood Protection/FoodCode/FoodCode2009/default.htm. Accessed September 7, 2010.

22. Burns S. A multiple evaluation study on artificial nails. *J Nurs Qual Assur.* 1988;2:77–79.

23. Wong E. The epidemiology of contact transmission: beyond Semmelweis. *Infect Control Hosp Epidemiol.* 2000;21:77–79.

24. Edel E, Houston S, Kennedy V, LaRocco M. Impact of a five-minute scrub on the microbial flora found on artificial, polished or natural fingernails of operating room personnel. *Nurs Res.* 1998;12:605–609.

25. Pottinger J, Burns S, Manske C. Bacterial carriage by artificial versus natural nails. *Am J Infect Control.* 1998;17:340–344.

26. Wynd CA, Samstag DE, Lapp AM. Bacterial carriage on the fingernails of OR nurses. *AORN J.* 1994;60:799–805.

27. Moolenaar RL, Crutcher JM, San Joaquin VH, et al. A prolonged outbreak of Pseudomonas aeruginosa in a neonatal intensive care unit: did staff fingernails play a role in disease transmission? *Infect Control Hosp Epidemiol.* 2000;21:80–85.

28. Mathus-Vliegen LM, Binnekade JM, de Hann RJ. Bacterial contamination of ready-to-use 1-L feeding bottles and administration sets in severely compromised intensive care patients. *Crit Care Med.* 2000;28:67–73.

29. Larson EL, Eke PI, Wilder MP, Laughon BE. Quantity of soap as a variable in handwashing. *Infect Control.* 1987;8:371–375.

30. Larson E. A causal link between handwashing and risk of infection? Examination of the evidence. *Infect Control Hosp Epidemiol.* 1988;9:28–36.

31. Karabey S, Ay P, Derbentli S, Nakipoglu Y, Esen F. Handwashing frequencies in an intensive care unit. *J Hosp Infect.* 2002;50:36–41.

32. Agostoni C, Axelsson I, Goulet O, et al. Preparation and handling of powdered infant formula: a commentary by the ESPGHAN Committee on Nutrition. *J Pediatr Gastroenterol Nutr.* 2004;39:320–322.

33. Anderton A, Aidoo KE. Decanting--a source of contamination of enteral feeds? *Clin Nutr.* 1990;9:157–162.

34. Padula CA, Kenny A, Planchon C, Lamoureux C. Enteral feedings: what the evidence says. *Am J Nurs*. 2004;104:62–69; quiz 70.

35. Schroeder P, Fisher D, Volz M, Paloucek J. Microbial contamination of enteral feeding solutions in a community hospital. *JPEN J Parenter Enteral Nutr*. 1983;7:354–368.

36. Centers for Disease Control and Prevention. Guidelines for hand hygiene in health-care settings: recommendations of the Healthcare Infection Control Practices Advisory committee and the HICPAD/SHEA/APIC/IDSA Hand Hygiene Task Force. *MMWR Morb Mortal Wkly Rep*. 2002;51:1–58.

37. Lawrence J. Home nursing. In: Lawrence J, ed. *Infection Control in the Community*. Philadelphia, PA: Elsevier Health Sciences; 2003:77–102.

38. Tudela E, Croize J, Lagier A, Mallaret MR. [Microbiological monitoring of milk samples and surface samples in a hospital infant formula room]. *Pathol Biol (Paris)*. 2008;56:272–278.

39. Matlow A, Wray R, Goldman C, Streitenberger L, Freeman R, Kovach D. Microbial contamination of enteral feed administration sets in a pediatric institution. *Am J Infect Control*. 2003;31:49–53.

40. Okuma T, Nakamura M, Totake H, Fukunaga Y. Microbial contamination of enteral feeding formulas and diarrhea. *Nutrition*. 2000;16:719–722.

41. McKinlay J, Wildgoose A, Wood W, Gould I, Anderton A. The effect of system design on bacterial contamination of enteral tube feeds. *J Hosp Infect*. 2001;47:138–142.

42. McLure HA, Talboys CA, Yentis SM, Azadian BS. Surgical face masks and downward dispersal of bacteria. *Anaesthesia*. 1998;53:624–626.

43. Black SR, Weinstein RA. The case for face masks—Zorro or zero? *Clin Infect Dis*. 2000;31:522–523.

Appendix 3-A

Sample Position Description: Infant Feeding Room Supervisor

Title

Feeding Preparation Room Supervisor

Position Summary

Under the direction of the administrative professional with expertise in feeding preparation room management: supervises, delegates, and coordinates the work of the infant feeding preparation room technician(s); ensures product integrity and safety through proper training and quality control. Develops, implements, and monitors compliance with policies and procedures, to comply with all regulating agencies and state laws and in accordance with the policies of the health care facility.

Key Responsibilities

1. Supervises daily operations of the infant feeding preparation room
    a. Maintains appropriate staffing for daily activities
    b. Handles disciplinary actions and solves problems
    c. Monitors inventory management
    d. Manages and monitors product formulary
    e. Performs employee evaluations

2. Develops, implements, and evaluates training program
   a. Employee training/orientation
   b. Evaluation and documentation of competencies/skills checklist
   c. Continuing education/in-service programs
   d. Conducts parent teaching programs
   e. Assists with student-supervised practice experiences

3. Reviews feeding orders for compliance with institution's ordering standards
   a. Reviews and revises enteral feeding order form used in the medical record
   b. Reviews computer-generated orders

4. Develops and monitors quality assurance activities
   a. Establishes written guidelines for the infant feeding preparation room
   b. Develops and implements an HACCP process for enteral feedings and establishes a monitoring system of the critical control points
   c. Ensures that equipment is in proper working order
   d. Conducts mock disaster drills for emergency preparedness

Appendix 3-B

Sample Position Description: Infant Feeding Room Technician

Title

Infant Feeding Room Technician

Position Summary

The infant feeding preparation room technician is responsible for the preparation and delivery of all infant feedings. Preparation techniques must adhere to all sanitary regulations and standards established by regulating agencies and the health care facility, which should include compliance with policies related to the institution's HACCP plan for enteral feedings. Duties include:

1. Maintaining adequate supplies that meet patient needs
2. Operating all equipment needed to prepare feedings for infants
3. Maintaining sanitation in the preparation room
4. Filing temperature records and feeding orders
5. Securing the feeding preparation room
6. Assisting with the training of ancillary personnel as necessary

Contact with Others

The infant feeding room technician will regularly interact with dietitians, nurses, patient care unit secretaries, housekeeping personnel, pharmacists, physicians, transportation staff, and parents.

Key Responsibilities

1. Prepares and delivers all infant feedings as ordered
   a. Verifies new or questionable infant feedings orders with a registered dietitian for accuracy and obtains standardized recipes as needed
   b. Prepares infant formula accurately according to established written formulations, following pre-established feeding preparation procedures and adhering to quality control standards
   c. Uses correct and accurate technique to measure powders and liquids
   d. Stores prepared infant feedings properly until delivery to the patient area
   e. Delivers prepared infant feedings to patient area refrigerators
   f. Maintains daily records of patient profiles or updates computerized patient profile regarding infant formula orders
   g. Uses clinical information system to update patient feeding orders and to print labels and production lists; communicates with allied health care personnel regarding feeding orders
   h. Completes daily batch records for prepared feedings
   i. Maintains a daily log of refrigeration and heating equipment temperatures, including refrigerators in the patient care unit
   j. Removes unused, previously prepared infant feedings from patient area refrigerators 24 hours after preparation time and discards according to established protocol

2. Inventories and maintains sufficient infant feeding room stock
   a. Completes daily tally or census sheets indicating formulas prepared
   b. Prepares storeroom or purchasing requisition for all infant formula, glassware, bottles, enteral feeding bags, nipples, and other supplies, as needed, to maintain adequate supply levels
   c. Orders products and supplies and notifies supervisor of any shortages
   d. Orders all enteral feeding products from an approved and reliable vendor
   e. Checks expiration dates on products
   f. Reports to supervisor when short-dated products are received from vendor
   g. Follows procedures for formula recalls at the direction of the supervisor

3. Maintains sanitation in preparation area
   a. Cleans and sanitizes all work surfaces in the infant feedings preparation room before and after each feeding preparation
   b. Cleans utensils, equipment, and storage areas used in the infant feeding preparation room according to established procedures
   c. Follows aseptic technique
   d. Follows department and infection control policies regarding feeding handling
   e. When appropriate, prepares samples for bacteria check according to established protocol
   f. Maintains daily appearance and personal hygiene according to departmental guidelines
   g. Reports to appropriate supervisor if ill

4. Calculates new formulations or standardized recipes manually or via the use of specifically designed software, and obtains verification of those formulations with the registered dietitian responsible for the nutrition care of that patient, as needed per protocol

5. Checks equipment for proper operation and reports problems to the appropriate supervisor

6. Assists in training other employees in infant feeding preparation and proper handling techniques, as needed
7. Communicates with patient's registered dietitian, nurse, physician, or unit manager regarding problems with feeding orders, formula storage, or administration
8. Prepares and maintains patient care unit batch or log sheets of prepared and dispensed feedings
9. Prepares monthly quality assurance report and production summaries
10. Performs additional duties as assigned

Appendix 3-C

Sample Competency Assessment Tool for Infant Feeding Room Technician

1. How many calories per ounce is the standard dilution for an infant formula?
    a. 15
    b. 20
    c. 24
    d. 30

2. Which of the following is not a commercially available form of infant formula?
    a. Ready-to-feed
    b. Powdered
    c. Half-strength
    d. Concentrate

3. A blender should be used whenever possible to make sure the ingredients are well mixed.
    a. True
    b. False

4. Which of the following needs to be included on the feeding label?
    a. Patient name and medical record number
    b. Room and bed number
    c. Feeding name and any additives
    d. Expiration date and time
    e. All of these

5. What is the expiration time for prepared feedings from the initial mixing time?

    _____

6. When do you need to wash your hands? Wear gloves? Wear a mask? Use a new gown?

    _____

7. When discarding expired feeding for a particular patient, you note that you are throwing out most of the volume prepared for the third day in a row. What should you do? _____

8. While mixing a batch of powdered formula, you notice a yellow-orange oily layer that will not mix into the formula. What should you do? _____

9. How often is the refrigerator cleaned and what do you use to clean it? What do you do with any items currently in the refrigerator? _____

10. If you receive a feeding order that you do not understand or for a product not on the formulary, what do you do? _____

11. If you have a bottle of human milk with a label that you cannot read clearly, what should you do?

    _____

Appendix 3-D

Demonstration Checklist

1. Demonstrate proper use of all equipment in the feeding preparation area, which may include, but is not limited to, the following:
    a. Gram scale
    b. Graduated cylinder or beaker
    c. Syringe
    d. Preparing a formula (from powder and concentrate) and labeling it
    e. Verification of human milk labels
    f. Dishwasher
    g. Other: _____

2. Give the recipe to prepare the following three orders. Tell which container you would use to deliver the feeding to the patient care unit. Prepare a label for the container.
    Example A: _____
    Example B: _____
    Example C: _____

3. Demonstrate how you would mix a feeding (use an order that will demonstrate familiarity with products, weighing and measuring skills, mixing technique, use of aseptic technique, proper labeling, and storage).

Chapter 4

Expressed Human Milk

Rachelle Lessen, MS, RD, IBCLC, and Amy Sapsford, RD, CSP, CLE

Except under rare circumstances, human milk is the preferred feeding for all infants, including those who are premature and hospitalized (1–7). The American Dietetic Association (ADA) and the American Academy of Pediatrics (AAP) recommend exclusive breastfeeding for the first 6 months of life and continued breastfeeding for at least the first year and beyond as long as desired by mother and child (1,2). The AAP, the World Health Organization (WHO), and the United Nations Children's Fund (UNICEF) support the Baby-Friendly Hospital Initiative, which promotes exclusive breastfeeding. Their 10 steps to successful breastfeeding have been outlined (8,9). Breastfeeding is supported by the Surgeon General (10,11) and Healthy People 2010, and the proposed 2020 objectives include increasing the proportion of mothers who breastfeed their babies (12,13).

Facilities providing maternity services for care of healthy newborns should be encouraged to adhere to published recommendations. Facilities providing care for high-risk newborns transferred by delivery hospitals should identify mothers who wish to provide milk for their infants within the first 24 hours in order to give these women the support they need to establish their milk supply. In addition, the Joint Commission has added exclusive human milk feeding as a measure for the expanded Perinatal Care measure set (14). Mothers of premature or high-risk newborns should be offered support and guidance to provide milk for their infants, even if they are not able to directly breastfeed. Benefits for use of human milk and clinical management of lactation have been described by the US Department of Health and Human Services and others (15–17).

Information is available on the development of a hospital-based lactation program and "mother's own" milk bank (18). Promotion and support of breastfeeding for vulnerable infants in pediatric health care institutions have been described as well (19,20). Lactation services may have a substantial impact on breastfeeding rates in the special care nursery, resulting in an increase in human milk feeding (18,21). Evidence-based interventions for hospitalized infants with medical problems have been described (22). Practice guidelines to support the use of human milk in hospitalized infants have been published (23,24).

Expression of Human Milk

Mothers of infants who are hospitalized must use hand or mechanical expression to establish and maintain their milk supply if their infants are unable to breastfeed (2,25–27). It is essential that mothers receive sufficient stimulation of the breast from either the baby or a breast pump in the first 2 weeks after delivery to produce an adequate milk supply (28). Expression of the milk should begin as soon as possible, usually within the first 6 hours following birth (17). Mothers are encouraged to use a hospital-grade electric breast pump that provides automatic intermittent suction with a double setup because this helps establish and maintain a sufficient milk supply. Hand massage and expression have been shown to be a useful adjunct to the use of an electric breast pump (29). Such pumping helps to express milk with maximum fat content. Ideally, mothers should express milk every 2 to 3 hours during the day and night, or at least 8 times in 24 hours, which approximates the feeding pattern of a newborn (17). This schedule is not always practical for some mothers who have been ill or who are enduring the stress of their infant being in an intensive care setting. Neonatal intensive care unit (NICU) mothers may need a lot of encouragement and support for this effort.

Hospital-grade electric breast pumps should be available for use by mothers while their infants are in the hospital. In addition, hospital staff should assist mothers with obtaining an appropriate breast pump for use at home, either through a hospital-based rental station; loaner program; Special Supplemental Nutrition Program for Women, Infants, and Children (WIC); independent rental station; or through their insurance provider (19,30). Objective independent evaluations of breast pump effectiveness, safety, acceptability, effect on milk composition, and cost implication are limited because most published research is funded by manufacturers (26). Research and technology continue to evolve to improve milk production and expression and to individualize it for specific situations. For example, a unique pumping pattern has been developed for mothers who initiate pumping at birth in the hospital setting. Additionally, new two-phase expression pumps first stimulate milk flow with fast and light expression and then move into the expression phase, which is slower with more vacuum (31). This two-phase pumping pattern was found to be as efficient and effective as single-phase pumping and was reported to be more comfortable and preferred by pump-dependent mothers of low-birth-weight infants (32). Other hospital-grade electric breast pumps that cycle with negative pressure and a rhythmic action are available.

Each mother should be given her own personal sterile or commercially clean collection kit to use with the pump. Use of a double kit, which allows the mother to express milk from both breasts at the same time, saves time and increases prolactin levels, leading to increased milk production (17). It is advisable and cost-effective for mothers to receive a reusable double kit; however, single-pump kits and disposable kits are also available. Hospitals should establish written policies for in-hospital sterilization of the kits in the event that the mother is unable to sterilize her kit daily at home. In-hospital sterilization may be achieved by sending the kit for sterile processing. There are also commercial products available to sterilize breast pump kits. One type of product uses steam generated in a special bag placed in a microwave oven. There are also special antibacterial wipes that are safe for use with the kit. Small electric and battery-operated pumps, hand pumps, and purchased double electric pumps should not be used exclusively by mothers of hospitalized infants. Hospital grade pumps are recommended for long-term use to establish and maintain milk supply; however, staff may need to be flexible in their recommendations if mothers do not have exclusive access to hospital grade pumps and must use either a manual pump or a pump designed for single users. It should be noted, however, that single user pumps cannot be adequately cleaned or sanitized because they lack backflow protection, and could lead to contamination of the milk. Multiple users should never share them.

The advantages of having a mother pump at the bedside are numerous. Women often are anxious about leaving their infant for 15 to 20 minutes every 2 to 3 hours to pump. This anxiety can inhibit the hormones that control milk production, and the mother may produce less milk. Milk expression in the hospital can take place in a designated private pumping room in a central location, in or adjacent to the patient care unit, or with the use of a portable pump on a trolley at the bedside. Skin-to-skin contact with the infant has been shown to increase milk production (33,34). Being close to the baby while pumping can promote maternal feelings and will help the mother relax, which helps facilitate milk flow. Mothers may also be inclined to pump more often if they do not have to leave their babies. Caregivers can assist the mother by providing privacy screens as well as by minimizing stressful noise at the bedside. Other strategies for overcoming barriers to breastfeeding in the NICU have been described (24,35). It is recommended that staff and mothers have easy, convenient access to pumps. Some mother/baby units or NICUs have their own supply of pumps stored in the unit. Large pediatric hospitals may benefit from central distribution of a large supply of pumps, similar to other pumps such as intravenous (IV), medication, or feeding pumps. Some NICUs provide a breast pump at each bedside, encouraging and facilitating mothers supplying human milk.

If mothers choose to pump in a more private environment, such as a separate pumping room, their wishes should be supported. These rooms need not be elaborate, but they do require careful planning and maintenance to ensure cleanliness and access to needed supplies. Examples of supplying a lactation room include the following suggestions:

- One or more hospital-grade electric pumps
- Appropriate cleaner for sanitizing the pump between uses
- Human milk storage containers
- Labels
- Hand-hygiene products
- Dishwashing soap
- Paper towels
- A comfortable chair or chairs for family members
- A table
- A sink
- Trash can
- Educational materials related to lactation
- A clock
- Telephone
- Signage to notify others that the room is occupied
- Appropriate lighting
- Privacy lock for the door
- Staff call system

Optional equipment may include a radio, television and video player, reading material, bulletin board, a mirror, pillows and pillowcases, foot rest, drinking water, breast pads, and linens. The room should be cleaned on a regular basis, including sanitization of the area around the pump as well as the pump itself. Mothers should be encouraged to clean the pump before they use it. The facility's biomedical engineering department must check electric breast pumps at least once a year, whenever they are not working properly, or if human milk accidentally enters the pump itself in an internal piston pump.

Parent Education

Mothers should be instructed, both in writing and verbally, about appropriate pumping technique. A log book, journal, or pumping diary provided by the hospital helps mothers monitor the frequency of their milk expressions and their daily milk production. Breast pumping and feeding logs or diaries may include: date, time, volume and minutes of pumping, volume goals, duration of breastfeeding session on each breast, wet diapers, stools, and formula supplement needed, if any. The following parent education information should be provided:

- Mothers should clean the hospital breast pump with an approved sanitizing agent before each use.
- Mothers should thoroughly wash their hands with soap and water before pumping to reduce the potential for contamination of their milk.
- Mothers do not need to clean the breast before pumping (36). In fact, unnecessary breast cleansing before pumping may lead to skin breakdown, which can provide a site for infection.
- Mothers should pump a minimum of 8 times in 24 hours to establish and maintain lactation. Use of massage and warm compresses may be beneficial for milk expression (23,37).
- Mothers should use a new container each time they pump to avoid adding warm milk to already refrigerated or frozen milk. This minimizes risk of contamination (28). Expressing milk directly into the storage container further reduces the risk of touch contamination.
- Containers designed specifically for colostrum may be used for small volumes collected in the first few days of lactation, whether the baby is premature or term.
- Mothers should not fill the bottle completely, allowing head space for freezing so that the bottle will not break or open.
- Mothers expressing milk for very-low-birth-weight (VLBW) infants may be advised to store small quantities of milk in multiple bottles to avoid waste and potential touch contamination from the nurses' hands (23).
- Mothers should pump for an additional 2 minutes after the milk flow stops to ensure that the breast is fully emptied.
- Collection kits should be cleaned after each use with soap and hot water and allowed to air dry on clean paper towels.
- Daily sterilization of parts of the collection kit that touch the milk is suggested. Kits can be sterilized by using a commercially available sterilizing bag, a special antibacterial wipe made for breast pump kits, boiling for 15 minutes, or washing in a dishwasher with a sanitation cycle. Sterilization is especially important for kits used by mothers of hospitalized infants (38).

Storage Containers

Human milk expressed for a mother's own infant in the hospital should be stored in a container that is suitable for food storage. Glass or food-grade plastic containers, such as those made from polypropylene (PP) (cloudy, hard plastic), are acceptable (36). Other plastics that are safe for food storage include polyethylene terephthalate (PETE) and high-density polyethylene (HDPE). Containers or bottles made of polycarbonate contain Bisphenol A (BPA or Bis A), a substance that may pose health risks. The Food and Drug Administration (FDA) is recommending reducing exposure to BPA (39,40). Bottles made with BPA should not be boiled or heated in the microwave or dishwasher because repeated exposure to high heat may cause the BPA to leach out (41). In addition, the plastics used to store human milk must withstand freezing for months at a time. Plastic containers not labeled as food grade, such as urine cups and centrifuge tubes, should not be used to store human milk.

Either sterile or aseptic containers may be used (36,42). Products are made sterile when manufacturers use sterilization processes such as gamma irradiation or ethylene oxide gas. Gamma irradiation results in no residue, and the product can be used immediately after sterilization. Use of ethylene oxide gas sterilization requires a period of time to allow the gas to be removed from the product (43).

Because expressed human milk is not sterile, the goal should be to minimize the risk for the growth of microbes and further contamination in order to provide the safest milk to infants, who are most at risk for infection. The containers should have a cap that provides an airtight seal to reduce the risk of contamination; a nipple is not a sufficient barrier (36). Risk can be further reduced if the milk is expressed using a collection kit that allows the milk to be expressed directly into the container in which it will be stored. Many commercially available storage containers are made with a universal thread so that the milk can be pumped directly into the storage container. Hard plastic or glass containers show the least loss of immunologic factors during storage, with glass seeming to maintain concentrations better than some plastics (25). The effects of the storage container type on the nutrient content of the expressed human milk have been summarized (25). Acceptable containers specifically made for human milk storage are available from various vendors (see Appendix 4-A).

Most hospitals provide new storage containers to mothers each time they express their milk. If mothers reuse their own human milk storage containers made from food-grade plastic, the containers should be carefully sterilized, following the same directions as those used for the collection kits. Milk should be stored in appropriate-size containers to prevent having to discard milk that has been thawed and not used. Smaller containers, holding 25 to 30 mL, with curved bottoms are available for use in the first few days of pumping for storing colostrum. Mothers gain confidence in their ability to produce adequate milk when they see that they are filling a small container. The curved bottom allows the milk to be easily removed with a syringe. They can transition to pumping into 60- to 80-mL containers as their milk volumes increase. Mothers who are filling more than one 60- to 80-mL container per breast at each pumping should express their milk into larger 120- to 240-mL containers so all the milk from one breast is expressed into one container, thus avoiding having the first bottle contain lower fat foremilk and the second bottle contain higher fat hindmilk. The mother can then pour the expressed milk into the appropriate size containers for storage.

Storage bags specifically designed for human milk are suitable for storing human milk for infants at home but not in the hospital. Storage bags do not provide a closed system, are prone to tearing and leaking, and are difficult to manage during human milk preparation. If the mother has already collected her milk in storage bags, they should be stored in the freezer in a double-zipped food storage bag, to be used in the hospital when no other human milk is available. Care must be taken to avoid contamination or spilling in the refrigerator where other milk is stored. Mothers should be instructed to use rigid human milk storage containers instead of storage bags. A policy should be developed to support this practice. The disposable polyethylene bags meant for formula feeding from bottles are not recommended for storage of milk for infants in the hospital. There may be increased loss of fat and fat-soluble vitamins with the polyethylene bags (28,44).

Labeling of Human Milk

Appropriate labeling of human milk stored in the hospital is essential to prevent errors in human milk delivery. The human milk stored in the hospital must be labeled with the following information:

- Infant's name
- Medical record/Identification number

- Date and time milk expressed
- Medications or supplements being taken by the mother
- The expiration date and time
- Any fortifiers added and caloric density
- If milk is pasteurized donor milk, this should be noted

Hospitals have developed novel approaches to labeling human milk. Unique identifiers such as bar codes, special colors, or alerts may be used to further identify the human milk. Hospitals may use either computer-generated or handwritten labels with duplicate information. If a mother is expressing milk and separating the foremilk from the hindmilk or making reduced-fat milk, this information may also be noted on the label. Some facilities also identify colostrum, transitional, or mature milk by using specially colored stickers and numbering the colostrum so it can be fed to the infant in the order it was expressed (28,45,46). Some units use basic labels; others use computerized labels. The latter may have bar code capabilities, or they may be formatted for placement in the chart to document milk that was fed. Computerized labels may sometimes be designed to track inventory (47–49). Nurses, designated hospital staff, or family members should double-check labels on milk prior to feeding to avoid the risk of feeding the wrong mother's human milk to an infant.

Transporting Milk

Mothers often express their milk at home and transport it to the hospital for storage and feeding to the infant. It is essential that milk remain chilled or frozen during transport. Hamosh et al reported that fresh, never-frozen milk stored in insulated bags with blue ice or gel bags can be safely maintained at 10°C to 15°C (50°F to 59°F) for 24 hours with relatively low rates of growth of primarily nonpathogenic bacteria; however, every effort should be made to keep the milk between 2°C and 6°C (35°F and 43°F) (50). Storage at room temperature of 25°C (77° F) should be limited to no more than 4 hours for hospitalized infants. Higher temperatures of 38°C (100°F) are not safe for storing milk even for 4 hours because bacterial growth is excessive at this temperature.

It is preferable to transport milk in a chilled state rather than frozen if the fresh milk can be readily used for the infant's feedings. If a mother is visiting the hospital daily, she can store her expressed milk in her home refrigerator until she visits the hospital. Otherwise, human milk should be frozen at home, transported frozen, and stored in the hospital freezer if the infant is unlikely to be able to use the fresh milk within 48 hours of expression. If extensive thawing occurs, the milk should be used within 24 hours or discarded. Rechtman et al report that milk that has undergone up to three repeated freeze-thaw cycles did not have higher microbial counts, suggesting that milk accidently thawed in the refrigerator for up to 8 hours may be safely refrozen (51). There was loss of as much as 50% of vitamin C. The six different milk samples tested had low colonization initially (10×1) and were still well (10×2) within guidelines for colonization of milk with nonpathogenic bacteria (51). In contrast, when Landers and Updegrove looked at 303 pools and 810 individual samples of frozen donor milk, 62% grew at least one gram-negative rod and many grew more than one species (52). Colonization load ranged from 10×1 to 8.6×4. Gram-negative rods are commonly pathogens, and not allowed in commercial milk supply. Pasteurizing effectively kills these organisms. Any protocol for refreezing unpasteurized milk used in health care facilities for immunocompromised infants should ensure that there is adequate control of the time milk is thawed and the number of refreezing cycles that are acceptable (52). To preserve the safety and quality of the milk, it is imperative that milk remains cold at all times and is labeled that it has been refrozen.

Milk that is transported to or from the hospital in a frozen state should be tightly packed in an insulated bag or a cooler without ice. A clean towel, newspaper, or foam beads can be used to fill dead air space (36). Because milk freezes at a lower temperature than water, ice is warmer than frozen milk and may actually thaw frozen containers of milk. Freezer gel packs are acceptable because they have a lower freezing temperature. Some centers report that wrapping frozen containers of milk in newspaper and packing them tightly in an insulated cooler will maintain a frozen state when traveling long distances by car or plane with the milk. If frozen milk will be in transit for more than 18 hours, it should be packed in a sturdy insulated container with dry ice (36). This will prevent milk from partial thawing and will minimize bacterial growth and deterioration of nutrient qualities (51). Careful handling of dry ice is required. Gloves can be worn to protect hands from frostbite, and tongs can be used to remove bottles of milk from dry ice. Only non-airtight Styrofoam containers should be used, to allow the escape of carbon dioxide gas. The dry ice should be allowed to evaporate in a safe well-ventilated space away from children and pets, and not disposed of in a sink or toilet. Some shipping companies limit dry ice to 5 pounds per container and will not be responsible for perishable goods. It is advisable for families to check policies of shipping companies or airlines before packing and transporting their milk. Special shipping labels may be needed.

A mechanism should be in place to ensure that milk is not left behind in the patient care unit when the infant is discharged to home or transferred to another facility. The bedside nurse, lactation consultant, or other designated hospital personnel should be aware that discharge is pending. Arrangements to safely transport the milk should be discussed with the family. This may include travel by plane, travel by car, or shipping with a commercial transport company. Families should be prepared to freeze the milk upon arrival at their home. Another option is for the mother to arrange to have her milk donated to a Human Milk Banking Association of North America (HMBANA) milk bank. The donor mother will need to contact the milk bank and be approved as a donor before the milk can be sent to the milk bank. Hospital staff may be able to help facilitate a milk donation.

Refrigeration and Freezing

Some sources suggest the use of dedicated freezers and refrigerators for storing human milk (36). Care should always be taken that any mother's fresh or frozen milk is not mixed with any other human milk, formula, or food source. As long as human milk is stored so that there is no spillage or dripping of thawing milk, it can be considered acceptably stored. One approach is to store human milk and infant formula in closed containers with lids in the same refrigerator, with human milk segregated and labeled in bins or resealable bags by patient and labeled with two identifiers such as name and medical record number. Local regulatory agency guidelines may supersede these guidelines. There is no federal government guideline on this issue to date. The Occupational Safety and Health Administration (OSHA) has stated that human milk does not constitute occupational exposure, based on lack of any evidence that any health care worker has acquired a viral infection via human milk (53). Still, as a precaution common to any body fluid handling, it is recommended that health care workers wear gloves when handling human milk. Because workers in milk banks have greater exposure to unpasteurized milk, they should consider wearing gloves.

Refrigerators and freezers must be cleaned regularly by hospital staff, and spilled milk should be promptly wiped up using a sanitizing wipe. Milk in the freezer and refrigerator should be stored in a separate bin for each breastfeeding mother to avoid misadministration of the feeding. Milk from mothers of multiples can be stored in the same bin and each bottle labeled with the names and medical record numbers of all multiples from the same mother so the milk can be fed to these infants. All bins should be clearly labeled with infant identifiers such as name and/or medical record number. To avoid mix-ups, bins should be specially flagged to alert health care workers when there is more than one infant in the unit with the same or similar surname. Stackable bins with lids are convenient to maximize storage space. Bins can be reused and should be thoroughly cleaned with soap and water and disinfectant and sanitized before being assigned to a new mother. Containers of milk within the bins should be organized by date so that the oldest milk is in the front of the bin to be used first. The hospital staff is responsible for storing and administering human milk to avoid any mix-ups among patients. Staff should inform parents when supplies are low so that mothers can bring stored milk from home.

Parents who are storing milk outside the hospital must be informed of possible adverse effects on the milk from less-than-optimal freezing temperatures in home freezer-refrigerator units. Milk stored at home will have a shorter shelf life than milk stored in a –20°C (–4°F) hospital or commercial freezer.

Unexpected thawing and loss of milk can occur when hospital freezers malfunction or the freezer door is not closed properly. An alarm triggered by temperatures greater than a safe level can be connected to the hospital's security system to prevent unnecessary loss of frozen milk. Installing freezers so that they are tilted slightly backward will help the doors close automatically. Temperatures should be checked regularly to ensure that refrigerator temperature is ≤ 4°C (≤ 40°F) and freezer temperature is at –20°C (–4°F). Some facilities elect to use colder freezers that maintain –70°C (–94°F). Hospital units should be plugged into the emergency power supply to prevent thawing during a power failure.

Recommendations for length of storage of human milk are described for home use for healthy full-term infants (54–56). Research on storage of human milk for hospitalized infants is limited. Refer to Table 4.1.

TABLE 4.1 *Recommendations for Human Milk Storage for Hospitalized Infants*

Storage Method	Recommended Storage Time
Freezer (home unit combined with refrigerator)	3 mo
Freezer (–20°C, –4°F)	6–12 mo
Freezer (–70°C, –94°F)	≥ 12 mo
Refrigerator (4°C, 40°F), fresh milk	48 h[a]
Refrigerator (4°C, 40°F), thawed milk	24 h
Refrigerator (4°C, 40°F), fortified milk	24 h
Refrigerator (4°C, 40°F), thawed pasteurized donor milk	48 h
Cooler with ice packs (15°C, 59°F), fresh milk	24 h
Room temperature (25°C, 77°F)	≤ 4 h

[a]Fresh milk that is unit-dosed at time of expression may be held at refrigerated temperatures for up to 96 hours if expressed under clean conditions and the container is not entered prior to infant feeding. This is particularly important for small volume, fresh milk feedings for ill or preterm high-risk infants.

A hospital policy on access to human milk freezers and refrigerators is recommended. When there are individual refrigerators or freezers in private rooms, parents are usually able to access their own infant's milk freely. When a patient care unit uses a community refrigeration or freezer storage system, it is recommended that access be limited to staff, in order to promote security of the milk. Facility staff has a responsibility to avoid human milk misadministration. Parents should not have access to human milk that does not belong to their infant.

Although milk should be fed to the baby as soon as possible after expression, fresh milk can be safely stored in the refrigerator for up to 48 hours. There is a recent report of a longer acceptable refrigerator storage time of 96 hours if the milk is only accessed once daily in an NICU setting. The authors found no significant changes in osmolality, total and gram-negative bacterial colony counts, or concentrations of sIgA, lactoferrin, or total fat (57). Milk pH, white blood cell count, total protein concentration, and total gram-positive colony counts decreased over 96 hours of refrigerator storage (57). There was a 3-fold increase in the concentration of free fatty acids during refrigerator storage due to active lipolysis. Milk retained an active host defense system as indicated by a decrease in gram-positive colony counts and no increase in gram-negative colony counts. Data also exist to support longer refrigerator storage of expressed human milk for healthy, term infants (54,58).

Numerous studies (25,44,59–62) have found that human milk can be safely refrigerated at 4°C (40°F) without any appreciable growth of bacteria. Pardou et al (59) found that refrigeration for up to 8 days has a greater inhibitory effect on bacteria than freezing. In fact, Pardou found that bacterial growth of lightly and heavily contaminated milk decreases over 24 hours at 4°C (40°F). Others (63) have found that the bacterial colony counts of expressed refrigerated milk decreased throughout a 5-day period. Martinez-Costa et al (64) found that human milk possesses bactericidal activity that remains stable during the first 48 hours of refrigeration, but is significantly reduced after 72 hours (64,65). Recommendations of 48 hours for refrigerator storage of human milk are within a bacteriologically safe range, even when taking into account variability in home refrigerator temperatures, collection techniques, and transport (65). Hamosh et al (50) reported that bacterial growth of milk was restricted to non-pathogens, such as *Lactobacilli*, and was minimal at 24 hours at 15°C (59°F), the approximate temperature of a cooler with ice packs. However, maintaining the safe food-handling temperature of 2°C to 6°C (35°F to 43°F) is always preferable. At 25°C (77°F), bacterial growth was low for the first 4 to 8 hours, and milk used within this time frame is considered safe. At 38°C (100°F), bacterial growth was considerable even at 4 hours, and storage at this temperature is not recommended for any length of time.

Cellular activity is greatly reduced at 0°C to 4°C (32°F to 40°F) for 48 hours. The number of macrophages and neutrophils is decreased, but the number of lymphocytes remains the same. Lactose, lipids, oligosaccharides, lactoferrin, lysozyme, and IgA are stable at refrigerator temperatures of 4°C (40°F) (25).

Major milk proteins are relatively stable for 24 to 48 hours at low or moderate temperatures because of minimal proteolysis during storage. The digestive enzymes lipase and amylase are stable at 24 hours. In contrast with the stability of milk proteins, milk fats are readily hydrolyzed into free fatty acids during storage. Accumulation of free fatty acids in human milk increases with the length of storage and with increased storage temperatures (66). This rapid lipolysis results in free fatty acids and monoglycerides, which have been shown to have antiviral, antimicrobial, and antiprotozoan effects, and it most likely prevents growth of microorganisms in stored milk.

The effect of freezing on milk constituents has been studied by many investigators. Lipolysis of milk fats occurs because lipoprotein lipase and bile salt–stimulated lipase remain active at –20°C (–4°F). At lower temperatures of –70°C (–94°F), only minimal lipolysis occurs (67). Lipolysis of milk fat that continues to occur during freezer storage may result in smells ranging from slightly soapy to rancid. Infants often are not bothered by this change in taste and smell, and it is not harmful. Three months of freezing was found to cause minimal loss of biologic activity in human milk. After 3 months of freezer storage at –20°C (–4°F), there was no significant change in lactoferrin, lysozyme, IgA, IgG, or C3 (67). The effects of refrigeration, freezing, and thawing on antioxidant activity have been described (68,69).

Home refrigerator-freezer units and some hospital freezers do not approach –20°C (–4°F) because of frequent door-opening, and the milk composition may change more rapidly in these cases (36). Freezing breaks the emulsion between milk fat globules and the aqueous fraction. Milk can safely be frozen at –20°C (–4°F) for 12 months and at –70°C (–94°F) indefinitely, with changes only in cell count and activity and some alterations in the fat globule (54,58,70,71).

Preparation of Human Milk

It is preferable for a baby to consume freshly expressed milk that was pumped within the past 48 hours. One study has shown that human milk maintained in a NICU environment for up to 96 hours was safe for use (57). The milk was stored in a NICU refrigerator where the refrigerator door was opened and closed often but the bottle of milk was not opened for 96 hours. This suggests that fresh unit-dosed milk may be safe for use for as long as 96 hours (57,72). Because this level of control of access is unusual in a NICU, and because there are high-risk infants, the conservative recommendation for the storage of fresh milk for up to 48 hours is suggested. Risk-benefit should always be evaluated; in some circumstances, unit-dosed fresh milk may be held longer.

If fresh milk is not available, frozen milk can be used, although many of the cellular immunologic components will not be active (25). When using frozen milk, the oldest milk should be used first. For example, feed the colostrum first, then the transitional milk, and so on. It is imperative that frozen milk be safely and fully thawed to prevent loss of nutrients and to minimize excessive bacterial growth. Milk that is partially thawed may not contain all the nutrients, particularly fat, that the entire bottle would contain. See Box 4.1 for steps for thawing human milk.

BOX 4.1 *Thawing Frozen Human Milk*

1. Use hand hygiene before handling human milk (see Chapter 5).
2. Label milk with date and time removed from freezer, as well as the expiration date.
3. Place in refrigerator in a labeled bin to thaw, or thaw under cool or warm running water or in a commercial human milk warmer. Do not submerse cap in water.
4. Do not use a microwave to thaw human milk.
5. Do not partially thaw milk; completely thaw and swirl the milk to promote even distribution of nutrients, especially fat.
6. Refrigerate and use milk within 24 hours after it is thawed.
7. Do not refreeze.

Frozen milk may be placed in the refrigerator to thaw gradually. The goal is to use the milk within 24 hours of thawing. The time needed to thaw the milk will vary from 2 to 24 hours, depending on the volume of milk in the container, the temperature of the freezer in which the milk was stored, and the temperature of the refrigerator in which the milk is thawed. It may be helpful to remove a container of frozen milk from the freezer to the refrigerator and observe the time required for thawing. Placing the milk in the refrigerator 8 to 12 hours before anticipated use is usually sufficient if the refrigerator is not used for thawing large volumes of frozen milk such as in a formula room. Rapid thawing may be done by holding the bottle of milk under cool or lukewarm running water or by placing the bottle of milk in a bowl of cold water in the refrigerator or in a cup of warm water with the water level below the lid of the container to prevent contamination. A plastic bag can be used to keep the bottle of milk from touching the water. Bottle warmers may be used as long as they thaw to refrigerator temperatures or warm milk to approximately no greater than body temperature. Frozen milk should never be thawed in the microwave because this can cause considerable loss of nutrients and many anti-infective factors, and it may cause hot spots that could burn the baby's mouth (70,73,74). Overheating milk by any method should be avoided. Box 4.2 describes safe milk warming.

BOX 4.2   *Warming Human Milk for an Oral or Bolus Feeding*

1. Use hand hygiene before handling human milk.

2. Place container of milk in a bowl or cup of warm water or under warm running water.

3. Do not submerse cap in water.

4. Do not place in hot or boiling water.

5. Do not heat in microwave.

6. Commercial warmers are available; care should be used to avoid cross-contamination if they are used for multiple patients.

According to the CDC and the Academy of Breastfeeding Medicine (ABM), once thawed, milk must be used within 24 hours (54,56). There is a paucity of data regarding the expiration of thawed milk. The California Perinatal Quality Care Collaborative states that completely thawed milk in the refrigerator can be stored for 48 hours for a term infant, or if the milk is heat-processed, banked donor milk (75). Because there are few published studies specifically for pasteurized donor milk, recommendations for storage of previously frozen, thawed donor human milk are based on recommendations of mother's own milk (36). However, milk banks routinely culture a sample of pasteurized milk from each batch at warm temperatures for 48 hours and only milk with no bacterial growth can be used. This supports the practice of using thawed refrigerated pasteurized milk for 48 hours.

To prevent contamination of milk during preparation, aseptic technique in handling milk should be used. The nurse or caregiver should wash his or her hands thoroughly with soap and water or use hand sanitizer. Gloves may be worn during milk preparation (76,77). The area where the milk will be prepared should be sanitized with soap and water, alcohol wipes, or disinfectant spray or it could be covered with a clean, disposable pad. Milk should not be prepared at a bedside table where diapers are placed or where medications are given. A separate area designated for milk preparation or sharing of space with an already existing formula preparation room adjacent to the patient care unit will provide the proper environment. Preparing milk in a clean, designated area of the patient care unit is acceptable as long as clean technique is used. When small volumes of milk must be removed from a single container for multiple feedings, the milk can be unit-dosed to single portions to avoid touch contamination. A human milk transfer lid is available that attaches to the storage container and allows milk to be transferred by sterile technique into an enteral syringe. Hospital staff's use of recommended techniques in handling human milk can be a valuable role model for teaching families good milk handling practices.

Fortification of Human Milk

Human milk may be stored and fortified in the feeding preparation room or on the patient care unit in a designated space for preparation of feedings. Fortification of human milk may be necessary to increase the calorie, protein, vitamin, and mineral content to meet the needs of the premature or sick infant. One strategy to get higher-calorie human milk is to ask mothers to separate the milk produced early in a pumping session from the later hindmilk that is higher in fat and therefore higher in calories. This hindmilk may be nutritionally adequate for a term baby who requires higher-calorie milk, but will need additional fortification to provide adequate protein, minerals, and other nutrients for a preterm infant. Commercially prepared human milk fortifiers enhance the nutritional intakes of premature infants. When available, liquid human milk fortifiers are preferable because they are sterile. Powdered human milk fortifiers are not sterile and have the same risk of contamination associated with formula powders (78,79). Alternatives to powdered human milk fortifiers include sterile liquid-concentrated formulas designed for term infants and ready-to-feed supplements that may be added to human milk. These sterile liquid alternatives do not provide an equivalent nutrient profile for preterm infants when compared to powdered human milk fortifiers.

Traditional human milk fortifiers (HMFs) available in the United States contain cow's milk protein and are in powdered form. At press time, liquid cow's milk–based fortifiers were in preparation for market. Susceptible infants may be sensitized to foreign proteins and this could lead to future intolerance to cow's milk protein. All powdered infant formula products are not sterile. These powdered HMFs have been widely used and are economical compared with a fortifier made from human milk. A fortifier made from human milk is advantageous because it contains only human milk proteins, thus minimizing or avoiding the issue of allergy and intolerance. An HMF made from human milk has been shown to significantly reduce the incidence of necrotizing enterocolitis (NEC) and of surgical NEC. This human HMF is a pasteurized liquid, and was shown to have good solubility, contained added minerals to meet the needs of VLBW infants, and was well tolerated (80). Vitamin and iron supplementation are indicated with this human milk fortifier. The cost of a human milk–based fortifier is considerably greater than for a cow's milk–based product, and has been a limitation to widespread use to date.

If no alternatives to a powdered product are available, care must be taken to minimize the risk of infection when using the powdered HMF product (78,79). Because of the risk of contamination, opened cans of powdered formula or modulars should not be stored at the bedside. A gram scale should be used for portioning powdered products that do not come in premeasured packets. Ideally, weighing powders should be done in the feeding preparation room or pharmacy, and premeasured packets sent to the patient care unit. Use of a scoop, teaspoon, syringe, or medicine cup is not accurate for measuring powdered infant formula for hospitalized infants and is not recommended. A liquid fortifier should be carefully measured with a liquid measure or with an oral syringe. Although preparation of a single feeding of human milk may prevent waste in the event that feeding orders change, up to a 24-hour supply may be prepared safely. Manufacturer's instructions should be followed.

Osmolality of the fortified milk may be greater at 24 hours compared to just after mixing (81). Use of commercially available fortifier mixed with human milk usually results in osmolality less than the recommended level; however, addition of some medications may exceed the recommended level of 400 mOsm/kg (82). Fortification of human milk increases the osmolality of the milk during storage because endogenous human milk amylase hydrolyzes glucose polymers in the fortifier. Storage of thawed and fortified milk for 12 hours in the refrigerator, followed by 15 minutes warming, resulted in significant increases in osmolality of the milk compared with unfortified human milk. Fenton and Belik found that the addition of Polycose (Abbott), Enfacare powder (Mead Johnson), and Nutramigen (Mead Johnson) powder to human milk resulted in osmolality exceeding the recommended 425 mOsm/kg (83).

Packets of premeasured powder used to fortify human milk should be labeled with the following information:

- Name
- Medical record number
- Unit
- Expiration date
- Ingredient name(s)
- Ingredient amount(s)
- Initials of the person preparing the packet

Alternatively, when the feeding preparation room is on or near the patient care unit, human milk can be fortified in the feeding preparation room. After the fortifier is added, the milk should be gently swirled to mix. Only gentle mixing should be used to avoid breaking the fat globules, which can cause fat to adhere to the sides of the container and result in loss of calories in the milk. The fortified milk must be relabeled with the infant's name and medical record number, date and time of milk preparation, expiration date, fortifiers added, and calorie content of milk. The addition of fortifiers to human milk can impair the anti-infective properties in the milk (84,85). Studies investigating the total bacterial colony count in fortified vs unfortified milk found that fortified milk had significantly greater counts from 0 to 72 hours than did unfortified milk (85). However, the change at 24 hours did not differ, supporting recommendations to use fortified refrigerated milk within 24 hours. Differences were also noted for fresh vs previously frozen milk. Fresh milk had significantly lower bacterial colony counts initially, but the increase at 24 hours was greater when compared with previously frozen milk. When milk was warmed per usual nursery practices and placed in a 34°C (93°F) infant incubator to simulate feeding procedures, the bacterial counts significantly increased. Total IgA concentration was not found to be affected by fortification, storage temperature, or duration of storage. However, lysozyme activity in milk was decreased. This decrease ranged from 41% to74%, and growth of *E. coli* was increased when formula was added to increase calories of human milk (85).

The effect of adding iron to human milk has been studied (84,86–89). In vitro studies of the addition of iron or fortifiers containing iron have shown a direct effect on lactoferrin, an iron-binding protein in human milk that deprives bacteria and fungus of this essential nutrient for growth. These studies have shown that the addition of iron to human milk inhibits the antimicrobial effect of human milk against *E. coli, Staphylococcus, Enterobacter sakazakii*, and Group B *Streptococcus* (84,86–88). The clinical effect of this impact is unknown. Research has shown no difference in incidence of confirmed or suspected NEC or sepsis in infants receiving human milk fortified with higher levels of iron compared to low iron fortification (89). It has also been shown that the addition of a human milk–derived fortifier did not affect the antibacterial activity of human milk (87).

Use of Skimmed Human Milk

Infants with chylous pleural effusions are treated with nutrition therapy that precludes the use of human milk due to its high long-chain fatty acid content. By removing the fat portion from human milk the infant would be able to receive the immune factors and other nutritional benefits from human milk without exacerbation of symptoms (90,91). Methods have been described to process human milk to remove the fat content using a refrigerated centrifuge. Alternately, if the facility does not have access to a refrigerated centrifuge, the refrigerated milk can be prepared by allowing the milk to sit without being disturbed so the fat can separate and rise to the top of the container (91). The fat-free lower portion can then be carefully removed with a feeding tube attached to a syringe that is threaded to the bottom of the container to draw up the fat-free milk. Freshly expressed milk can also be drawn into a 60-mL syringe and placed upright in the refrigerator with the tip down in a breast milk storage container to allow for fat separation. The skimmed milk in the lower portion of the syringe can easily be removed by pushing on the plunger, leaving the fat behind. The skimmed milk was found to be well tolerated and did not result in re-accumulation of chylous pleural effusion (90). Because half of the calories in human milk are provided as fat, the calories must be made up some way. One method would be to use medium-chain triglyceride (MCT) oil or an appropriate formula containing MCT oil. Essential fatty acids may be provided as an intravenous fat emulsion or through enteral boluses of essential fatty acid–containing oils (91).

Feeding of Expressed Human Milk

It is often necessary to feed hospitalized infants their mother's milk using nasogastric (NG), orogastric (OG), nasojejunal (NJ), or, in some cases, gastrostomy (GT) tube feeding. Bolus feeding using fresh milk from the infant's own mother is recommended. A major concern when human milk is delivered via tube feeding is loss of fat due to separation and adherence to the sides of the feeding tube (92–94). A 34% reduction in fat availability was observed during continuous drip feeds vs 17% loss during intermittent bolus feeds (93). Slow flow rates were also associated with greater fat loss, which can be significant for small, low-birth-weight babies. The position of the syringe affects the delivery of fat during continuous feeds because the fat rises within the syringe toward the end of the feeding. Tilting the pump upward to between 25° and 40° can be effective in reducing fat losses during continuous feedings (92). Whenever possible, the following should be considered for tube feeding human milk: (*a*) use of a small-bore, short feeding tube and connecting set; (*b*) complete emptying of the syringe at the end of each feeding; and (*c*) early initiation of bolus feeds (92).

There are some unique issues to tube feeding human milk. Tube feeding of human milk can significantly lower the availability of macronutrients to the baby, which is of concern because low-birth-weight infants have high nutrient requirements. Tube feeding may reduce vitamin C concentration by 44% and vitamin B-6 concentration by 19% (95). This may need to be considered when tube feeding human milk that is not fortified. Growth of bacteria can be substantial when milk is held at warm temperatures for 4 hours during continuous feeding (46,50,96). If continuous feedings are used, the syringe and tubing should be changed every 4 hours to avoid unacceptable levels of bacteria in the milk. It is not necessary to warm milk for tube feeding. Excessive warming can destroy components of the milk that are heat sensitive, such as IgA and enzymes; it can also initiate bacterial proliferation. Only the amount of milk needed for a bolus feeding should be warmed, and milk that has been warmed but not used should be discarded (34,46). See Box 4.3 for a summary list of procedures involved in continuous tube feeding.

Although there are no known studies on bacterial contamination of human milk when feeding bags are used, infectious complications have been associated with bacterial contamination of enteral tube feeds (97). Expressed human milk is never sterile and contains a variety of normal skin flora such as *Staphylococcus epidermis* as well as *Lactobacilli*. Pathogens such as *Bacillus coliformis, Enterococci,* and *Staphylococcus aureus* may also be present in expressed human milk (50). Contamination can occur during milk expression and storage, during the preparation and mixing of ingredients, and while assembling and handling feeding systems. See the Hazard Analysis and Critical Control Point (HACCP) plan for handling human milk in Chapter 8.

BOX 4.3   *Continuous Tube Feeding of Human Milk*

1. Hang only 4-hour portion of milk at one time.

2. Change syringe and tubing at least every 4 hours.

3. Orient syringe at a 25° to 40° angle for continuous tube feedings to enhance fat delivery.

4. Do not overfill syringe more than necessary to ensure baby receives nearly all the milk in the syringe and tubing, including the fat.

Note: Always check the manufacturer's recommendations regarding hang time for fortified human milk.

Use of nonsterile ingredients, inadequate hand-washing, inadequate cleaning and disinfecting of feeding equipment, and reuse of enteral feeding systems are key factors in the contamination of enteral tube feeds (96). To reduce potential for contamination, feeding systems that include bags, syringes, or tubing should never be reused, and feeding systems should not be used for more than 4 hours for neonates or immunocompromised infants. Attempts to clean or disinfect feeding containers or bags are not effective in removing bacteria (96).

Colonization of enterostomy tubes in the NICU has been reported (98). These colonization loads exceed the standards for sale of milk for the healthy population (99). This is a practical dilemma because feeding tubes may need to stay in place for days or weeks but may become heavily colonized. Limiting hang time and use of external feeding equipment may promote feeding tolerance. Even with these precautions, colonization of the enterostomy tube may be high. The clinical impact of this is unknown.

When bottles are used to feed an infant, any milk left in the bottle should be discarded. Refeeding partially fed bottles is not recommended because of bacterial contamination of the milk from oral flora. Thawed milk that has not been warmed or fed to the infant should be stored in the refrigerator and used within 24 hours (46).

Prevention and Management of Misadministration of Human Milk   A multidisciplinary task force that developed a quality assurance protocol for handling human milk safely in the hospital has been described (100). Preventing errors and improving safety for patients require a systems approach to modify the conditions that contribute to errors (101). Prevention of human milk errors requires attention of staff to complete all steps accurately in the process or system of handling human milk, including labeling, storage, and verification of correctly matched infant and feedings at the bedside. Hospitals have implemented use of labeled bins, special labels for the bottles, bar coding, and systems of double-checking to attempt to prevent human milk misadministration.

Neonatal and pediatric units have had incidents in which a baby was fed another mother's human milk. This type of error may or may not be a sentinel event; reporting systems for sentinel events have been developed and mandated by the Joint Commission (102). If misadministration of milk occurs, hospitals should have procedures to respond quickly to the event; written procedures facilitate management of this type of occurrence (102). It is important that staff know the relative risk of this type of exposure to reassure the family whose baby was fed the wrong milk (103).

There is a national movement toward improving patient safety in the hospital and setting performance standards (101). The Joint Commission implemented additional patient safety standards for hospitals in

July 2001, including a program to encourage patients to get involved in their own care (104). Although most hospitals have a standard for open, nonpunitive reporting of errors, the new standards outline the hospital's responsibility to inform a patient if he or she has been harmed by care provided (102). Reporting systems provide a tool for gathering data from multiple sites to learn more about the error (105). Once an error occurs, hospitals should have procedures to respond quickly to the event (102,105). Recommendations for addressing misadministration of human milk have been published (106–110). Appendixes 4-B and 4-C present a sample family education sheet and hospital policy.

Contraindications to Use of Human Milk

There are few situations in which a mother's own milk may not be suitable for her high-risk infant. Breast-feeding is contraindicated for infants with galactosemia (2,111). Mothers who are receiving antimetabolites, chemotherapy, radioactive isotopes, certain other medications, or use drugs of abuse may need to wait to breastfeed until these substances have cleared from the milk (2). Women who have HIV, human T-cell lymphotropic virus (HTLV) I, or HTLV II are advised in the United States to use an alternative to mother's own milk (2,110,112). Women with active untreated tuberculosis will need to express their milk to feed to their infants and avoid direct contact with the infant (110,112,113). Mothers with herpes simplex lesions on the breast can breastfeed on the unaffected breast and pump the affected breast (2,110,112). Mothers who have hepatitis B or C, are febrile, have mastitis, have been exposed to low level chemical agents, are carriers of cytomegalovirus (CMV) (see below for further information regarding CMV and high-risk infants), smoke tobacco, drink moderate amounts of caffeine, or drink an occasional alcoholic beverage, may safely breastfeed their own infant (2,110,112). AAP's Red Book (110) and the 7th edition of Lawrence and Lawrence (114) also discuss other viruses known to be transmitted into human milk, including rubella, varicella, and West Nile virus, and do not recommend limiting breastfeeding in these situations (110). When a mother of an immunocompromised infant such as an extremely low-birth-weight infant is known to have acute infection with one of these viral illnesses, caution and/or consultation with infectious disease physicians is recommended before the human milk is fed. In some cases, mother's milk may be withheld temporarily.

Donor Human Milk

UNICEF (115) and WHO (116) have issued a joint resolution supporting the use of banked donor milk as the "first alternative" for infants whose mothers are unable to breastfeed. The most recent policy statement of the AAP states that banked human milk may be a suitable feeding alternative for infants whose mothers are unable or unwilling to provide their own milk (2). At the time of publication, there are 10 HMBANA-member milk banks in the United States and Canada (36), and one commercial milk bank. (See Appendix 4-A.) Use of donor milk should be considered for the infant with feeding intolerance or for the high-risk infant whose mother is not able to breastfeed or to maintain an adequate supply. Clinical uses of banked donor milk have been described (117–121). Some conditions in which donor human milk may be beneficial include prematurity, malabsorption, allergy, short gut, and chronic lung disease.

There is no federal regulation of human milk banks. Human milk is exempt from FDA regulations of human cells and tissue. Only human milk fortifiers, including those derived from human milk, fall under FDA regulation and inspection for infant formula. Three states—New York, California, and Maryland—require a tissue license for human milk banks.

On December 6, 2010, the FDA Pediatric Advisory Committee held a meeting to discuss current practices in human milk donation, banking, and distribution; to identify the risks and benefits associated with use of donated human milk; and consider risk migration. As described on the FDA Web site (122):

> The purpose of this meeting was to explore potential risks of exposure to human breast milk from sources other than maternal, to understand state-level regulatory approaches to risk mitigation, and to describe current practices of human milk banking and human milk processing. Overall, the committee agreed that the infectious disease risk associated with the process of collection and donor screening is minimal when taken from HMBANA member banks or Prolacta Bioscience Inc. The committee did not express concerns regarding the distribution of milk via HMBANA or Prolacta Bioscience Inc., however, they were highly concerned with the growing practice of Internet and person-to-person milk exchange. The practice of Internet milk exchange was highly discouraged. The committee noted that the current state regulations are not consistent with each other and are only present in three states (California, New York, and Maryland). Although they would like more regulatory consistency, they noted the difficulty associated with the task. The greatest concern was the absence of a mechanism which could monitor and stop illegitimate milk banking operations. Therefore, the committee noted that some federal oversight or guidelines might be beneficial. The committee stressed that the trafficking of human milk over the Internet is the greatest concern. The committee stated that there is not enough data available to completely address concerns regarding the risks and benefits of banked human milk. The committee suggested some of the studies could be obtained through collaborative efforts between FDA and NIH [National Institutes of Health]. However, the committee also challenged HMBANA and Prolacta Bioscience Inc. to develop a donor registry and generate an outcome profile which would identify the benefits of banked milk, mother's milk, infant formula, and cow's milk as well as determine the ideal composition associated with growth.

HMBANA has developed guidelines for establishing and operating milk banks (36,123,124). Only human milk obtained from facilities that screen donors and pasteurize the milk should be used because of the risk of disease transmission to the recipient. Use of human milk from anyone other than the patient's own mother if not obtained from an HMBANA milk or the licensed for profit milk bank is strongly discouraged. This includes milk that families obtain informally from friends or relatives or procure via the internet. Human milk banking through HMBANA is a service that screens and tests donors, collects and processes milk, and dispenses by prescription human milk donated by nursing mothers who are not biologically related to the recipient infant. All HMBANA member milk banks use Holder pasteurization (62.5°C for 30 minutes) to treat human milk. This virtually eliminates the threat of many viral contaminates such as HIV, HTLV-1, and CMV, in addition to common bacterial contaminants (118). Pasteurized milk retains antimicrobial activity, although some antimicrobial properties are lost in processing (121,125). Pasteurization using high-temperature short-time (HTST) (72°C for 16 seconds) (126) is used by a for-profit commercial milk bank in the United States. This method of pasteurization is common in the dairy industry in which large quantities of milk are processed quickly. It has been found to be effective in the elimination of bacteria and pathogenic viruses (126).

All HMBANA milk banks must complete a yearly self-assessment based on HMBANA guidelines that are reviewed and updated annually. Because the milk is dispensed to unrelated recipients, precautions are taken to provide a safe product (118,123). Bacteriological testing on each batch of processed milk confirms no growth of bacteria after pasteurization. Only milk with no bacterial growth is distributed. The milk is frozen for storage and transported to users in a frozen state. The cost-effectiveness of donor milk for premature babies has been reviewed (127,128).

Hospitals that obtain donor human milk should develop policies related to the ordering, receiving, storage, labeling, and feeding of donor human milk (see Appendix 4-D).

Transmission of CMV, MRSA, and Other Pathogens in Human Milk

Very-low-birth-weight (VLBW; ie, < 1,500 g) infants have been shown to be at high risk of acquiring symptomatic CMV infection via human milk when their mothers are CMV-seropositive, although CMV is not typically included in prenatal screening (129–133). Mothers who are CMV-seropositive shed CMV into their milk by 2 to 8 weeks postpartum, but usually within the first month (134). Storage of human milk at –20°C (–4°F) for variable time periods decreases the viability of CMV in human milk, but there is concern regarding mothers with a high viral load and a question about what period of freezing is necessary to achieve 100% deactivation (135). Holder pasteurization (30 minutes at 62.5°C) and short-term pasteurization (5 seconds at 72°C) destroy viral infectivity, with the latter preserving more bioactive components of the milk (136). These strategies can be considered for protection of VLBW infants from CMV. Risk/benefit of reduction of exposure to CMV vs loss of some beneficial components of human milk need to be weighed. Practical aspects should be considered as well, including whether colostrum will be fed fresh and whether the hospital or family's freezer is consistently in the recommended temperature range to ensure the virus is eliminated.

Cases of transmission of methicillin-resistant *Staphylococcus aureus* (MRSA) from human milk to infants in the NICU have been reported (137,138). MRSA can be transmitted into milk by touch contamination by anyone handling milk, or can be transmitted into the milk from a mother's MRSA mastitis. MRSA can be passed from the mother into the human milk even in the absence of maternal infection and can lead to colonization or clinical disease with severe outcomes. Analysis of human milk samples can determine the presence of MRSA, although guidelines for universal screening have not been established. Individual institutions must explore strategies to prevent transfer of MRSA to patients via human milk. This should include use of community human milk pump rooms and facilities within the hospital, and any special precautions that may be needed for isolation storage of MRSA–positive human milk at the hospital. Transmission of other infectious agents in human milk has been described (110). Mastitis and breast abscesses have been associated with bacterial pathogens present in milk; however, infectious mastitis generally resolves with continued lactation during antibiotic use (110). Milk expressed from a mother with a breast abscess is safe when expressed from the unaffected breast (110). These mothers should maintain lactation by expressing their milk while their infection is being treated. The mother should be advised about discarding vs storing for later use the milk from the affected breast. The presence of tuberculous mastitis, although uncommon, has been associated with transmission of that organism in human milk (113). It has been recommended that women with tuberculosis who have been treated appropriately for 2 or more weeks and who are otherwise considered not contagious may breastfeed (110). In the event of misadministration of milk from a mother with tuberculosis or other possible pathogens, the health care team caring for the recipient infant may consider whether the milk increased the child's risk for tuberculosis or other pathogens and alter the plan of care accordingly (110,139). Transmission of infectious disease through human milk and breastfeeding has been recently reviewed in depth (114).

REFERENCES

1. James DC, Lessen R. Position of the American Dietetic Association: promoting and supporting breastfeeding. *J Am Diet Assoc.* 2009;109:1926–1942.

2. American Academy of Pediatrics. Section on Breastfeeding. Breastfeeding and the use of human milk. *Pediatrics.* 2005;115:496–506.

3. Fomon S. Feeding normal infants: Rationale for recommendations. *J Am Diet Assoc.* 2001;101:1002–1005.

4. American Academy of Pediatrics, American College of Obstetricians and Gynecologists. Neonatal nutrition. In: *Guidelines for Perinatal Care.* 6th ed. Elk Grove Village, IL: American Academy of Pediatrics; 2007:235.

5. Ip S, Chung M, Raman G, et al. Breastfeeding and maternal and infant health outcomes in developed countries. *Evid Rep Technol Assess (Full Rep).*2007;(153):1–186.

6. Horta BL, Bahi R, Martines JC, Victoria CC. Evidence on the long-term effects of breastfeeding: systematic reviews and meta-analyses. http://whqlibdoc.who.int/publication/2007/9789241595230_eng.pdf. Accessed December 22, 2010.

7. National Association of Neonatal Nurses. The Use of Human Milk and Breastfeeding in the Neonatal Intensive Care Unit. Position Statement #3046. http://www.nann.org/pdf/09nicu_milk.pdf. Accessed December 22, 2010.

8. UNICEF and the Global Strategy on Infant and Young Child Feeding (GSIYCF). Understanding the Past—Planning the Future. http://www.unicef.org/nutrition/files/FinalReportonDistribution.pdf. Accessed December 22, 2010.

9. World Health Organization. The Optimal Duration of Exclusive Breastfeeding: A Systematic Review. http://www.who.int/nutrition/publications/optimal_duration_of_exc_bfeeding_review_eng.pdf. Accessed December 22, 2010.

10. Galson SK. Mothers and children benefit from breastfeeding. *J Am Diet Assoc.* 2008;108:1106.

11. US Surgeon General. Surgeon General's Perspectives: The 25th Anniversary of the Surgeon General's Workshop on Breastfeeding and Human Lactation: The Status of Breastfeeding Today. http://www.surgeongeneral.gov/library/publichealthreports/sgp124–3.pdf. Accessed December 22, 2010.

12. US Department of Health and Human Services. Healthy People 2010. http://www.healthypeople.gov/document/html/objectives/16–19.htm. Accessed September 10, 2009.

13. US Department of Health and Human Services. Proposed Healthy People 2020 Objectives. http://www.healthy people.gov/hp2020/Objectives/TopicAreas.aspx. Accessed March 19, 2010.

14. The Joint Commission. Specifications Manual for Joint Commission National Quality Core Measures. http://manual.jointcommission.org/releases/TJC2010A1. Accessed December 22, 2010.

15. US Department of Health and Human Services. Health professionals with comprehensive knowledge of lactation and use of human milk are vital to the care of hospitalized infants. http://www.womenshealth.gov/breastfeeding. Accessed January 14, 2011.

16. United States Breastfeeding Committee. Core competencies in breastfeeding care for all health professionals. http://www.usbreastfeeding.org/AboutUs/PublicationsPositionStatements/tabid/70/Default.aspx. Accessed September 10, 2009.

17. Spatz DL. State of the science: use of human milk and breast-feeding for vulnerable infants. *J Perinat Neonatal Nurs.* 2006;20:51–55.

18. Hurst N, Myatt A, Schanler R. Growth and development of a hospital-based lactation program and mother's own milk bank. *J Obstet Gynecol Nurs.* 1998;27:503–510.

19. Spatz DL. Report of a staff program to promote and support breastfeeding in the care of vulnerable infants at a children's hospital. *J Perinatal Educ.* 2005;14:30–38.

20. Arnold L. Human milk in the NICU: In: *Policy into Practice.* Sudbury, MA: Jones and Bartlett Publishers; 2010:123–190.

21. Castrucci BC, Hoover KL, Lim S, Maus KC. Availability of lactation counseling services influences breastfeeding among infants admitted to neonatal intensive care units. *Am J Health Promot.* 2007;21:410–415.

22. Meier P. Breastfeeding in the special care nursery. *Pediatr Clin N Am.* 2001;48:425–442.

23. Lemons P. Breast milk and the hospitalized infant: guideline for practice. *Neonatal Netw.* 2001;20:47–52.

24. Spatz DL. Ten steps for promoting and protecting breastfeeding for vulnerable infants. *J Perinat Neonatal Nurs.* 2004;18:385–396.

25. Lawrence R, Lawrence R. The collection and storage of human milk and human milk banking. In: Lawrence R, Lawrence R, eds. *Breastfeeding: A Guide for the Medical Profession.* 6th ed. St. Louis, MO: Mosby; 2005:761–796.

26. Becker GE, McCormick FM, Renfrew MJ. Methods of milk expression for lactating women. *Cochrane Database Syst Rev.* 2008(4):CD006170.

27. Slusher T, Slusher IL, Biomdo M, Bode-Thomas F, Curtis BA, Meier P. Electric breast pump use increases maternal milk volume in African nurseries. *J Trop Pediatr.* 2007;53:125–130.

28. Meier P, Brown L, Hurst N. Breastfeeding the preterm infant. In: Riordan J, Wambaugh K, eds. *Breastfeeding and Human Lactation*. 4th ed. Sudbury, MA: Jones and Bartlett; 2009:425–470.

29. Morton J, Hall JY, Wong RJ, Thairu L, Benitz WE, Rhine WD. Combining hand techniques with electric pumping increases milk production in mothers of preterm infants. *J Perinatology*. 2009;29:757–764.

30. Chamberlain LB, McMahon M, Philipp BL, Merewood A. Breast pump access in the inner city: a hospital-based initiative to provide breast pumps for low-income women. *J Hum Lact*. 2006;22:94–98.

31. Kent JC. Response of breasts to different stimulation patterns of an electric breast pump. *J Hum Lact*. 2003;19:179–186.

32. Meier PP, Engstrom JL, Hurst NM, et al. A comparison of the efficiency, efficacy, comfort, and convenience of two hospital-grade electric breast pumps for mothers of very low birthweight infants. *Breastfeed Med*. 2008;3:141–150.

33. Hurst NM. The 3 M's of breast-feeding the preterm infant. *J Perinat Neonatal Nurs*. 2007;21:234–239; quiz 240–231.

34. Hurst N, Valentine C, Renfro L, Burns P, Ferlic L. Skin-to-skin holding in the neonatal intensive care unit influences maternal milk volume. *J Perinatology*. 1997;17:213–217.

35. Lessen R, Crivelli-Kovach A. Prediction of initiation and duration of breast-feeding for neonates admitted to the neonatal intensive care unit. *J Perinat Neonatal Nurs*. 2007;21:256–266.

36. Jones F, Tully MR. *Best Practice for Expressing, Storing and Handling Human Milk in Hospitals, Homes and Child Care Settings*. 2nd ed. Fort Worth, TX: Human Milk Banking Association of North America; 2006.

37. Hurst NM, Meier P. Breastfeeding the preterm infant. In: Riordan J, ed. *Breastfeeding and Human Lactation*. 3rd ed. Sudbury, MA: Jones and Bartlett; 2005:367–408.

38. Cincinnati Children's Hospital. Breastfeeding and Related Topics. http://www.cincinnatichildrens.org/health/info/newborn/breastfeed/default.htm. Accessed September 13, 2009.

39. US Food and Drug Administration. Bisphenol A. http://www.bisphenol-a.org/whatsNew/20080205.html. Accessed September 13, 2009.

40. US Food and Drug Administration. Draft Assessment of Bisphenol A for Use in Food Contact Applications. http://www.fda.gov/Food/FoodIngredientsPackaging/ucm166145.htm. Accessed September 13, 2009.

41. Biedermann-Brem S, Grob K. Release of bisphenol A from polycarbonate baby bottles: water hardness as the most relevant factor. *Eur Food Res Technol*. 2009;229:679–684.

42. Pittard W, Geddes K, Brown S. Bacterial contamination of human milk: container type and method of expression. *Am J Perinatology*. 1991;8:25–27.

43. Sterilisation Services (Isotron). Synergy Health Web site. http://www.isotron.co.uk. Accessed December 11, 2009.

44. Hamosh M. *Breastmilk Storage: Review of the Literature and Recommendations for Research Needs*. San Diego, CA: Wellstart International; 1994.

45. The Joint Commission. Facts about Patient Safety. http://www.jointcommission.org/patientsafety. Accessed September 13, 2009.

46. Arnold L. *Recommendations for Collection, Storage and Handling of a Mother's Milk for Her Own Infant in the Hospital Setting*. 3rd ed. Denver, CO: Human Milk Banking Association of North America; 1999.

47. SafeBaby Breast Milk Tracking. http://www.safebabybmt.com. Accessed September 13, 2009.

48. MobilityScan Solutions. Mother's Best Breast Milk Tracking system. http://www.mobilityscan.com/scanonline/pdf/NEW%20brochure%20MOTHERS%20BEST%205.pdf. Accessed December 27, 2010.

49. Huber C, Blanco ME, Davis MM. Expressed breastmilk: safety in the hospital. *Am J Nurs*. 2009;109:54–55.

50. Hamosh M, Ellis L, Pollock D, Henderson T, Hamosh P. Breastfeeding and the working mother: effect of time and temperature of short-term storage on proteolysis, lipolysis, and bacterial growth in milk. *Pediatrics*. 1996;97:492–498.

51. Rechtman DJ, Lee ML, Berg H. Effect of environmental conditions on unpasteurized donor human milk. *Breastfeed Med*. 2006;1:24–26.

52. Landers S, Updegrove K. Bacteriological screening of donor human milk before and after pasteurization. *Breastfeed Med*. 2010;5:117–121.

53. Occupational Safety and Health Administration. Breast milk does not constitute occupational exposure as defined by Standard No. 1910.1030 Interpretation and compliance letters. http://www.osha.gov/pls/oshaweb/owadisp.show_document?p_table=INTERPRETATIONS&p_id=20952. Accessed December 27, 2010.

54. Centers for Disease Control and Prevention. Proper Handling and Storage of Human Milk. October 2009. http://www.cdc.gov/breastfeeding/recommendations/handling_breastmilk.htm. Accessed December 16, 2009.

55. Lawrence R, Lawrence R. Appendix H. The storage of human milk . In: *Breastfeeding: A Guide for the Medical Profession*. 6th ed. St. Louis, MO: Mosby; 2005:1018–1024.

56. The Academy of Breastfeeding Medicine Protocol Committee. ABM Clinical Protocol #8: Human Milk Storage Information for Home Us for Full-Term Infants. *Breastfeed Med*. 2010;5:127–130.

57. Slutzah M, Codipilly CN, Potak D, Clark RM, Schanler RJ. Refrigerator storage of expressed human milk in the neonatal intensive care unit. *J Pediatr*. 2010;156:26–28.

58. Academy of Breastfeeding Medicine. Human Milk Storage. http://www.bfmed.org/Resources/Protocols.aspx. Accessed September 10, 2009.

59. Pardou A, Serruys E, Mascart-Lemone F. Human milk banking: influence of storage processes and of bacterial contamination on some milk constituents. *Biol Neonate*. 1994;65:302–309.

60. Alowe SA AI, Lawal SF, Ransome-Kuti S. Bacteriological quality of raw human milk: effect of storage in a refrigerator. *Ann Trop Pediatric*. 1987;7:233–237.

61. Ogundele MO. Effects of storage on the physicochemical and antibacterial properties of human milk. *Br J Biomed Sci*. 2002;59:205–211.

62. Ogundele MO. Techniques for the storage of human breast milk: implications for anti-microbial functions and safety of stored milk. *Eur J Pediatr*. 2000;159:793–797.

63. Sosa R, Barness L. Bacterial growth in refrigerated human milk. *Am J Dis Child*. 1997;141:111–112.

64. Martinez-Costa C, Silvestre MD, Lopez MC, Plaza A, Miranda M, Guijarro R. Effects of refrigeration on the bactericidal activity of human milk: a preliminary study. *J Pediatr Gastroenterol Nutr*. 2007;45:275–277.

65. Silvestre D, Lopez MC, March L, Plaza A, Martinez-Costa C. Bactericidal activity of human milk: stability during storage. *Br J Biomed Sci*. 2006;63:59–62.

66. Lavine M, Clark RM. Changing patterns of free fatty acids in breast milk during storage. *J Pediatr Gastroenterol Nutr*. 1987;6:769–774.

67. Evans TJ, Ryley HC, Neale LM, Dodge JA, Lewarne VM. Effect of storage and heat on antimicrobial proteins in human milk. *Arch Dis Child*. 1978;53:239–241.

68. Hanna N, Ahmed K, Anwar M, Petrova A, Hiatt M, Hegyi T. Effect of storage on breast milk antioxidant activity. *Arch Dis Child Fetal Neonatal Ed*. 2004;89:F518–F520.

69. Miranda M, Muriach M, Almansa I, et al. Oxidative status of human milk and its variations during cold storage. *Biofactors*. 2004;20:129–137.

70. Lawrence R. Storage of human milk and the influence of procedures on immunological components of human milk. *Acta Paediatrics*. 1999;88:14–18.

71. Berkow SE, Freed LM, Hamosh M, et al. Lipases and lipids in human milk: effect of freeze-thawing and storage. *Pediatr Res*. 1984;18:1257–1262.

72. Meier P, Brown L. Breastfeeding for mothers and low birth weight infants. *Nurs Clin N Am*. 1996;31:351–365.

73. Quan R, Yang C, Rubinstein S. Effects of microwave radiation on anti-infective factors in human milk. *Pediatrics*. 1992;89:667–669.

74. Nemethy M, Clore ER. Microwave heating of infant formula and breast milk. *J Pediatr Health Care*. 1990;4:131–135.

75. California Perinatal Quality Care Collaborative. Nutritional Support for the VLBW Infant. December 2008. http://www.cpqcc.org/quality_improvement/qi_toolkits/nutritional_support_of_the_vlbw_infant_rev_december_2008. Accessed December 18, 2009.

76. Centers for Disease Control and Prevention. Update: universal precautions for prevention of transmission of HIV, hepatitis B virus and other bloodborne pathogens in health-care settings. *MMWR Morb Mortal Wkly Rep*. 1988;37:377–382,387–388.

77. Nommsen-Rivers L. Universal precautions are not needed for health care workers handling breast milk. *J Human Lact*. 1997;13:267–268.

78. US Food and Drug Administration. Health professional's letter on *Enterobacter sakazakii* infections associated with use of powdered (dry) infant formulas in neonatal intensive care units revised October 10, 2002. http://www.fda.

gov/Food/FoodSafety/Product-SpecificInformation/InfantFormula/AlertsSafetyInformation/ucm111299.htm. Accessed October 4, 2010.

79. Centers for Disease Control and Prevention. *Enterobacter sakazakii* infections associated with the use of powdered infant formula—Tennessee 2001. *MMWR Morb Mortal Wkly Rep.* 2002;51:297–300.

80. Sullivan S, Schanler RJ, Kim JH, et al. An exclusively human milk-based diet is associated with a lower rate of necrotizing enterocolitis than a diet of human milk and bovine milk-based products. *J Pediatr.* 2010;156:562–567.

81. De Curtis M, Candusso M, Pieltain C, Rigo J. Effect of fortification on the osmolality of human milk. *Arch Dis Child Fetal Neonatal Ed.* 1999;81:F141–F143.

82. Srinivasan L. Increased osmolality of breast milk with therapeutic additives. *Arch Dis Child Fetal Neonatal Ed.* 2004;89:F514–F517.

83. Fenton TR, Belik J. Routine handling of milk fed to preterm infants can significantly increase osmolality. *J Pediatr Gastroenterol Nutr.* 2002;35:298–302.

84. Quan R, Yang C, Rubinstein S. The effect of nutritional additives on anti-infective factors in human milk. *Clin Pediatr.* 1994;33:325–328.

85. Jocson MAL, Mason E, Schanler RJ. The effects of nutrient fortification and varying storage conditions on host defense properties of human milk. *Pediatrics.* 1997;100:240–243.

86. Chan GM. Effects of powdered human milk fortifiers on the antibacterial actions of human milk. *J Perinatol.* 2003;23:620–623.

87. Chan GM, Lee ML, Rechtman DJ. Effects of a human milk-derived human milk fortifier on the antibacterial actions of human milk. *Breastfeed Med.* 2007;2:205–208.

88. Ovali F, Ciftci IH, Cetinkaya Z, Bükülmez A. Effects of human milk fortifier on the antimicrobial properties of human milk. *J Perinatol.* 2006;26:761–763.

89. Berseth CL, Van Aerde JE, Gross S, Stolz SI, Harris CL, Hansen JW. Growth, efficacy, and safety of feeding an iron-fortified human milk fortifier. *Pediatrics.* 2004;114:e699–e706.

90. Chan GM, Lechtenberg E. The use of fat-free human milk in infants with chylous pleural effusion. *J Perinatol.* 2007;27:434–436.

91. Lessen R. Use of skim breast milk for an infant with chylothorax. *Infant Child Adolesc Nutr.* 2009;1:303–310.

92. Narayanan I, Singh B, Harvey D. Fat loss during feeding of human milk. *Arch Dis Child.* 1984;59:475–477.

93. Martinez FE, Desai ID, Davidson AG, Nakai S, Radcliffe A. Ultrasonic homogenization of expressed human milk to prevent fat loss during tube feeding. *J Pediatr Gastroenterol Nutr.* 1987;6:593–597.

94. Tacken KJ, Vogelsang A, van Lingen RA, Slootstra J, Dikkeschei BD, van Zoeren-Grobben D. Loss of triglycerides and carotenoids in human milk after processing. *Arch Dis Child Fetal Neonatal Ed.* 2009;94:F447–F450.

95. Van Zoeren-Grobben D, Schrijver J, Van den Berg H, Berger HM. Human milk vitamin content after pasteurisation, storage, or tube feeding. *Arch Dis Child.* 1987;62:161–165.

96. Anderton A. Reducing bacterial contamination of enteral tube feeds. *Br J Nurs.* 1995;4:368–376.

97. Mehall J, Kite C, Saltzman D, Wallett T, Jackson R, Smith S. Prospective study of the incidence and complications of bacterial contamination of enteral feeding in neonates. *J Pediatr Surg.* 2002;37:1177–1182.

98. Hurrell E, Kucerova E, Loughlin M, et al. Neonatal enteral feeding tubes as loci for colonisation by members of the *Enterobacteriaceae. BMC Infect Dis.* 2009;9:146.

99. US Food and Drug Administration. Pasteurized Milk Ordinance (2007 Revision). http://www.fda.gov/Food/FoodSafety/Product-SpecificInformation/MilkSafety. Accessed February 21, 2010.

100. Dougherty D, Giles V. From breast to baby: quality assurance for breast milk management. *Neonatal Network.* 2000;19:21.

101. Committee on Quality of Health Care in America. Setting performance standards and expectations for patient safety. In: Kohn lT, Corrigan JM, Dondaldson MS, eds. *To Err Is Human.* Washington, DC: National Academy Press; 2000:153.

102. The Joint Commission. Sentinel Event Policy and Procedures. http://www.jointcommission.org/sentinel_event.aspx. Accessed December 27, 2010.

103. Warner B, Sapsford A. Misappropriated human milk: fantasy, fear and fact regarding infectious risk. *Newborn Infant Nurs Rev.* 2004;4:56–61.

104. The Joint Commission. Speak Up: Help Prevent Errors in Your Child's Care. http://www.jointcommission.org/NewsRoom/NewsRelease/nr_080509.html. Accessed January 4, 2009.

105. Committee on Quality Health Care in America. Why do errors happen? In: Kohn L, Corrigan JM, Donaldson MS, eds. *To Err Is Human*. Washington, DC: National Academy Press; 2000:49.

106. Robbins S, Beker L, eds. *Infant Feedings: Guidelines for Preparation of Formula and Breastmilk in Health Care Facilities*. Chicago, IL: American Dietetic Association; 2003.

107. Barry C, Lennox K. Management of expressed breast milk. Is the right breast milk being fed to infants? *Canadian J Infect Control*. 1998(Spring): 16–19.

108. New South Wales Government. Breast Milk—Safe Management. NSW Health. November 6, 2006. http://www.health.nsw.gov.au/policies/pd/2010/pdf/PD2010_019.pdf. Accessed December 27, 2010.

109. Centers for Disease Control and Prevention. What to Do if an Infant or Child Is Mistakenly Fed Another Woman's Expressed Breastmilk. October 20, 2009. http://www.cdc.gov/breastfeeding/recommendations/other_mothers_milk.htm. Accessed December 27, 2010.

110. Pickering L. Section 2: recommendations for care of children in special circumstances. In: Pickering L, ed. *Red Book 2009: Report of the Committee on Infectious Diseases*. 28th ed. Elk Grove Village, IL: American Academy of Pediatrics; 2009:118–124.

111. Lawrence R, Lawrence R. Breastfeeding the infant with a problem. In: Lawrence R, Lawrence R, eds. *Breastfeeding: A Guide for the Medical Profession*. 6th ed. St. Louis, MO: Mosby; 2005:525–527.

112. Lawrence R. *A Review of the Medical Benefits and Contraindications to Breastfeeding in the United States*. Arlington, VA: National Center for Education in Maternal and Child Health; 1997.

113. Lawrence R, Lawrence R. Transmission of infectious diseases through breast milk and breastfeeding. In: Lawrence R, Lawrence R, eds. *Breastfeeding: A Guide for the Medical Profession*. 6th ed. St. Louis, MO: Mosby; 2005:637–640.

114. Lawrence R, Lawrence R, eds. *Breastfeeding: A Guide for the Medical Profession*. 7th ed. St. Louis, MO: Mosby; 2011.

115. United Nations Children's Fund. *Innocenti Declaration on the Protection, Promotion and Support of Breastfeeding*. Florence, Italy; 1990. http://www.unicef.org/programme/breastfeeding/innocenti.htm. Accessed December 27, 2010.

116. World Health Organization. Protecting, promoting and supporting breastfeeding: the special role of maternity services. Geneva, Switzerland: WHO/UNICEF; 1989.

117. Arnold L. The case for banked donor human milk in the NICU. In: *Human Milk in the NICU: Policy into Practice*. Sudbury, MA: Jones & Bartlett; 2010:309–447.

118. Tully D, Jones F, Tully M. Donor milk: What's in it and what's not. *J Hum Lact*. 2001;17:152–155.

119. McGuire W, Anthony MY. Donor human milk versus formula for preventing necrotising enterocolitis in preterm infants: systematic review. *Arch Dis Child Fetal Neonatal Ed*. 2003;88:F11–F14.

120. Quigley MA, Henderson G, Anthony MY, McGuire W. Formula milk versus donor breast milk for feeding preterm or low birth weight infants. *Cochrane Database Syst Rev*. 2007(4):CD002971.

121. Bertino E, Giuliani F, Occhi L, et al. Benefits of donor human milk for preterm infants: current evidence. *Early Hum Develop*. 2009;85(10 Suppl):S9–S10.

122. US Food And Drug Administration Pediatric Advisory Committee. Flash Minutes (for meeting held at Bethesda Marriott; Bethesda, MD, December 6, 2010). http://www.fda.gov/downloads/AdvisoryCommittees/CommitteesMeetingMaterials/PediatricAdvisoryCommittee/UCM238627.pdf. Accessed January 17, 2011.

123. Arnold L. Donor human milk banking: more than nutrition. In: Riordan J, Auerbach K, eds. *Breastfeeding and Human Lactation*. 2nd ed. Sudbury, MA: Jones and Bartlett Publishers; 1998:775–799.

124. Centers for Disease Control and Prevention. Human Milk Banks. http://www.cdc.gov/mmwr/preview/mmwrhtml/00031670.htm. Accessed December 30, 2009.

125. Silvestre D, Ruiz P, Martinez-Costa C, Plaza A, Lopez MC. Effect of pasteurization on the bactericidal capacity of human milk. *J Hum Lact*. 2008;24:371–376.

126. Terpstra FG, Rechtman DJ, Lee ML, et al. Antimicrobial and antiviral effect of high-temperature short-time (HTST) pasteurization applied to human milk. *Breastfeed Med*. 2007;2:27–33.

127. Arnold L. The cost-effectiveness of using banked donor milk in the neonatal intensive care unit: prevention of necrotizing enterocolitis. *J Hum Lact*. 2002;18:172–177.

128. Wright N. Donor human milk for preterm infants. *J Perinatol*. 2001;21:249–254.

129. Maschmann J, Hamprecht K, Dietz G, Speer C. Cytomegalovirus infection of extremely low-birth weight infants via breast milk. *Clin Infect Dis.* 2001;33:1998–2003.

130. Jim WT, Shu CH, Chiu NC, et al. Transmission of cytomegalovirus from mothers to preterm infants by breast milk. *Pediatr Infect Dis J.* 2004;23:848–851.

131. Miron D, Brosilow S, Felszer K, et al. Incidence and clinical manifestations of breast milk-acquired Cytomegalovirus infection in low birth weight infants. *J Perinatol.* 2005;25:299–303.

132. Schleiss MR. Role of breast milk in acquisition of cytomegalovirus infection: recent advances. *Curr Opin Pediatr.* 2006;18:48–52.

133. Omarsdottir S, Casper C, Zweygberg Wirgart B, Grillner L, Vanpee M. Transmission of cytomegalovirus to extremely preterm infants through breast milk. *Acta Paediatr.* 2007;96:492–494.

134. Vochem M, Hamprecht K, Jahn G, Speer CP. Transmission of cytomegalovirus to preterm infants through breast milk. *Pediatric Infect Dis J.* 1998;17:53–58.

135. Lawrence RM. Cytomegalovirus in human breast milk: risk to the premature infant. *Breastfeed Med.* 2006;1:99–107.

136. Hamprecht K, Maschmann J, Muller D, et al. Cytomegalovirus (CMV) inactivation in breast milk: reassessment of pasteurization and freeze-thawing. *Pediatr Res.* 2004;56:529–535.

137. Behari P, Englund J, Alcasid G, Garcia-Houchins S, Weber SG. Transmission of methicillin-resistant Staphylococcus aureus to preterm infants through breast milk. *Infect Control Hosp Epidemiol.* 2004;25:778–780.

138. Gastelum DT, Dassey D, Mascola L, Yasuda LM. Transmission of community-associated methicillin-resistant Staphylococcus aureus from breast milk in the neonatal intensive care unit. *Pediatr Infect Dis J.* 2005;24:1122–1124.

139. Kerrey BT, Morrow A, Geraghty S, Huey N, Sapsford A, Schleiss MR. Breast milk as a source for acquisition of cytomegalovirus (HCMV) in a premature infant with sepsis syndrome: detection by real-time PCR. *J Clin Virol.* 2006;35:313–316.

Appendix 4-A

Human Milk Resources

Supplies

Abbott Nutrition
Columbus, OH 43215–1724
800/551–5838   http://www.abbottnutrition.com
Human milk storage bottles (2-oz and 4-oz, BPA–free, commercially sterile, universal thread), sterile water bottles.

Ameda
475 Half Day Rd
Lincolnshire, IL 60069
866/992–6332   http://www.ameda.com
Breast pumps and kits, breastfeeding supplies, 4-oz collection containers without BPA.

Hygeia II Medical Group
1370 Decision Street, Suite C
Vista, CA 92081
888/789–7466   www.HygeiaBaby.com
Breast pumps and kit, BPA–free 4-oz and 8-oz breast milk storage containers.

Medela
PO Box 660/1101 Corporate Dr
McHenry, IL 60051–0660
800/435–8316   http://www.medela.com

Breast pumps and kits, 80-mL and 35-mL collection containers (sterile pathway, universal thread with lid, dishwasher safe, autoclavable, bulk pack 100 per box), microwave steam bags and wipes for pump cleaning, human milk transfer lids, breast shells, nipple shields, educational materials, scales, supplemental feeding device. Products are all BPA–free.

Snappies Human Milk Containers
Capitol Vial, Inc
2039 McMillan St
Auburn, AL 36832
800/772–8871   http:www.capitolvial.com
Sterile BPA–free 35-mL colostrum containers and 70-mL human milk containers with hinged flip-top lid and universal thread. These containers are also available through Mead Johnson Nutritionals.

Mead Johnson Nutritionals
Evansville, IN 47721
847/832–2420   www.meadjohnson.com

Publications and Online Resources

Academy of Breastfeeding Medicine. http://www.bfmed.org.

Arnold LD. *Human Milk in the NICU: Policy and Practice.* Sudbury, MA: Jones and Bartlett Publishers; 2010.

Drugs and Lactation Database (LactMed). http://toxnet.nlm.nih.gov/cgi-bin/sis/htmLgen?LACT. (A peer-reviewed and fully referenced database of drugs to which breastfeeding mothers may be exposed. Among the data included are maternal and infant levels of drugs, possible effects on breastfed infants and on lactation, and alternate drugs to consider.)

Hale T. *Medications and Mothers' Milk.* 14th ed. Amarillo, TX: Hale Publishing; 2010.

Human Milk Banking Association of North America. *Best Practice for Expressing, Storing and Handling Human Milk in Hospitals, Homes and Child Care Settings.* Raleigh, NC: HMBANA; 2005.

Lawrence R, Lawrence R, eds. *Breastfeeding: A Guide for the Medical Profession.* 7th ed. St. Louis, MO: Mosby; 2011.

Nonprofit Human Milk Banks in the United States and Canada

The following are nonprofit milk banks affiliated with the Human Milk Banking Association of North America:

California
Mothers' Milk Bank
751 South Bascom Ave
San Jose, CA 95128
Phone: 408/998–4550   Fax: 408/297–9208
E-mail: mothersmilkbank@hhs.co.santa-clara.ca.us
Web site: www.milkbanksj.org

Colorado
Mothers' Milk Bank
Presbyterian/St. Luke's Medical Center and Rocky Mountain Hospital for Children
1719 E 19th Ave
Denver, CO 80218
Phone: 303/869–1888
E-mail:
Laraine.Lockhart-Borman@healthonecares.com

Florida
Mothers' Milk Bank of Florida (developing)
2520 N. Orange Ave, Suite 103
Orlando, FL 32804
E-mail: milkbankofflorida@gmail.com

Indiana
Indiana Mothers' Milk Bank, Inc
Methodist Medical Plaza II
6820 Parkdale Place, Suite 109
Indianapolis, IN 46254
Phone: 317/329–7146   Fax: 317/329–7151
E-mail: inmothersmilkbank@clarian.org
Web site: http://www.immilkbank.org

Iowa

Mother's Milk Bank of Iowa

Department of Food and Nutrition Services

University of Iowa Hospitals and Clinics

University of Iowa at Liberty Square

119 2nd St, Suite 400

Coralville, IA 52241

Phone: 319/356–2652

Fax: 319/384–9933

E-mail: jean-drulis@uiowa.edu

Web site: www.uihealthcare.com/milkbank

Michigan

Bronson Mothers' Milk Bank

601 John St, Suite N1300

Kalamazoo, MI 49007

Phone: 269/341–8849

Fax: 269/341–8918

E-mail: Duffc@bronsonhg.org

Mississippi

Mothers' Milk Bank of Mississippi (developing)

PO Box 1538

Madison, MS 39130–1538

E-mail: MilkBankofMS@gmail.com

Missouri

Kansas City Regional Human Milk Bank (developing)

E-mail: mcross@saint-lukes.org

New England

Mothers' Milk Bank of New England (developing)

PO Box 600091

Newtonville, MA 02460

or

225 Nevada St, Room 201

Newtonville, MA 02460

Phone: 781/535–7594

E-mail: info@milkbankne.org

Web site: www.milkbankne.org

North Carolina

WakeMed Mothers' Milk Bank and Lactation Center

3000 New Bern Ave

Raleigh, NC 27610

Phone: 919/350–8599

E-mail: Suevans@wakemed.org *or* MBradshaw@wakemed.org

Web site: http://www.wakemed.com/body.cfm?id=135

Ohio

Mothers' Milk Bank of Ohio

Grant Medical Center at Victorian Village Health Center

1087 Dennison Ave

Columbus, OH 43201

Phone: 614/544–0810

Fax: 614/544–0812

E-mail: gmorrow@ohiohealth.com

Oregon

Northwest Mothers' Milk Bank (developing)

3439 NE Sandy Blvd, #130

Portland, OR 97232

E-mail: info@nwmmb.org

Texas

Mothers' Milk Bank at Austin

900 E 30th St, Suite 214

Austin, TX 78705

Phone: 512/494–0800 *or* 877/813–6455 (toll-free)

Fax: 512/494–0880

E-mail: info@mmbaustin.org

Web site: www.mmbaustin.org

Mothers' Milk Bank of North Texas

1300 W Lancaster, Suite 108

Fort Worth, TX 76102

Phone: 817/810–0071 *or* 866/810–0071 (toll-free)

Fax: 817//810–0087

E-mail: mmbnt@hotmail.com

Web site: http://www.mmbnt.org

British Columbia, Canada

BC Womens' Milk Bank

C & W Lactation Services

4500 Oak St, IU 30

Vancouver, BC V6H 3N1

Phone: 604/875–2282

Fax: 604/875–2871

E-mail: fjones@cw.bc.ca

Ontario, Canada

Ontario Human Milk Bank (developing)

Toronto, ON

For-Profit Milk Bank

Prolacta Bioscience
605 E Huntington Dr, Suite 101
Monrovia, CA 91016
Phone: 888/776–5228
Fax: 626/599–9269
Website: www.prolacta.com
E-mail: info@prolacta.com

Appendix 4-B

Hospital Policy on Misadministration of Human Milk

Human Milk Post-Exposure Procedure

Introduction   Human milk has been recognized as a potential source of transmission of Human Immunodeficiency Virus (HIV), Human T-cell Lymphotrophic Virus (HTLV I/II) and cytomegalovirus (CMV). In addition, there is a theoretical risk of transmission of other microbial pathogens, possibly including, but not limited to, hepatitis B virus (HBV), hepatitis C virus (HCV) and West Nile Virus (WNV).

Purpose   The purpose of this procedure is to provide guidelines for assessing the possibility of transmission of a microbial pathogen to an infant if human milk from other than that infant's mother is accidentally ingested.

Definitions

- Recipient patient: the infant who received the incorrect human milk.
- Recipient parent/guardian: the parent of the infant who received the incorrect human milk.
- Donor mother: the mother whose human milk was given to the incorrect infant.

Procedure   1. The individual who recognizes that a patient has received human milk from other than his or her mother should immediately inform the charge nurse, and if available, the unit nurse manager/ supervisor. The nurse is responsible for notifying the attending physician or designee of the patient who received the incorrect milk (recipient patient).

Either the charge nurse or the nurse manager/supervisor will notify the attending physician(s) of the recipient and donor patients and the Medical Director of Infection Prevention and Control (IP&C). The Medical Director of IP&C, or his/her designee, will review the event and assist in evaluation of the exposure. If the Medical Director of IP&C is unavailable, contact the Infectious Disease Attending on call.

- Complete an Incident Report as per incident reporting policy.
- Document the incident in the recipient's chart.

Nursing personnel should follow these additional instructions:

- Do not attempt to remove human milk from the baby's stomach, even if a nasogastric tube is in place. Attempting to remove the milk will irritate the lining of the esophagus and stomach and increase the risk of transmission of organisms if they are present.
- Respect patient confidentiality. The nurse may not release the name of the human milk donor or recipient to either family.
- Distribute the patient family education sheet to parents/guardians of each family (Caring for Your Child: What are the Concerns if my Baby is Fed the Wrong Human milk?)

2. The attending physician of the recipient patient, or his/her designee, after consultation with the Medical Director of Infection Prevention and Control, or his/her designee, may choose to request the donor mother's consent to test her blood for specific pathogens. The discussion with the donor mother of the risks and benefits of testing must include the need to release test results to the attending physician or designee of the recipient patient and the recipient parents. This discussion needs to be documented in the medical record and the donor mother must sign the HIPAA—Authorization to Use and Share Medical Information. Section 4–3 [not reprinted here].

Source: This sample policy was generously shared by The Children's Hospital of Philadelphia and can be used as a model by other facilities to develop their own policy. Reprinted by permission of The Children's Hospital of Philadelphia.

Appendix 4-C

Family Education on Use of Donor Milk

Caring for Your Child—Donor Human Milk: The Next Best Thing to Mother's Own Milk

Why Donor Milk?   Human milk is the very best food for your baby. Your own milk is usually best but if you are not able to provide enough milk for your baby or choose not to pump, donor human milk is the next best thing. Your baby's doctor will decide if donor milk is right for your baby. Donor milk has been safely used in Europe for over a century, and in the United States for over sixty years. Donor human milk is a way to give your baby human milk when your own milk is not available. Human milk strengthens the baby's immune system and may help your baby fight disease and infection. It also contains growth hormones that help your baby grow. Human milk is easier to digest than most formulas. According to some studies, human milk may also increase intelligence and reduce allergies and illness later in life.

Where Does Donor Milk Come From?   Donor milk is ordered from a milk bank that is a member of the Human Milk Banking Association of North America (HMBANA). The website for HMBANA is www.hmbana.com. Milk bank donors are mothers who care about helping others by providing their extra milk to babies who need it. They are volunteers who are nursing their own babies and generously pump for the milk bank. They receive no payment or compensation, only the satisfaction of knowing they have improved the health of another baby. The milk bank screens all donors to make sure that they are healthy and meet the

HMBANA's donor strict criteria. (See attached HMBANA donor screening criteria [not reprinted here].) All donors receive instructions on proper hand washing, pumping technique, and cleaning of equipment.

Quality of Donor Milk   All donor milk is pasteurized (heat-treated) to eliminate bacteria or viruses that may have been present in the milk. The milk is tested after pasteurization to make sure there are no bacteria in the milk. Although some nutrients are lost in pasteurization, donor milk is still better for your baby than infant formula. Preterm infants need extra special nutrition. For the first month of life, milk from mothers of preterm infants is higher in some nutrients than milk of mothers who deliver full term babies. Therefore, preterm milk will be ordered for preterm infants whenever it is available.

Safety of Donor Milk   In addition to completing a medical history and lifestyle questionnaire, prospective donors are required to obtain their doctors' approval to donate milk. Moreover, donors are tested for HIV, Hepatitis B and syphilis. A mother is accepted as a donor only if she has no risk factors for AIDS and the blood tests are negative for the virus. These rules are set by the HMBANA, the Food and Drug Administration, and the Centers for Disease Control and Prevention. These rules are almost identical to the rules for blood donation.

Source: This sample policy was generously shared by The Children's Hospital of Philadelphia and can be used as a model by other facilities to develop their own policy. Reprinted by permission of The Children's Hospital of Philadelphia.

Appendix 4-D

Example of a Hospital Policy on Use of Donor Milk

Patient Care Manual: Use of Donor Human Milk

Policy   The Hospital supports the use of donor human milk from milk banks approved by The Human Milk Banking Association of North America (HMBANA) for patients.

Scope   This policy applies to the care of patients at (the "Hospital") who receive donor human milk.

Related Policies

- Patient Care Manual: Patient Care Order Processing
- Nursing Procedure Manual: Pumping and Storage of Human milk
- Nursing Procedure Manual: Administration and Fortification of Human milk
- Nursing Procedure Manual: Transport or Disposal of Human milk
- Patient-Family Education Manual: Donated Human Milk: The Next Best Thing to Mother's Own Milk

Definitions

A. *Donor Milk Bank*: A service established for the purpose of collecting, screening, processing and distributing donated human milk to meet the specific medical needs of patients for whom it is prescribed.

B. *The Human Milk Banking Association of North America (HMBANA)*: The professional association founded in 1985 for human milk banks in Canada, Mexico and the United States. The website for HMBANA is www.hmbana.com.

Guidelines

A. Patients receive donor human milk only with a patient care order (See Patient Care Policy IM-2-01 Patient Care Order Processing [not reprinted here]). Some reasons for prescribing donor human milk may include but are not limited to:

    1. Prematurity
    2. Allergies
    3. Feeding/formula intolerance
    4. Immunologic deficiencies
    5. Post-operative nutrition
    6. Treatment of some infectious diseases
    7. Treatment of certain inborn errors of metabolism; and/or
    8. Parental preference

B. With a patient care order, the Nutrition Services Department obtains and stores donor human milk only from an HMBANA approved donor milk bank. See Appendix A [at end of this example] for information regarding HMBANA donor screening guidelines.

C. The Nutrition Services Department distributes labeled, thawed, donor human milk to patient refrigerators on patient care units on a daily basis according to the patient care orders. Labels indicate:

    1. Patient name
    2. Patient medical record number
    3. Donor human milk batch number
    4. Expiration date/time
    5. Whether the milk is pre-term or term milk
    6. The name and amount of any fortifiers added and whether additive is made from powder or concentrate
    7. Hang time of four hours and
    8. Signature of Formula Technician who prepared the label and the solution

D. Clinicians provide information regarding the use of donor human milk to parents/legal guardians when appropriate (See Patient Family Education materials under Related Documents [not reprinted here]) and obtain parent/legal guardian consent to use donor human milk prior to its administration.

E. Nurses and other staff who administer feedings to patients utilize the same techniques for storage, handling and administration of donor human milk as is used for mother's own milk (See nursing references listed under Related Policies [not reprinted here].)

Responsibility for Maintenance of This Policy

Senior Vice President—Support Services
Approved by the Nutrition Committee 12/3/2009

Appendices/Attachments: Appendix A: Information Regarding Donor Screening for Human Milk

Policy TX-21-01 Use of Human Donor Milk

Milk banks screen human milk donors very much like blood donors. As per the HMBANA screening criteria, a candidate for donation may not donate human milk if she:

- Has been told that she cannot give blood for a medical reason, unless the reason was low body weight, pregnancy or breastfeeding
- In the last 12 months has had a blood transfusion, blood products, an organ or tissue transplant
- In the last 12 months had, ear or body part piercing, tattooing, permanent make-up applied with non-sterile needles or an accidental hypodermic needle stick
- Has ever received human pituitary growth hormone, a dura mater or brain covering graft, or had intimate contact with someone who has Creutzfeldt-Jakob disease
- Was born in, lived in, or traveled in any African country since 1977
- Since 1977, donor or an intimate partner of the donor's was born in, lived in, received medical treatment in, or traveled in, any of the following African countries: Cameroon, Central African Republic, Chad, Congo, Equatorial Guinea, Gabon, Niger, Nigeria
- Between 1980 and 1996 lived in the United Kingdom (England, North Ireland, Scotland, Wales, The Isle of Man, the Channel Islands, Gibraltar or the Falkland Islands) for more than 3 months
- Between 1980 and 1996 spent time that adds up to a total of 5 years in Europe (includes Albania, Austria, Belgium, Bosnia-Herzegovina, Bulgaria, Croatia, Czech Republic, Denmark, Finland, France, Germany, Greece, Hungary, Republic of Ireland, Italy, Liechtenstein, Luxembourg, Macedonia, Netherlands, Norway, Poland, Portugal, Romania, Slovak Republic, Slovenia, Spain, Sweden, Switzerland, UK and Federal Republic of Yugoslavia)
- Had a blood transfusion given to the baby during pregnancy
- Has ever had hepatitis or yellow jaundice, or in the last 12 months had close contact with someone with viral hepatitis or yellow jaundice (lived together or had sexual contact)
- Within the last 12 months has been exposed to hepatitis A or received a gamma globulin shot
- Has ever, even once, had sex with someone who is at risk for HIV/AIDS, including hemophiliacs, IV drug users, prostitutes and men who have had sex, even once, with another man
- Has exchanged sex for money or drugs, even one time
- Has ever injected drugs, or had sex with a man who has injected drugs
- Is on regular medication other than vitamins, thyroid replacement hormones, insulin, iron or progestin-only birth control pills while she is pumping
- Is taking herbal supplements or vitamins containing herbal supplements
- Smokes, uses tobacco products or uses a nicotine patch or gum
- Has a chronic health condition such as MS [multiple sclerosis] or a history of cancer
- Consumes more than 24 ounces of caffeinated drinks per day, or regularly consumes alcohol (there is a 12 hour waiting period after consuming alcohol before pumping for the bank)
- Has ever tested positive for tuberculosis—the milk bank discusses the circumstances
- Has had acupuncture or electrolysis with non-sterile needles

In addition, milk banks serologically screen potential donors for HIV-1, HIV-2, HTLV, Hepatitis C, Hepatitis B surface antigen and syphilis.

Source: This sample policy was generously shared by The Children's Hospital of Philadelphia and can be used as a model by other facilities to develop their own policy. Reprinted by permission of The Children's Hospital of Philadelphia.

Chapter 5

Formula Preparation and Handling

Sandra Robbins, RD, CSP, and Robin Meyers, MPH, RD

Important Note: Requirements for infant formula are found in the Federal Food, Drug, and Cosmetic Act. The Food and Drug Administration (FDA) has been charged with the implementation of the Infant Formula Act of 1980, which was amended in 1986. This law regulates the infant formula industry in ways intended to make infant formula adequate in nutrients, safely produced, accurately labeled, and recallable. Current good manufacturing practice, quality control procedures, quality factors, notification requirements, and records and reports for the production of infant formula are addressed (1). For each new infant formula product or addition of a major change to an existing product, the FDA requires assurances that the standards for infant formula are met prior to marketing.

The FDA includes an infant formula section on its Web site (http://www.fda.gov/Food/default.htm), which includes regulatory information affecting infant formulas. The Web site contains information for health care providers regarding letters of warning about formulas, recalls, how to report an adverse event, and other pertinent information about the FDA's interests in infant formula (1,2).

Appropriate preparation and handling of formula for infants in the health care facility are essential for the delivery of a safe and nutritious food product. Although specific procedures for safe handling and preparation may differ according to the size and type of health care facility, the recommended basic techniques are the same.

Stock Control Procedures

Written guidelines to ensure safe storage of infant formula products and ingredients should be available. Formula should be handled and stored in a manner that ensures product integrity, proper food sanitation, and the preservation of its nutritional value. Commercially prepared formula for infants (liquids and powders) should be stored at room temperature in the original unopened container.

Any guideline regarding the storage of commercially prepared formula for infants should include a discussion of appropriate storage times, temperatures, and the relationship between the two. Freezing commercial formula may cause curdling and separation of some products. Storage at high temperatures for long periods may cause nutrient degradation, browning, and physical change. The following procedures are recommended:

- Product should be ordered and received only from approved and reliable vendors. Donated products from individuals or groups other than the designated vendor should not be used. Dented, rusted, or water-damaged canned products should not be accepted, but should be returned to the manufacturer or distributor. Product containers should not be damaged in any fashion, and labeling should be intact. Products received with an expiration date within 3 months (short-dated) should not be accepted unless needed for immediate use.
- The manufacturer should be consulted if commercially prepared liquid formula for infants has been frozen during shipping and delivery.
- Lot numbers of received products should be recorded and maintained as part of the inventory control system to facilitate response to product recalls. A bar-coding system would be helpful to accomplish inventory control. At the time of publication of this document, manufacturers' bar codes on containers do not contain batch codes. Pharmacy practices in tracking lot numbers could be considered as a model. The documentation of recalled lot numbers should include sampled products such as in gift bags distributed at discharge or from outpatient facilities. The use of such sample products or gift bags has been discouraged by the World Health Organization's (WHO) The Baby-Friendly Hospital Initiative USA (3).
- Formula for infants should be rotated using a first-in, first-out inventory method, with attention to expiration dates. The feeding preparation room technician(s) or designated staff should monitor the inventory routinely to remove outdated stock. Batch or lot numbers should be accessible in case of a recall.
- Expired formula for infants should be discarded in such a manner as to prevent its use. Storage at room temperature 13°C to 24°C (55°F to 75°F) in a dry area with relatively low humidity is most desirable. The outside limits on storage temperatures should be no more than 35°C (95°F) and no less than 0°C (32°F). The room should be well-ventilated.

Staff should be encouraged to report any suspicious or unusual physical qualities of formula. Some physical separation may occur during storage, but once shaken well the formula should appear homogeneous. Any foreign particulate matter needs to be investigated. Outdated formula may appear grainy or lumpy, or may have separation of constituents. Any concerns should be reported according to the health care facility's established procedure.

The health care facility should establish a process to follow for identifying a suspected problem with a product's physical appearance or integrity. Manufacturers should be notified using the toll-free telephone number located on the product's original container, or by contacting the manufacturer's local representative. In the event of a product recall, procedures of the health care facility should be followed to identify and remove the product based on lot number, and detailed documentation of the amount of recalled formula recovered should be completed. The Infant Formula Act of 1980 gives FDA the authority to track mandatory recalls.

Procedures for manufacturers' product marketing, including leaving samples in patient care areas, should be established and managed by the individual health care facility. The recording or tracking of product codes and lot numbers of nutritional products that are distributed as samples is not required by the Joint Commission at the time of this publication.

Ordering Formulas for Infants

Health care facilities should adopt written guidelines for ordering formula for infants and transmitting those orders to the infant feeding preparation room. These guidelines should include the following items:

- Designation of individuals who may order formula for infants.
- Transmission of orders for infant formulas using electronic (computer order entry) or a written form. Telephone orders should be followed with written orders.
- Assignment of responsibility for the transmission of routine orders to the infant feeding preparation room within an established time limit as well as prompt transmission of urgent or STAT orders.
- Format of the order should be as follows:
  - Patient's name
  - Patient's medical record/identification number
  - Patient's location
  - Name of base formula plus additives
  - Caloric density/volume/feeding frequency and/or infusion rate

- In addition, the following items can be useful and may be desirable:
  - Date and time of order
  - Food allergy (may be included in the patient's computer profile)
  - Route of administration
  - Name of authorizing physician

- Formula orders should be retained in a designated way (such as electronic or written). Long-term retention of formula orders should be consistent with the policies of the health care facility. The use of the electronic medical record provides for the retention of all orders by virtue of the design.
- Regarding rapid expedition of urgent or STAT orders, orders for a simple increase or decrease in the concentration or volume of formula for infants are not considered "urgent." However, new admissions, initial feeding orders, and orders for patients on some specialized feedings, such as formulas for patients with inborn errors of metabolism or who are on a ketogenic formula, may need to be addressed quickly. In urgent situations, infant feeding preparation room personnel should make every effort to provide for the needs of the patient without compromising the integrity of the hastily prepared formula. STAT formula changes should be processed within the period established by the health care facility once the electronic or written order is received.
- An after-hours procedure should be defined (see After-Hours Operation section later in this chapter).

Aseptic Technique (Clean or "No-Touch")

Aseptic technique must be practiced in the preparation of all infant formula in the health care facility to control the microbiological quality of the formula. Aseptic technique, as described by the Centers for Disease Control and Prevention (CDC) and others (4,5), incorporates hand hygiene in conjunction with "no-touch" technique. Aseptic technique provides stringent control of all actions to exclude contact contamination from personnel (eg, skin and clothing), work surfaces, equipment, and the environment (5). This technique prevents nutrient loss that may occur with terminal sterilization methods.

Gowning and Hand Antisepsis

All personnel working in the infant feeding preparation room must follow the gowning and hand antisepsis techniques approved by the appropriate committees of the health care facility (eg, infection control). A detailed description of the uniform code and of gowning is provided in Chapter 3 (6).

The CDC has published standards for hand hygiene (5). Written guidelines for hand hygiene techniques for infant formula preparation should include the following:

- Hand washing with an antiseptic hand wash is recommended for infant feeding room personnel whenever entering the feeding preparation room and whenever hands are visibly soiled (5). Hands and arms should be rinsed (using water control blades that do not require the use of hands, wrists, or elbows) and dried on single-use paper towels from a dispenser. Specific hand-washing procedures should be developed in conjunction with the facility's infection control program.
- Antibacterial agents, such as an alcohol-based, hand-rub gel, may be used at other times (5,7–10). Fingernails must be short and unpolished. Artificial nails are not allowed (7,11).
- Nonsterile gloves may be used while preparing formula. They must be changed whenever soiled.
- Infant formula preparation room personnel may use only hand lotions that are approved for use by the health care institution. Hand care products that contain oils or petroleum are ideal mediums to support microbial growth and should not be used. Consult infection control in each facility.
- A face mask may be used during formula preparation when the employee has any minor respiratory illness, depending on the guidelines of the facility's infection control committee. To be effective, face masks should be changed frequently (every 15 minutes or when they become saturated with moisture) (12).
- Hair should be covered with a surgical-type hat or hair cover.

Work Area for Formula Preparation

- Before infant formula is prepared, all work surfaces must be cleaned with an antibacterial sanitizing solution that is appropriate for food contact surfaces.
- The solution should be wiped off with individual paper towels from a dispenser.
- Surfaces should be cleaned after any spills during the preparation process and again at the end of the day's formula preparation.
- Cleaning supplies must be stored separately from infant formula products and ingredients.

Sanitation of Equipment   Large equipment located in the infant feeding preparation room must meet sanitation standards of the National Sanitation Foundation (13). All equipment and utensils used in the preparation of formula for infants must be properly sanitized or sterilized (14). Autoclaving or a thermal disinfection process (eg, commercial dishwasher) is recommended for effectively cleaning equipment used in feeding preparation (14). Sterilized equipment and utensils should be dated and kept wrapped until use. Sterilized equipment and utensils not used within 3 weeks must be sterilized again before use. Equipment may be sanitized in a commercial-grade dishwasher (13). Alternatively, in emergencies, sanitized equipment should be assembled, and all ingredient containers should be washed with an appropriate food-grade antibacterial solution, rinsed with clean water, and placed in a final rinse solution designed for a final rinse in a three-compartment sink used in food service facilities. Equipment that is hand-washed should be allowed to air dry or be dried with clean towels.

Facility-prepared formula for infants should be made with single-use containers; nipple assemblies; and disposable, commercial, tube-feeding sets that do not require additional sanitation. Reuse of bottles and nipples should be restricted to specialty feeding devices such as a Special Needs Feeder (formerly Haberman Feeder; manufactured by Medela Inc). Each infant is provided a specialty feeding device, which may be reused by that infant. Specialty feeding devices should be sterilized daily and can be cleaned after each feeding throughout the day. Guidelines should also be written for the sanitizing of any reused equipment, including bottles, nipple assemblies, and specialty feeding devices.

Laminar Airflow Hood   A laminar airflow is optional for a feeding preparation room; the hood provides

an additional barrier to potential contaminants. Laminar airflow hoods are commonly used in the preparation of sterile products (15,16). Use of a laminar flow hood for preparation of nonsterile products, such as powdered formulas, will *not* result in a sterile final product. See Appendix 5-A for sample procedures for use of a laminar flow hood. The hood should remain in operation continuously (15). If turned off for any reason, the blower of the laminar airflow hood should be turned on for 30 to 60 minutes before the bench area can be considered clean. Arms or hands should not rest on or touch the surface of the laminar flow hood. The manufacturer's guidelines for use always should be followed. When using a laminar flow hood, formula preparation should be done while working downstream and parallel to small- or large-volume containers (see Appendix 5-A).

Recipes, Records, and Labeling

Written formulations and instructions for the preparation of all formulas for infants should be available in the feeding preparation room. See Appendix 5-B for standardized recipes to prepare commonly needed formulas from concentrated liquids and a sample calculation for preparation of formula from powder. Specific composition of powdered formulas, including calories per gram, may change whenever ingredients are updated for these formulas. These changes can occur often and the timing is unpredictable. Label declaration of composition should be used to calculate formula recipes. Formula manufacturers can be contacted for current information when there are specific questions about their products. See Table 5.1 for contact information for major infant formula distributors.

TABLE 5.1   *Contact Information for Major Infant Formula Distributors*

Formula Company	Web Site	Professional Services Phone
Abbott	www.abbottnutrition.com	800/227–5767
PBM/Perrigo	www.brightbeginnings.com	800/485–9969
Mead Johnson	www.meadjohnson.com/professional	812/429–6399
Nestlé	http://medical.gerber.com/products	800/628–2229
Nutricia	www.neocate.com	800/365–7354

Manipulation of formula concentration with modules should be done with knowledge of final nutrient density of all nutrients, not only calories. Published guidelines for composition of infant feedings are referenced here; these guidelines should be followed unless there are specific clinical contraindications (17–19). New or specialized formulations must be verified for accuracy and appropriateness and must be updated as changes occur, preferably by a registered dietitian who is knowledgeable in the preparation of formula for infants. It is important that the specific written instructions for formula preparation be followed each time formula for infants is prepared.

Forms of Infant Formula

Ready-to-Feed and Concentrated Liquid Infant Formulas   Ready-to-feed and concentrated liquid infant formulas are commercially sterile products and should be used when available and nutritionally appropriate.

Powdered Infant Formulas   *Powdered formulas are not sterile.* Powdered infant formulas should only be used in health care facilities when clinically necessary and when alternative commercially sterile liquid products are not available. When there are no other alternatives to infant formula powder, clinicians need to be aware of potential risks with use of powdered formulas for immunocompromised patients (20–23). For a discussion of the potential risks, see Chapter 7.

Ingredient Water

> **Important note:** In this publication, all references to ingredient water should be understood to mean the use of commercially prepared sterilized water for oral use or water that has been boiled and chilled in the manner explained in this section.

Commercially prepared, chilled, sterilized water, such as that supplied by manufacturers of formula for infants, is recommended for reconstituting concentrated or powdered formula (24). Chilling ingredient water promotes quickly achieving holding temperatures $\leq 4°C$ ($\leq 40°F$) (25,26). Alternatively, a blast chiller can be used to achieve safe holding temperatures within 1 hour of feeding preparation.

If commercially sterile water is unavailable, any local water used in the preparation of formula for infants in the health care facility should meet federal drinking water standards required by the Safe Drinking Water Act of 1974 and Amendments of 1996 (27). Municipal, distilled, or other bottled waters cannot be assumed to be sterile. Potable water can be sterilized by using a heat-tempered glass or stainless steel container and bringing the water to a full rolling boil for 1 to 2 minutes. Water is then covered with a sterilized lid during cooling (26). As a result of the outbreak of *Cryptosporidium* in the water supply in Milwaukee in 1993, the American Academy of Pediatrics (AAP) recommended using water that had been boiled for 1 to 2 minutes. Once cooled, this water can be used for preparation of infant formula (26,28). Chemically softened water is not appropriate for use in the preparation of formula for infants because the chemicals used to soften water bind calcium and magnesium and increase sodium in the water in the process (29).

Preparation of formula using very hot water is not recommended. Problems with physical stability of the formula (clumping or separation), nutrient degradation, and safety of staff handling boiling water prompted the FDA to withdraw a suggestion to use very hot water in reconstitution of powdered formula (30). The WHO (23) has recommended preparing powdered formula with water at exactly 70°C (158°F); however, this practice has not been shown to be safe in a clinical setting and has not been adopted in the United States.

Formula Mixing

Preparation in the Infant Feeding Preparation Room
Formula and feeding containers should be handled under aseptic technique and in a location where there is little risk of contamination with pathogenic microorganisms or undesirable environmental substances (14,30,31). This requires a clean room with restricted access and healthy personnel (14). During the time designated for preparation of formula for infants, no other activity should be permitted in the room.

Only authorized personnel should have access to the infant feeding preparation room at any time. Chemicals used for cleaning should be stored away from any formula or feeding ingredients and away from the preparation area. Drugs or food not used in the preparation of infant feedings should not be stored or used in the room. Human milk may be stored and fortified in the feeding preparation room as long as care is taken to avoid any cross-contamination of human milk with feedings. The infant feeding preparation room should not be used for patient care. Formula should not be prepared at the bedside. Doors to the infant formula preparation room must be kept closed and secured during the mixing of formulas. Formulas should be prepared by trained staff using at least the standards established for safe food handling (14).

Steps in formula mixing include the following:

1. Sanitize surfaces to be used in formula preparation.
2. Check compounding recipe.
3. Assemble needed equipment and ingredients.
4. Use hand antisepsis.
5. Open and handle formula per specific procedures described by type of formula.
6. Measure ingredients using sterilized equipment and aseptic (clean or no-touch) technique (see specific procedures for various types of formulas later in this chapter).
7. Mix formula, using whisk or stick or immersion blender as needed. Upright blenders are not recommended (See Chapter 2).
8. Pour into clean or sterile container(s).
9. Label each container with at least the following: patient name, medical record number, formula name, formula dilution, and expiration time and date.
10. A new or sanitized container should be used to prepare each formula type to prevent possible exposure of the patient to allergens. For example, an extensively hydrolyzed formula should not be prepared in the same mixing container as an intact cow's-milk–based formula without first sanitizing it thoroughly. It is not sufficient to simply rinse the container with water.
11. Per facility policy, batch records may be recorded.

Refer to Box 5.1 for information on preparing formula in facilities that lack a feeding preparation room.

The preparation of a single feeding immediately before administration of the formula is recommended on the label of at least one powdered formula. This recommendation may be made because the product label was developed in another country where this practice is common. Infant feeding preparation rooms are generally not staffed 24 hours per day in the United States. To allow for the addition of water immediately before feeding, a measured amount of formula powder can be dispensed in a feeding bottle and labeled with the appropriate amount of water to be added. When the feeding is to be administered by continuous drip, chilled sterile water may be added to this measured unit of formula powder immediately before feeding. This preparation should be done away from the bedside, after hand antisepsis, and in a manner that minimizes risk of contamination. If the feeding is to be done immediately as a bolus feeding, the sterile water used can be at room temperature.

BOX 5.1   *Procedures for Preparing Infant Formula If There Is No Feeding Preparation Room*

When developing procedures, facilities without a designated infant feeding preparation room need to follow the principles and techniques described in this publication for safe preparation and handling infant formula. Anyone preparing formula must do so away from the bedside and after hand antisepsis. Accurate compounding recipes and sterile equipment and ingredients should be used. Powdered formula products should not be used when alternative sterile liquid products are available. If it is necessary to use powdered formula, it should be portioned by weight rather than scoop or household measuring utensils because there is a large range of measurement variation caused by packing of powdered formulas. This range of error can be as much as 25% because of the variation in technique among individuals.

Prepared human milk or formula must be adequately labeled as described previously in this chapter. Opened cans of concentrated liquid or powdered formula must be covered and labeled with expiration date and must be stored to ensure security and cleanliness during storage. If this is not feasible at the site of formula preparation, unit doses of concentrated liquid or powdered formula modules can be prepared using the appropriate measuring techniques in an alternate site such as the pharmacy. These additive modules must be labeled with instruction for adding them to ready-to-feed (RTF) formula or sterilized water and with the formula label requirements, including name of formula, instructions for mixing, and expiration date and time. Staff preparing formula should have specific training regarding safe food-handling practices. A related competency should be administered to help ensure safety and quality of the formula product (see Chapter 3). Achieving consistent safe food-handling technique may be difficult if many bedside personnel are required to prepare feedings.

Ready-to-Feed Formula

- Check expiration date.
- Shake formula well; clean and sanitize the top of the can before decanting or feeding.
- Open can by puncturing the can top in two places with a sanitized can opener. Care must be taken to prevent contact of the point of the can opener with the table surface or hands. The top of the can should not be touched with hands during this process.
- Opened commercial liquid formula can be stored in the original container for 24 hours in the refrigerator. The container must be covered and should be labeled with expiration date and time. Any unused formula should be discarded after 24 hours. Liquid formula held for longer periods is at risk for bacterial growth and loss of vitamin C and some B vitamins.

Concentrated Liquid Formula

- Check expiration date.
- Shake can well before opening.
- Clean and sanitize the top of the can.
- Open can by puncturing the top in two places with a sanitized can opener. Care must be taken to prevent contact of the point of the can opener with the table surface or hands. The top of the can should not be touched with hands during this process.
- Pour formula into a sanitized mixing container.
- Add chilled sterile ingredient water in the required proportion to the formula, following written instructions.

- If the formula is not prepared in a pitcher or another container used for pouring into individual bottles, transfer it to a sterile pitcher to be used to pour formula into bottles. Alternatively, a sanitized funnel may be used to pour formula into bottles or feeding bags.
- Cover prepared formula and immediately put it in a refrigerator used only for infant feedings (16).
- Use a new set of mixing equipment with each batch of formula to avoid cross contamination and to ensure that clean mixing conditions are maintained.
- Rinse all residue from equipment, and then sanitize equipment by autoclave or commercial dishwasher.
- See Chapter 6 for hang time of continuous feedings.

Powdered Formula

- Use powdered formula only when nutritionally comparable sterile liquid formula is not available.
- Check the expiration date. If the entire contents of the container will not be used, label the container with the date it was opened.
- Carefully remove the plastic scoop from inside the can, using a gloved hand or sanitized equipment, to prevent touch contamination.
- Weigh powdered formula on a gram scale, in a new disposable or sanitized container. Although formula scoops and household measuring utensils may be acceptable for formula preparation in the home, they are not reliable or accurate enough for hospital preparation.
- Measure ingredient water with a graduated liquid measuring device. Pour the specified amount of chilled ingredient water required for formula dilution into an appropriate mixing container.
- Transfer the weighed formula powder to the container and mix until all lumps disappear. A whisk, electric beater, or stick blender may be helpful.
- Once opened, label containers of powdered formula with the expiration date based on the opening time and date. The container should be covered and kept in a cool (room-temperature), dry area (*not* in the refrigerator) and discarded 1 month after the date it was opened. Refer to manufacturer's directions for storage. Powdered formula stored longer than 1 month (or the period stated by the manufacturer on the container) may become rancid and suffer excessive loss of vitamins A and C.
- When formulas are produced from manufacturer's unit-dosed pouches or packets, the instructions for preparation of an entire packet of powdered formula should be followed.
- Transfer formula from the mixing container to a sanitized, covered pitcher or container used for pouring the formula into individual bottles. A sanitized funnel may be used for this purpose.

Mixtures of Ready-To-Feed Formula

- Mixtures of 30 or 40 kcal/oz formulas with lesser concentrations of formula, such as 20 to 24 kcal/oz formulas, provide more energy-dense feedings while still using all sterile ingredients. This method is preferred to the use of nonsterile formula powders or modules as long as the final feeding product meets nutrient goals for all nutrients, including macronutrients and micronutrients.
- Recipes for these mixtures should be prepared by a source knowledgeable in formula compounding. See Appendix 5-B for examples.
- Use the same procedures described earlier for RTF formulas and for measuring, mixing, and labeling concentrated liquid formulas.

Additions to Formula in the Feeding Preparation Room   The Joint Commission standards for handling food and food modules are different from standards for handling medications. Macronutrient modules, such as carbohydrates, protein, or fats, are most appropriately added in the feeding preparation room, supervised by staff familiar with formula manipulation. Additives that are typically dispensed by the pharmacy, such as electrolytes or calcium, are considered medications in a health care environment and therefore should be administered by staff certified for that job.

Each facility should develop written guidelines governing acceptable ingredients that may be added to formulas for infants. Modules and additives added to formulas for infants may affect the physical and chemical stability of the formula. For example, medium-chain triglyceride (MCT) oil is known to interact with some plastics (see discussion later in this chapter). Written guidelines governing acceptable ingredients that may be added to formulas for infants should be developed with someone knowledgeable in physical-chemical compatibilities (32). Manufacturers of formula for infants should be consulted for specific product information. Honey, syrup, raw eggs, or unpasteurized milks must *never* be used in the preparation of formula for infants (26,33). Issues related to the addition of modules to human milk are considered in Chapter 4.

Use of Facility-Allowed Additives in the Infant Feeding Preparation Room

- Check expiration dates on modular or additive products.
- Follow written formulation instructions. The precise amount of module (carbohydrate, protein, or fat source) required should be poured or injected into the base formula. A medicine cup or single-use measuring device, such as a syringe, graduated feeder, or oral liquid dispenser, can be used for measuring liquid additives. Powdered additives should be portioned by weight.
- Use separate measuring devices for different modules and additives.
- Label formulas mixed with modulars or additives. The label should include the name of the formula and the added ingredients.
- Label opened additive containers and discard them within 1 month of opening or in accordance with the manufacturer's guidelines.

Freezing   Facility-prepared formulas for infants should not be frozen and thawed because freezing may cause irreversible physical changes.

Special Concerns

Administering Medications and Adding Micronutrients   Medications should *not* be added to formulas for infants at the time of formula preparation in the feeding preparation room. The mixing of medication with a formula increases the potential for physical and chemical interactions between the drug and the formula (34–37). Micronutrients, such as sodium or calcium, should be measured and dispensed by a registered pharmacist or registered nurse based on the policies and procedures of the health care facility. Practice may vary among institutions, but the following points should be considered:

- The addition of micronutrients (eg, calcium, sodium, or other vitamin or mineral additives) may change the osmolality, nutrient availability, and physical qualities of the formula.
- The risk of contamination may be increased by interrupting the feeding system to allow the addition of these products.
- Electrolytes, vitamins, or mineral additives are considered medications, and the addition of these to formula is outside the scope of practice of a feeding preparation room technician and *must* be dispensed in compliance with state licensure and the Joint Commission standards.

Medium-Chain-Triglyceride Oil MCT oil can soften or break certain types of plastic containers and utensils. The suppliers of MCT oil recommends that nonplastic containers and utensils be used in the preparation and handling of formulas with supplemental MCT oil. MCT oil added in the manufacturing of commercially prepared formula for infants has been placed in a stable emulsion and no longer acts on plastic.

If supplemental MCT oil is added to infant formula in the health care facility, the supplier or manufacturer of single-use disposable containers and graduated feeders used by the facility should be contacted to determine its stability when exposed to MCT oil. Polystyrene containers should not be used when MCT oil is added to formula for infants. Limited exposure to bottles made of other plastics may not be a problem if the infant formula containing MCT oil is held less than 24 hours. Once opened, the bottle of MCT oil should be labeled with the date opened and stored in a cool, dry area, but not refrigerated, for a maximum period of 90 days.

Colorants Colorants, such as blue food coloring, should *not* be added to infant formula for detection of aspiration (38). There is little evidence to support the sensitivity and specificity of colorants as a method to detect aspiration of enteral feedings in intubated patients (38–41). Systemic absorption of FD&C blue no. 1 has been documented in septic patients and is caused by enhanced gut permeability during sepsis (42,43).

Aside from the risk of systemic absorption and adverse reactions to the dye itself, colorants also are a potential source of bacterial contamination if doses are taken from a bulk container (44). *Pseudomonas aeruginosa* has been identified as a source of infection from contaminated food coloring containers (39).

Contaminants: Melamine and Bisphenol A Melamine is a synthetic chemical widely used in plastics, adhesives, countertops, and dishware. It does not occur naturally in food. Trichloromelamine is approved for use as a sanitizing agent on food processing utensils and equipment except for milk containers and equipment. Trichloromelamine decomposes to melamine. The Tolerable Daily Intake (TDI) for melamine for infants was determined with a 10-fold safety factor and has been established to be less than 1.0 ppm in infant formula (45).

Melamine was recently discovered in foodstuffs, including infant formula from China. The melamine was possibly added to inflate the perceived protein level of the diluted milk since melamine is high in nitrogen. Melamine is not an approved food additive in the United States (46,47). In light of this discovery the FDA issued a Health Information Advisory to reassure the public that there is no known threat of contamination in infant formula manufactured by companies that have met the requirement to sell infant formula products in the United States. No Chinese manufacturers of infant formula have fulfilled the requirements to sell formula in the United States (47). The FDA continues to conduct studies to assess the toxicity of melamine and the risk from melamine and its analogues.

Bisphenol A (BPA) is a chemical used primarily in polycarbonate plastics and epoxy resins. Polycarbonates are found in food and drink containers, such as baby bottles and water bottles. Epoxy resins are used in lacquers to coat the inside of food cans, bottle tops, and water pipes. Human exposure is generally through diet. BPA can migrate into food from containers made from polycarbonate plastic or with epoxy resin interior coatings, but it is not intentionally added to any foods. Estimated exposure is higher in infants than adults (due to the higher BPA-to–body weight ratio in infants and children). Based on ongoing review, the FDA has determined that BPA-containing products currently on the market are safe (48). However, given that exposure is higher for infants, and because it is difficult to establish a safe level of exposure, many institutions have implemented practices to reduce BPA exposure by, for example, purchasing baby bottles and other products that are BPA-free whenever possible.

Terminal Heating   Terminal heating (pasteurization) is *not recommended* as a routine method for preparation of infant formulas in health care facilities because of potential alteration of the nutritive and physical characteristics of the prepared formula. To kill vegetative forms of microorganisms, terminal heating is a method of heat processing in which the formula is heated to a temperature of 82°C (180°F) and then rapidly cooled to a safe temperature. Most facilities are not able to pasteurize milk. Some formulas for infants, such as those containing free amino acids or small peptides, will be nutritionally compromised by terminal heating. Unless oxygen is eliminated from the head space of the bottles, the degradation of vitamin C will slowly continue, even though the formula is refrigerated. Other potential problems include changes in the physical qualities of the product and other nutrient degradation with extreme (> 100°C, > 212°F) and prolonged heating.

Some health care facilities use autoclaves (steam under pressure) for terminal heating of infant formulas. This method frequently exposes the product to excessive heat, which may result in the caramelization of sugars, physical changes, chemical changes, and nutrient loss. Manufacturers of infant formulas recommend that autoclaves not be used to prepare formula in health care facilities. Autoclaves may be appropriately used only to sanitize empty bottles or equipment.

It is not recommended that formula be prepared with boiling hot water (31). See the Formula Preparation and Handling section earlier in this chapter.

Labeling Infant Formula   All units of prepared formula for infants must carry an identifying label. The use of preprinted labels or standardized label formats is recommended. Labels are often prepared at the time individual patient orders are reviewed and recipes to be used are identified. The container of facility-prepared formula or individual units of formula for infants should be labeled with the following information:

- Patient's name
- Patient's medical record/ID number
- Patient's location
- Base formula name plus additives
- Caloric density/volume
- Volume in container
- Expiration date and time
- Route of administration
- Frequency or rate of administration
- "For enteral use only"
- "Refrigerate until used"
- "Shake well" also may be included as a reminder to nursing staff to agitate the formula before decanting it into an individual unit or graduated feeder.

The expiration date and time for facility-prepared formula for infants should be 24 hours after formula preparation. To avoid confusion, the 24-hour clock (military time) is recommended for designating expiration times.

Preprinted labels for "shake well," "enteral use only," and "keep refrigerated" are commonly available for purchase and may be used in addition to labels generated through the patient information system of the health care institution. See Appendix 5-C for a sample label. The label may also have printed directions to discard contents within a designated hang time (see Chapter 6).

Packaging Infant Formula

Unit dosing for individual patients in quantities required for one feeding or per allowed hang-time is recommended. However, facility-prepared formula for infants may be packaged in bulk containers (eg, liter bottles) in up to 24-hour supplies. If prepared formula is packaged in bulk containers, additional precautions are warranted because of the increased risk of inoculating the formula with bacteria from the multiple openings of the container to access the formula.

Unit-of-Use Packaging   Formula for infants should be dispensed in unit-of-use containers. Formula for infants should be filled to the appropriate mark on a scaled container (taking the facility's policy on overfill into account.) Containers should be capped when filled, then a label affixed to the container. Safety tabs, if used, may be affixed over the container closure. If not used immediately, unit-of-use containers should be refrigerated to maintain safe food temperature (1°C–4°C, 33°F–40°F) during delivery and storage.

Bulk Container Packaging   When formula is prepared and delivered to the patient care unit in a 24-hour volume batch, a storage container made from food-grade plastic or other food-grade material must be used. Prepared formula that is delivered in bulk containers (eg, 1-liter or larger bottles) to the patient care unit should be decanted into graduated feeders or single-use bottles in the amount for one feeding or bolus. The prepared formula should be decanted using aseptic technique, proper hand antisepsis methods, and infection control precautions in a designated, clean area (see Chapter 3 and Chapter 7).

Bulk-packaged formula (eg, 32 oz cans of RTF liquid formula) should be repackaged in the infant formula preparation room. When packaged in unit-dose quantities, the amount of formula required for one bolus feeding or per 4-hour period is dispensed. If packaged in bulk quantities, the amount required for a 24-hour period should be dispensed. Unused formula should not be stored in opened, uncovered cans; it should be in a container with a tight lid. Any opened bottle must be labeled with expiration date and time and must be refrigerated between uses.

Packaging of Feedings for Continuous (Pump-Assisted) Feedings   Feedings may be administered using a syringe pump or enteral feeding pump device. Neonatal intensive care units (NICUs) often use syringe pumps for administration of continuous feedings. This type of pump-assisted device is used to facilitate optimal delivery of human milk. Human milk is not homogenized; fat separates and rises to the top. When milk is fed via a syringe pump, the pump can be positioned so that the tip of the syringe points up, thereby delivering the fat first. A syringe leaves little space for milk to coat the syringe as it empties, and the tubing used with a syringe is of smaller caliber than that used with feeding bags. A syringe pump also accommodates very slow feeding rates sometimes needed by extremely low-birth-weight infants. Use of a feeding bag increases calorie losses from human milk substantially because the bag drains from the bottom, leaving fat coating the bag and the tubing.

After several reports of administration of enteral feedings into intravenous or other medical devices, the Joint Commission issued a warning about misconnection of feeding sets (49). This warning suggested several strategies to avoid misconnections and improve safety. Unique syringe pumps designed for enteral feedings are just coming onto the market at the time of this publication. Health care facilities should make every effort to comply with safety practices designed to avert misadministration of enteral feedings.

Packaging of formula for infants receiving pump-assisted, continuous enteral feedings may be through a system consisting of a syringe and extension tubing designed for this use. Unit-of-use preparation of this feeding container and administration tubing set can be completed in the formula preparation room (50). Feeding containers with pre-attached tubing sets may be beneficial because the amount of manipulation of the device is decreased, thus reducing the potential for touch contamination (51). These containers vary in size from 100 to 1,500 mL. Feeding syringes range in size from 10 to 100 mL. The quantity of formula should be appropriate to that which will be administered during a designated acceptable hang-time. In NICUs or in other situations when small volumes of feedings are delivered by continuous drip, a syringe pump may be used. Extension tubing designed for the delivery of enteral feedings is recommended. This tubing has safety features to reduce the risk of accidental infusion of enteral feedings into an intravenous line. Color-coding of tubing has been proposed; at this time there is no standard enteral or intravenous (IV) color established in the US market. There should be written guidelines for the filling of containers or administration sets. These guidelines should be approved by appropriate committees, including the facility's infection control committee. Chapter 6 discusses issues related to hang time and should be considered when establishing policies related to hang time.

Work Area for Formula Packaging   All equipment used in the packaging of formula for infants should be organized on a counter near the preparation area. The feeding preparation room technician should use hand antisepsis (usually hand gel) and "no-touch" technique before packaging feedings. When a face covering is needed (see Chapter 3), a clean face mask should be used (8).

Storage and Handling of Infant Formula Units

Opened commercial formula for infants should be stored according to the manufacturer's instructions on the product label. Health care facilities should not store opened commercial formula for longer than 24 hours maximum. (Note: some manufacturers suggest that formula can be stored up to 48 hours; this practice may be safe in the home setting.)

If the health care facility is unable to ensure that opened containers are tightly closed and containers labeled with expiration date and time, unused portions of formula for infants should be immediately discarded. All personnel should be instructed and monitored regarding the proper storage of formula for infants. The use of can openers on the patient care unit should be discouraged unless there is a specific process and mechanism for sanitizing them after each use by thermal processing or autoclaving.

Refrigerator in Infant Feeding Preparation Room   Commercial refrigerators designed for the volume use they serve and that have an alarmed temperature gauge should be used in feeding preparation rooms (see Chapter 2).

Label Verification   Labels should be checked against the individual patient's feeding order before dispensing the formula or human milk to the patient care unit. If a formula is prepared based on an unconfirmed or verbal request, confirmation using the facility's order transmission system should be required.

Delivery to Patient Units   Feedings for infants must be transported in accordance with written guidelines of the health care facility and with local and state health guidelines (14). Equipment that prevents contamination of the formula and maintains formula temperature safe for food storage must be used to distribute formula to patient units. Safe food-handling temperature ranges can be maintained during the delivery process to patient units if chilled ingredient water is used, prepared formula is quick-chilled in a freezer for 20 minutes, and the formula is transported in coolers with ice packs. Depending on the distance traveled and the length of delivery time, a refrigerated cart may be required to maintain correct formula storage temperatures. A system to monitor the adequacy of temperature control of formula at the time of delivery should be established.

Infant formula unit-of-use containers should be placed in designated refrigerators on patient units immediately on arrival. Units should not touch one another to limit the possibility of cross-contamination. There must be integrated guidelines for the storage and handling of all infant formula by nutrition service and nursing personnel on the patient care units (see Chapter 6).

Refrigerator on Patient Units   Commercial refrigerators that maintain temperatures suitable for safe food handling should be used for infant feedings. There should be a separate refrigerator for infant feedings. Medications or employee items should never be stored in the same refrigerator. Feeding units stored in the refrigerator, both in the infant feeding preparation room and near patient units, should be slightly separated to allow circulation of air and promote safe food storage temperature.

State and local regulations on storage of human milk and infant formulas must be followed. Human milk and formula may be stored in the same refrigerator, as long as there are procedures in place to ensure that no feedings become mixed. To date, there are no federal guidelines addressing storage of human milk and formula together. The Occupational Safety and Health Administration (OSHA) has written an interpretation of their standards to exclude any regulation addressing human milk (52). Currently, other federal agencies have not published a position on this issue. Of primary concern are the prevention of errors and the maintenance of infection control procedures. A reasonable approach is to use a separate bin for each mother's human milk and to store formula on a shelf above human milk in the refrigerator. That practice would prevent human milk leakage onto formula containers. All feedings and bins must be clearly labeled to prevent misadministration. Consideration should be given to the need for additional control of access to refrigerated feedings for infants. The feedings storage area or refrigerator should be securable to prevent unauthorized access to the feedings and possible adulteration of infant feedings during storage in the nursery or pediatric unit.

Discarding Formula   Any facility-prepared infant formula units remaining in the refrigerator more than 24 hours after preparation should be discarded, as indicated on the label for expiration date and time (see Chapter 6). There must be written procedures for disposal of expired formula or human milk for infants on patient care units, including identification of responsible personnel and times to perform tasks. Expired feedings should be removed from the refrigerator on the patient care unit and discarded at a designated time each day. Any time a new formula is mixed for a patient, the old formula should be discarded. Infant formula containers can be recycled in compliance with the facility recycling policies. Human milk and containers that contact human milk should be disposed of in compliance with the facility policy for disposal of body fluids and medical waste; this includes any recycling.

Care and Maintenance of Facilities and Equipment   At all times the work area and equipment in the infant formula preparation room should be kept neat, clean, and organized. Written guidelines should be established for the maintenance of a clean unit, and daily checks should be made by the immediate supervisor to verify that directions are followed. Heavy cleaning (mopping, disinfecting, cleaning of refrigerator) in the feeding preparation room should be done at a time when human milk and formula are *not* being prepared.

All equipment and furnishings should be thoroughly cleaned after use (15). Spills should be wiped up immediately with clean paper towels. Brushes used in the cleaning of bottles, nipples, and utensils should be sanitized. Stationary equipment (eg, countertops and telephones) should be routinely washed with appropriate cleaning solution before and after the preparation of formula. Refrigerator interiors should be sanitized daily.

Work surfaces should be washed with cleaning solution appropriate for food contact surfaces before and after use. Floors should be cleaned at least daily with clean warm water and detergent; and only wet mopping or wet vacuum pickup should be permitted. If mops are used, they should be changed daily and either discarded or laundered. For wet mopping, a double bucket should be used to minimize contamination of the wash solution by dirty water. Under no circumstances should sweeping, dusting, or dry mopping be done during human milk or formula preparation (14).

Walls, ceiling, windows, and doors should be washed at scheduled intervals to ensure a clean room. All cleaning equipment and supplies should be clearly labeled and designated for use in the infant formula preparation room only (see Chapter 2). These materials should be stored in a cleanup area *outside* the preparation room (see Chapter 1).

Opening and Closing the Infant Feeding Preparation Room

Opening the Infant Feeding Preparation Room   Only authorized personnel should go into the infant feeding preparation room. The anteroom should contain clean scrub suits, gowns, disposable bonnets, and face masks for use by personnel in the infant feeding preparation room. The anteroom should be equipped with a sink and antibacterial solution for hand-washing before entry into the clean room.

Closing the Infant Feeding Preparation Room   At the close of operations, the infant feeding preparation room should be cleaned with a sanitizing solution, according to a prescribed procedure described earlier. At the close of daily operations, the door to the infant feeding preparation room should be securely locked.

After-Hours Operation   Procedures should be established for human milk and formula orders made after normal hours of operation of the infant feeding preparation room. Whenever possible and medically appropriate, RTF products should be dispensed and administered until modulated formula or formula concentrations that must be prepared from concentrate or powder can be made by the feeding preparation room technician. A written policy for situations requiring a formula that should be substituted (eg, formulas for metabolic disorders) should be established in each facility. Some facilities prepare approved formula substitution lists for after-hours interchange of similar formulas. Limited quantities of commonly ordered facility-prepared formulas may be prepared and labeled daily for after-hours use. Alternatively, a measured amount of powdered formula can be available and labeled as to volume of sterile water to add. Expiration dates should be labeled and products discarded when expired.

Irregularities in Infant Formula

Written guidelines should be in place for systems to report and follow-up in cases of any flaws in facility-prepared infant formula (eg, formula is defective, adulterated, or contaminated; a preparation error is suspected; or the label does not match the current order).

Infant Formula Recall

Under federal law, infant formula manufacturers must remove from the market all adulterated or misbranded formula that the FDA has determined may present a risk to human health (31,53). Recalls voluntarily initiated by a manufacturer must be conducted in a manner consistent with FDA requirements. Manufacturers are required to have specific recall procedures. Formula products recalled by the manufacturer or a regulatory agency should be handled in the health care facility in accordance with the recalling agency's instructions.

Tracking of batch numbers could facilitate response to recalls. However, batch numbers are currently printed on cartons and units of infant formula but are not included in bar coding. Any tracking would therefore need to be done by manual recording.

The facility should have written guidelines governing its response to recall of either facility-prepared or manufacturer's formulas for infants. All recalled products, including those used in the facility, those available as samples in clinics, or discharge supplies, must be considered in the event of a recall. The following items should be included in those guidelines:

- Notification of appropriate medical, nursing, purchasing, central distribution, and feeding preparation room personnel, as well as the administrative staff
- A system for reporting and follow-up
- Retention of recall records

WHO Guidelines for Safe Preparation, Storage, and Handling of Powdered Infant Formula

The Codex Alimentarius Commission was created in 1964 by the Food and Agriculture Organization of the United Nations (FAO) and the WHO to develop food standards, guidelines, and related texts such as codes of practice under the Joint FAO/WHO Food Standards Programme. The main purposes of the Programme are protecting health of the consumers and ensuring fair trade practices in food trade, and promoting coordination of all food standards' work done by international governmental and nongovernmental organizations (54). The Codex Committee on Food Hygiene requested that the FAO and the WHO review scientific research and give advice on *Cronobacter* (*Enterobacter sakazakii*) and *Salmonella* in powdered infant formula.

Expert meetings held in 2004 in Geneva yielded guidelines for preparation of powdered infant formula (55). In 2006 another meeting on this topic convened in Rome (56), and recommendations were made to Codex, member countries, industry, and FAO and WHO. In 2007 WHO published *Safe Preparation, Storage, and Handling of Powdered Infant Formula: Guidelines* (23). These guidelines are divided into two sections: one part for institutions preparing large quantities of formula for large numbers of infants and one part for home use.

It was recognized that serious illness from *Cronobacter* (*E. sakazakii*) and *Salmonella* have been transmitted to infants from powdered formula in several countries around the world, and that infants are at higher risk for infections compared with children older than 1 year of age. Reports of illness acquired through formula are rare (estimated to be 1 to 9.4 cases per 100,000 infants (57), but cases may be underreported.

The WHO guidelines provided detailed procedures for powdered formula preparation (23). Feedings made fresh for each feed are preferred, but the guidelines also acknowledge this is not always practical either in health care facilities or at home. Although the formula preparation procedures described in this publication are largely in agreement with the WHO guidelines, there are at least two notable differences. In contrast to the recommendations in this book, WHO advocates the following:

- Water for formula preparation be boiled. It should then be cooled to no less than 70°C (158°F) for mixing with powdered infant formula. This temperature should be verified with a sterile thermometer at the time of formula mixing. The feeding should be cooled to a safe feeding temperature; the temperature should be verified with a thermometer before feeding the infant.
- Hang time for continuous feedings should not exceed 2 hours. There is no recommendation about change of feeding reservoir and tubing.

At this time, the WHO guidelines for preparation of infant formula (23) have not been adopted in the United States. Problems identified with the use of hot water for formula preparation include risk of burn to staff during formula preparation or to the infant being fed, stability of nutrients, and clumping of powdered formula products.

REFERENCES

1. US Food and Drug Administration. 21 CFR Parts 106 and107 (1996). Current Good Manufacturing Practice, Quality Control Procedures, Quality Factors, Notification Requirements, and Records and Reports, for the Production of Infant Formula. http://www.fda.gov/OHRMS/DOCKETS/98fr/95n-0309-nec0002.pdf. Accessed November 21, 2009.
2. Center for Food Safety and Applied Nutrition. Infant Formula. http://www.cfsan.fda.gov. Accessed September 3, 2009.
3. Turner-Maffei C, Cadwell K. The Baby-Friendly Hospital Initiative USA Overcoming Barriers to Implementing the Ten Steps to Successful Breastfeeding. http://www.babyfriendlyusa.org/eng/docs/BFUSAreport_complete.pdf. Accessed October 3, 2010.
4. Centers for Disease Control and Prevention. Guidelines for prevention of intravascular catheter–related infections. *MMWR Morb Mortal Wkly Rep.* 2002;51:16.
5. Boyce JM, Pittet D. Guideline for hand hygiene in health-care settings: recommendations of the Healthcare Infection Control Practices Advisory Committee and the HICPAC/SHEA/APIC/IDSA Hand Hygiene Task Force. *Infect Control Hosp Epidemiol.* 2002;23(12 Suppl):S3–S40.
6. Saloojee H, Steenhoff A. The health professional's role in preventing nosocomial infections. *Post Grad Med J.* 2001;77:16–19.
7. Larson E. A causal link between handwashing and risk of infection? Examination of the evidence. *Infect Control Hosp Epidemiol.* 1988;9:28–36.
8. Jones R. Moisturizing alcohol hand gels for surgical hand preparation. *AORN J.* 2000;71:589–590,592.
9. Pittet D, Hugonnet S, Harbarth S, et al. Effectiveness of a hospital-wide programme to improve compliance with hand hygiene. Control programme. *Lancet.* 2000;10;357:479–480.
10. Pittet D. Compliance with hand disinfection and its impact on hospital-acquired infections. *J Hosp Infect.* 2001;48(Suppl A):S40–S46.
11. Pottinger J, Burns S, Manske C. Bacterial carriage by artificial versus natural nails. *Am J Infect Control.* 1998;17:340–344.
12. McLure H, Talboys C, Yentis S, Azadian B. Surgical face masks and downward dispersal of bacteria. *Anaesthesia.* 1998;53:624–626.
13. Joint Committee on Food Service Equipment. *National Sanitation Foundation Standard No. 3: Commercial Spray-Type Dishwashing Machines.* Ann Arbor, MI: National Sanitation Foundation; 1990.
14. US Food and Drug Administration. FDA Food Code 2009. http://www.fda.gov/Food/FoodSafety/RetailFood Protection/FoodCode/FoodCode2009/default.htm. Accessed December 10, 2010.
15. Avis K, Levchuk J. Special considerations in the use of vertical laminar flow workbenches. *Am J Hosp Pharm.* 1984;41:81–86.
16. Crawford S, Narduccin W, Augustine S. National survey of quality assurance activities for pharmacy-prepared sterile products in hospitals. *Am J Pharm.* 1991;48:2398–2413.

17. 21 CFR 107.100. Nutrient Requirements for Infant Formulas. 2001. http://www.fda.gov/Food/FoodSafety/Product-SpecificInformation/InfantFormula/GuidanceRegulatoryInformation/RegulationsFederalRegisterDocuments/ucm106547.htm. Accessed November 9, 2010.

18. Assessment of nutrient requirements for infant formulas. *J Nutr.* 1998;128(suppl 11):S2059–S2294.

19. Klein C. Nutrient requirements for preterm formulas. *J Nutr.* 2002;132(suppl):S1395–S1577.

20. Anderton A. Reducing bacterial contamination of enteral tube feeds. *Br J Nurs.* 1995;4:368–376.

21. 21 CFR 106. Subpart D. Standards of Identity. Part 106 Infant formula quality control procedures. Washington, DC; 2001. http://edocket.access.gpo.gov/cfr_2005/aprqtr/pdf/21cfr106.1.pdf. Accessed January 14, 2011.

22. ASPEN Board of Directors. Standards for hospitalized pediatric patients. *Nutr Clin Pract.* 1996;11:217–228.

23. Food and Agriculture Organization of the United Nations/World Health Organization. *Safe Preparation, Storage, and Handling of Powdered Infant Formula.* http://www.fao.org/ag/agn/agns/files/pif_guidelines.pdf. Accessed March 19, 2010.

24. Safe Drinking Water Act, 42 USC§ 300f et seq (1974) http://www.aaronline.com/documents/42_usc_300f.pdf. Accessed January 3, 2011.

25. Stehlin I. Infant formula: second best but good enough. *FDA Consumer.* June 1996. http://permanent.access.gpo.gov/lps1609/www.fda.gov/fdac/features/596_baby.html. Accessed January 3, 2011.

26. Committee on Nutrition, the American Academy of Pediatrics. *Pediatric Nutrition Handbook.* 6th ed. Elk Grove Village, IL: American Academy of Pediatrics; 2009.

27. Environmental Protection Agency. The Safe Drinking Water Act. http://www.epa.gov/safewater/sdwa/sdwa.html. Accessed January 21, 2003.

28. MacKenzie W, Hoxie N, Proctor M. A massive outbreak in Milwaukee of Cryptosporidium infection transmitted through the public water supply. *N Engl J Med.* 1994;331:161–167.

29. Lenntech Water treatment & purification Holding B.V. Water treatment solutions. http://www.lenntech.com. Accessed January 3, 2011.

30. US Food and Drug Administration. Health professional's letter on enterobacter sakazakii infections associated with use of powdered (dry) infant formulas in neonatal intensive care units. Revised October 10, 2002. http://www.fda.gov/Food/FoodSafety/Product-SpecificInformation/InfantFormula/AlertsSafetyInformation/ucm111299.htm. Accessed October 4, 2010.

31. Boyce J, Pittet D. Guidelines for hand hygiene in health-care settings: Recommendations of the healthcare infection control practices advisory committee and the HICPAD/SHEA/APIC/IDSA hand hygiene task force. *MMWR Morb Mortal Wkly Rep.* 2002;51(RR–16):1–58.

32. Davis A, Baker S. The use of modular nutrients in pediatrics. *JPEN J Parenter Enteral Nutr.* 1996;20: 228–236.

33. Rowan N, Anderson J. Effectiveness of cleaning and disinfection procedures on the removal of enterotoxigenic Bacillus cerus from infant feed bottles. *J Food Prot.* 1998;61:196–200.

34. Epps D, Feagans B, Joch L, Miller S, Behe K. Drug stability/compatibility in enteral formulations. In: Mohler P, ed. *Nutrition and Drug Therapy: Clinical Pharmacology Drug Compatibility and Stability.* Silver Spring, MD: American Society for Parenteral and Enteral Nutrition; 1992:23–40.

35. Crowther R, Bellanger R, Szauter K. In vitro stability of ranitidine hydrochloride in enteral nutrient formulas. *Ann Pharmacother.* 1995;29:829–862.

36. Stom JJ, Miller S. Stability of drugs with enteral nutrient formulas. *DICP.* 1990;24:130–134.

37. Udeani G, Bass J, Johnston T. Compatibility of oral morphine sulfate solution with enteral feeding products. *Ann Pharmacother.* 1994;28:451–455.

38. Maloney J, Ryan T, Brasel K, et al. Food dye use in enteral feedings: a review and a call for a moratorium. *Nutr Clin Pract.* 2002;17:169–181.

39. Potts R, Zarovkian M, Guerrero P, Baker C. Comparison of blue dye visualization and glucose oxidase test strip methods for detecting pulmonary aspiration of enteral feedings in intubated adults. *Chest.* 1993;103:17–21.

40. Thompson-Henry S, Braddock B. The modified Evan's blue dye procedure fails to detect aspiration in the tracheostomized patient: five case reports. *Dysphagia.* 1995;10:172–174.

41. Dahl M. HACCP and enteral feedings. The blue dye controversy. *Health Care Food Nutr Focus.* 2001;17:10–11.

42. Maloney J, Halbower A, Moss M. Systemic absorption of food dye in patients with sepsis. *N Engl J Med*. 2000;343:1047.

43. Ryan T, Batchelder S, Maloney J. FD&C blue no. 1 food dye absorption from enteral tube feeding in sepsis: a summary of five cases (four deaths) linked to systemic absorption. *J Am Diet Assoc*. 2001;101:A49.

44. Fellows L, Miller E, Frederickson M, Bly B, Felt P. Evidence-based practice for enteral feedings: aspiration prevention strategies, bedside detection and practice change. *Medsurg Nurs*. 2000;9:27–31.

45. US Food and Drug Administration. Update: Interim Safety and Risk Assessment of Melamine and Its Analogues in Food for Humans. http://www.fda.gov/Food/FoodSafety/FoodContaminantsAdulteration/ChemicalContaminants/Melamine/ucm164520.htm. Accessed January 1, 2011.

46. US Food and Drug Administration. Food Ingredients and Colors. October 7, 2009. http://www.fda.gov/Food/FoodIngredientsPackaging/ucm094211.htm. Accessed January 16, 2011.

47. US Food and Drug Administration. Melamine Contamination in China. September 2008; updated October 2009. http://www.fda.gov/NewsEvents/PublicHealthFocus/ucm179005.htm. Accessed January 2, 2011.

48. US Food and Drug Administration. Bisphenol A (BPA). February 19, 2010. http://www.fda.gov/NewsEvents/PublicHealthFocus/ucm064437.htm. Accessed March 1, 2010.

49. The Joint Commission. Tubing misconnections—a persistent and potentially deadly occurrence. Sentinel Event Alert; 2006. http://www.premierinc.com/all/safety/topics/tubing—misconnections/downloads/jcaho-sentinel-event-issue-36.pdf. Accessed January 16, 2011.

50. Centers for Disease Control and Prevention. Enterobacter sakazakii infections associated with the use of powdered infant formula—Tennessee 2001. *MMWR Morbid Mortal Wkly Rep*. 2002;51:297–300.

51. Mathus-Vliegen L, Binnekade J, de Hann R. Bacterial contamination of ready-to-use 1-L feeding bottles and administration sets in severely compromised intensive care patients. *Crit Care Med*. 2000;28:67–73.

52. Occupational Safety and Health Administration. Breast milk does not constitute occupational exposure as defined by Standard No. 1910.1030. Interpretation and compliance letters. http://www.osha.gov/pls/oshaweb/owadisp.show_document?p_table=INTERPRETATIONS&p_id=20952. Accessed October 13, 2010.

53. Electronic Code of Federal Regulations: 21 CFR 107.200–107.280. Infant formula recall requirements. 2001. http://ecfr.gpoaccess.gov/cgi/t/text/text-idx?c=ecfr;rgn=div6;view=text;node=21%3A2.0.1.1.7.5;idno=21;cc=ecfr. Accessed January 16, 2011.

54. Food and Agriculture Organization of the United Nations/World Health Organization. Food Standards. Codex alimentarius. http://www.fao.org/UNFAO/Bodies/codex/28/index_en.htm. Accessed January 16, 2011.

55. Food and Agriculture Organization of the United Nations/World Health Organization. Joint FAO/WHO Workshop on Enterobacter Sakazakii and Other Microorganisms in Powdered Infant Formula. Geneva, Switzerland. February 2004. http://www.who.int/foodsafety/publications/micro/pif2007/en. Accessed March 19, 2010.

56. Food and Agriculture Organization of the United Nations/World Health Organization. FAO/WHO Expert Meeting on Enterobacter sakazakii and Salmonella in Powdered infant Formula. Rome, Italy. January 16–20, 2006. http://www.who.int/foodsafety/publications/micro/pif2007/en. Accessed March 19, 2010.

57. World Health Organization. Enterobacter sakazakii and Other Micro-organisms in Powdered Infant Formula. http://www.who.int/entity/foodsafety/publications. Accessed February 15, 2010.

Appendix 5-A

Proper Use of a Laminar Flow Hood

Manufacturer guidelines for proper use of their laminar flow hood should be used.

Note parallel bottles in straight, horizontal line, not staggered in front of each other. Hands are "downstream."

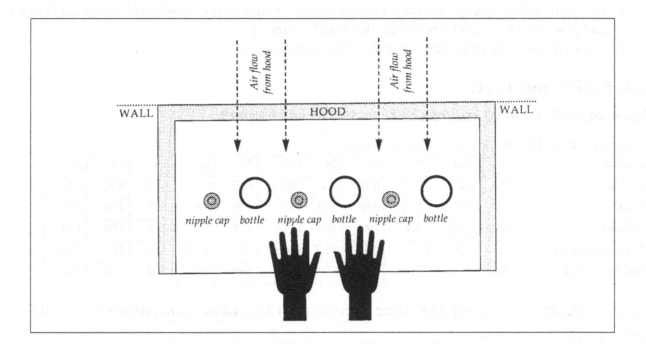

Appendix 5-B

Sample Infant Formula Recipe Instructions for Use in Health Care Facilities

Please read General Information prior to using recipe charts.

General Information

- The charts were developed using selected products, calorie concentrations, and volumes.
- There are recipe charts for:
  - Concentrated liquid formula (40 kcal/oz)
  - 24 kcal/oz formula mixed with 40 kcal/oz concentrated formula
  - 24 kcal/oz formula mixed with 30 kcal/oz concentrated formula
  - 22 kcal/oz formula mixed with 30 kcal/oz concentrated formula
  - 20 kcal/oz formula mixed with 40 kcal/oz concentrated formula

- The recipe charts for powdered formulas can be found on the manufacturers' Web sites. Powdered formulas are not commercially sterile and should not be used in the neonatal intensive care setting unless there is no nutritionally comparable alternative available. When available, a sterile ready-to-feed or concentrated liquid formula is recommended for use with all infants.
- If you are using a product that is not on a recipe chart included here, refer to product literature to determine kcal/g for powdered formulas or kcal/oz for liquid products and then use the appropriate chart, or contact the manufacturer.
- When altering formula concentration, analyze nutrient composition to ensure desired nutrient levels are obtained.
- In the hospital setting, use of accurate measurements for liquids (graduated liquid measuring devices) and powders (gram scale) is recommended. (See Chapter 2.)
- The recipe charts have not been reviewed by the manufacturers.

Sample Recipe Charts

Formula Made from 40 kcal/oz Concentrated Liquid Formula

1 can concentrated liquid formula = 13 oz = 390 mL

kcal/oz	20	21	22	23	24	25	26	27	28	29	30
kcal/mL	0.67	0.7	0.73	0.76	0.8	0.83	0.87	0.9	0.93	0.97	1.0
1 can (mL)	390	390	390	390	390	390	390	390	390	390	390
Add mL water	390	355	320	290	260	235	210	190	170	150	130
Final volume (oz)	26	24.8	23.7	22.6	21.7	20.8	20	19.3	18.7	18	17.3
Final volume (mL)	780	745	710	680	650	625	600	580	560	540	520

Formula Made from Mixing 24 kcal/oz Formula with 30 kcal/oz Concentrated Formula

Final concentration (kcal/oz)	26	27	28
Volume (mL) of 24-kcal/oz formula	60	60	60
Volume (mL) to add of 30-kcal/oz formula	30	60	120
Final volume (mL)	90	120	180
Proportion of 24 kcal/oz formula to 30 kcal/oz formula	2:1	1:1	1:2

Formula Made from Mixing 24 kcal/oz Formula with 40 kcal/oz Concentrated Formula

Final concentration (kcal/oz)	26	27	28	29	30
Volume (mL) of 24 kcal/oz formula	60	60	60	60	60
Volume (mL) to add of 40 kcal/oz concentrated formula	10	15	20	30	35
Final volume (mL)	70	75	80	90	95
Proportion of 24 kcal/oz formula to 40 kcal/oz formula	6:1	4:1	3:1	2:1	NA

Formula Made from Mixing 22 kcal/oz Formula with 30 kcal/oz Concentrated Formula

Final concentration (kcal/oz)	24	26	27	28
Volume (mL) of 22 kcal/oz formula	60	60	60	60
Volume (mL) to add of 30 kcal/oz concentrated formula	30	60	120	180
Final volume (mL)	90	120	180	240
Proportion of 22 kcal/oz formula to 30 kcal/oz formula	2:1	1:1	1:2	1:3

Formula Made from Mixing 20 kcal/oz Formula with 40 kcal/oz Concentrated Formula

Final concentration (kcal/oz)	24	26	27	28	29	30
Volume (mL) of 20 kcal/oz formula	60	60	60	60	60	60
Volume (mL) to add of 40 kcal/oz concentrated formula	15	25	30	40	50	60
Final volume (mL)	75	85	90	100	110	120
Proportion of 20 kcal/oz formula to 40 kcal/oz formula	4:1	2.4:1	2:1	3:2	1.2:1	1:1

Concentrated Formula Using a Powdered Infant Formula

This method can be used with any powered formula, at any concentration, and any final volume.

1. Refer to can or manufacturer to obtain kcal per gram in powdered product to be used:
   - *Example*: Neocate Infant: 4.2 kcal per gram of powder
2. Determine final calorie concentration and the final volume desired.
   - *Example*: Neocate Infant 24 kcal/oz; 24 oz (720 mL)
3. Determine the number of calories in the final volume. Multiply concentration by final volume.
   - *Example*: 24 kcal/oz × 24 oz (720 mL) = 576 total kcal
4. Determine the amount of powdered formula needed. Divide total calories by the kcal/g in the product.
   - *Example*: 576 kcal ÷ 4.2 kcal/g = 137 g Neocate Infant powder
5. Determine the displacement from the powdered formula. First, contact the formula manufacturer, check the product can, or check the Pediatric Nutrition Practice Group Web site or the *PNPG Post* for the displacement factor (1). Then multiply the grams of formula in the recipe by the displacement factor.
   - *Example*: Neocate Infant displacement factor = 0.7 mL/g
     137grams × 0.7 mL/g = 95.9 mL (round off as 96 mL)
6. Determine the volume of water to add to powder by subtracting the amount of powdered formula displacement from the final volume desired.
   - *Example*: 720 mL – 96 mL = 624 mL of water needed to make the formula

Final recipe: 137 g of Neocate Infant powder plus 624 mL water to make 720 mL of 24 kcal/oz Neocate.

Note: If the displacement factor is unknown, an alternative is to mix powdered formula in water up to the final total volume goal.

Household Recipes for Powdered Formula Preparation

Refer to the can for preparation of standard formula recipes using a scoop.

Refer to information on manufacturers' Web sites for instructions for preparation of formula from household measures.

Editor's Note: Product-specific recipes for facility or home preparation of powdered formulas are not included in this edition because changes in products make these recipes obsolete on an unpredictable schedule. The Pediatric Nutrition Practice Group of the American Dietetic Association published recipes for home use in their newsletter, *PNPG Post*, in April 2010 (1,2). These were current as of January 2010.

Due to frequent changes to products and the introduction of new products, any published data must be verified before use to see whether the information is current.

REFERENCES

1. Hustler D, Neiman Carney L. Formula recipe tables. *PNPG Post*. 2010(Apr);(20):3. http://www.pnpg.org/post/archives/20/3. Accessed October 3, 2010.
2. Hustler D, Neiman Carney L. Calorically dense infant formulas using household measurements. *PNPG Post*. 2010(Apr);(20):3. http://www.pnpg.org/post/archives/20/3. Accessed October 3, 2010.

Appendix 5-C

Formula Label Template

Patient name: _____

        MR #: _____

        Room: _____

Formula expiration date/time: _____

Administration route: _____ Volume: _____ mL Rate: _____ mL/hr

Frequency: _____

Base formula: _____

Nutrient additives: _____

_____

Final concentration: _____ kcal/oz

Mixture contains _____ mL plus _____ mL overfill

Keep refrigerated until ready to use. Shake well before using.

FOR EXTERNAL USE ONLY

Chapter 6

Delivery and Bedside Management of Infant Feedings

Deborah Hutsler, MS, RD, and Laura Benson-Szekely, MS, RD

Careful handling of feedings and the feeding delivery system at the bedside—including feeding tube, extension tubing, and feeding reservoir—is important. Retrograde colonization from the patient and/or their environment into the feeding in the feeding system is well documented and may have serious consequences (1,2). This chapter focuses on bedside management. Once the feeding has been delivered to the patient care unit and is safely refrigerated, the nursing staff is primarily responsible for ensuring that proper handling techniques are used. Written policies are necessary to ensure that safe and appropriate procedures for feeding tube care, product handling, and administration are in place and monitored.

Storage on Patient Unit

To avoid possible tampering or contamination, all formulas and expressed human milk, as well as feeding additives and supplies, should be stored on the patient unit in either a secured area or an area with limited access. Temperatures in refrigerators must be suitable for safe food handling and should be used for patient food only, not medications or employee items. Ready-to-feed (RTF) formulas, feeding supplies, and any additives not requiring refrigeration should be stored on clean, dry, covered shelves or in cabinets with protection from any environmental contaminants such as water splashes, dust, or cleaning supplies. Any items taken into an individual patient room should not be returned to the storage area or used for other patients.

Thawed or fresh expressed human milk, prepared formulas, and any additives requiring refrigeration must be stored in patient unit refrigerators. Ideally, expressed human milk and formula should be in separate refrigerators. If this is not possible, expressed human milk must be stored in an individual bin labeled for a patient and on the lower shelves to avoid any possibility of leakage onto prepared formula containers. If prepared items are to be stored on shelves attached to the inner door space, temperatures should be monitored to ensure that the refrigeration unit is maintaining a safe temperature. A temperature tracking system provides an added measure for maintaining safe storage temperatures.

A freezer must be available for frozen expressed human milk. Separate bins or sealable plastic bags must be provided to separate the expressed human milk for individual infants. For additional storage guidelines, see Chapter 4.

To avoid cross-contamination, other foods should not be stored in the patient unit refrigerators or freezers designed for expressed human milk and prepared formula storage, unless there is no other option available. Frequent opening of unit refrigerators and freezers may result in temperatures that are unsafe for food or infant feeding storage.

Bottle Preparation

Whenever human milk is transferred from one container to another and relabeled, authorized staff must verify that patient identification on the new label matches the original. Some facilities use bar-coding systems, whereas others use verification by two people; many facilities require that this verification is documented.

When preparing individual units for nipple or tube feeding, the following should be considered:

- Feedings should be handled on a clean, dry, disinfected surface. This area may not be used for potentially infectious wastes, such as weighing soiled diapers.
- Hand hygiene should be used before handling feedings, bottles, or other feeding devices.
- Bulk containers must be checked for the patient's name, identification number, and the expiration date. The label information should be checked to make sure it matches the current order. If there is any discrepancy, the feeding preparation room staff or a dietitian should be contacted for the appropriate feeding.
- When pouring specially prepared feedings from a bulk container, the feeding should be removed from the refrigerator immediately before pouring and returned as quickly as possible to the refrigerator. Container and lid integrity should be evaluated for cleanliness.
- For bottle or tube feedings, a graduated feeder should be used for feedings of 60 mL or less, and a standard single-use bottle with ounce or milliliter markings should be used for larger amounts. For tube feedings, a syringe, feeding bag, or bottle may be attached to the feeding set.
- After the desired amount is poured into the feeding container, it should be covered immediately with the appropriate cap or nipple, leaving the protective covering intact until ready to feed. Feeding should never be poured back into the bulk container once it has been poured into another container. Instead, it should be discarded.
- In the event that feedings are poured for more than one infant or that the container will be set down before delivery to the patient's bedside, the individual container should be labeled with the patient's name, identification number, full feeding name and any additives, time poured, and date.
- All bottles, nipples, syringes, feeding bags, and graduated feeders should be used only once. Home bottles should not be permitted, unless they are for special feeding purposes, such as the Special Needs Feeder (formerly Haberman Feeder), manufactured by Medela.
- If using a specialized feeding devices such as a bottle or nipple that is not disposable and is meant to be reused, the feeding unit should be washed in warm, soapy water in the unit, rinsed well between each use, and sterilized at least daily. Specialized feeding devices should be designated for the specific infant and should not be shared unless sterilized.

Warming

Although milk is traditionally warmed before feeding, bringing the feeding to a warm temperature will promote accelerated bacterial growth. Feeding that is to be tube-fed via continuous drip usually does not need to be warmed because it will assume room or body temperature as it travels through the tube. Warming of feedings for full-term infants before feeding may not be necessary (3–6). Warming bolus feedings for preterm infants is needed, and some infants may show preference for warmed feedings.

Acceptable methods for warming human milk or formula include electric warming units, warm water baths, and warm running water. The water should not reach the level of the nipple ring, and the lid should not be submersed in the water. Warm water baths should be cleaned and replaced with fresh water on a regular basis, according to institutional policy, as well as any time contamination occurs. If feedings are warmed, the process should take less than 15 minutes. Feedings should not be stored in milk warmers because extended warming time has been associated with bacterial growth (7,8). Devices designed to safely thaw and warm human milk commercially are available.

Microwave ovens should *never* be used to warm infant feeding because of the danger of overheating and the creation of hot spots. Feeding an infant overheated milk can burn the infant and the caregiver (9–12). When microwaved, the bottle may remain cool while the feeding inside is heated, and it is easy to overheat the feeding unintentionally (13). Overheating also causes vitamin loss.

Label Verification

Before feeding human milk or infant formula, the appropriate nursing personnel must verify the label for the correct patient name and identification number. The current feeding order should be verified with the feeding name on the label, including kilocalories per ounce and all additives. The seal on an RTF formula should pop or break when the bottle is opened. The expiration date should be checked for both prepared and RTF formulas.

If the formula appears curdled after shaking or has any foreign particles present, it should not be used. The cause of the problem should be investigated, and if a commercial formula or modular is involved, the manufacturer should be contacted.

Bottle Feeding

The appropriate designated personnel or family member/caregiver should wash their hands or use an approved hand-hygiene method before feeding an infant (14). The nipple cover should be removed only after all preparations for feeding are made, immediately before inserting the nipple into the infant's mouth. All formula for infants should be shaken before feeding. This will not only distribute heat, if the formula has been warmed, but will ensure that all components of the formula are in suspension. Before placing the nipple in the infant's mouth, the temperature of the warmed feeding should be checked by testing a few drops on the inside of the caregiver's wrist to confirm that the feeding is near body temperature.

Prepared feeding units that are removed from the refrigerator should be fed immediately. Ready-to-feed individual bottles should be opened just before use and either used within 2 hours or discarded. Once the infant has started to nipple feed, any feeding remaining in the bottle after 1 hour should be discarded because of the risk of bacterial contamination (15). Among older infants, an increased incidence of diarrhea has been associated with ambient holding of formula (16).

A policy for administering medications in infant feeding should be developed. In general, it is suggested that medications not be added to infant feedings. If medication is added to expressed human milk or formula, special precautions and aseptic technique are necessary. Properly trained personnel in compliance with facility guidelines for medication administration should do the addition of any medication to a feeding for infants. The medication must be compatible with the feeding (17). With certain medications, potential changes in osmolar load must be considered. Depending on the medication, addition to a small aliquot of feeding may ensure that a complete and maximally effective dose is administered to the patient.

Tube Feeding

The guidelines for this section are based on best evidence currently available and on consensus of experienced practitioners in the field. Manufacturers' recommendations for product use should also be considered.

The following steps should be taken when administering tube feeding:

- Use hand hygiene before handling feedings or administration systems. Using clean, disposable gloves may be beneficial (14,18,19).
- Assemble feeding system on a clean, dry, disinfected surface (not on the patient's bed or top of incubator). Avoid touching any portion of the feeding system that will come into contact with milk (eg, tubing ends, syringe tips, or feeding ports).
- Keep house-prepared feeding refrigerated until ready to use. If RTF formula is used, open containers immediately before use. Use good hand hygiene and aseptic technique when filling, refilling, or changing feeding containers (14).
- Limit hang time of prepared human milk and formula to a maximum of 4 hours (20,21) or less, with the expiration time clearly marked on the feeding container. If the feeding is interrupted or held or the feeding volume is reduced, there will be milk left in the feeding container beyond the hang-time limit. Replace the entire setup with a new supply of human milk or formula every 4 hours.
- Limit maximum hang time of decanted, RTF formulas to 8 hours. Longer hang times may be permitted for immune-sufficient patients. However, 4-hour hang times are appropriate for immunocompromised infants, newborns, and premature infants. With commercial closed systems that are available for a limited number of pediatric tube feedings, longer hang times may be considered. Refer to manufacturers' recommendations.
- Per manufacturer advice, do not give probiotic formulas by continuous infusion until there are data to support safety of this method (oral communication between this publication's editors and representatives of Mead Johnson and Nestlé; 2009).
- Flush the tube with sterile water after intermittent feeds and any medication additions.
- Replace feeding bags, containers, and tubing every new hang time, or follow the schedule in Table 6.1 for patients *older than 12 months* who are not immunocompromised (21,22–27). For the purposes of enteral feeding management, there is no clear definition of who is considered immunocompromised, and the decision is left to the individual care provider's discretion. Retrograde colonization of feeding systems is well documented (2,28–30). Policies regarding expiration time of feeding tubes and extension sets, feeding reservoirs, and the feeding itself all potentially play a role in enteral feeding safety.

The set up and manipulation of the feeding system in the patient care unit can be responsible for some of the contamination with potential pathogens. One study of pediatric burn patients found no increased incidence of infections when the feeding was added to the bag every 4 hours and the feeding bag and tubing were changed every 8 hours (31). When a new feeding solution, container, or extension set is hung, the expiration time should be clearly marked.

- Confine refilling bags to the home setting. Allow the feeding containers to empty completely before adding more human milk or formula. Rinsing the bag or tubing between feeds has not been proven to decrease microbial contamination (32).

Feeding Administration Systems

There are several options for feeding administration systems for intermittent or continuous feedings. Smaller disposable feeding sets (100 mL, 500 mL) are available with pre-attached pump tubing and non–IV-compatible mating adaptors for pump feeding. For gravity feeding, a gravity feeding set with screw top/drip chamber that can be attached to a graduated feeder or baby bottle is an option. Drip chambers were associated with prevention of retrograde bacterial contamination in two studies (33,34). Retrograde contamination occurs when bacteria residing in the patient ascend the feeding tube and contaminate the formula (28–30). This has been shown to occur in up to 85% of feeding systems in the neonatal intensive care unit (NICU), and gram-negative organisms are common (2). An open syringe connected to the feeding tube may also be used for intermittent feeding. Open systems should not be used to deliver enteral feeds unless it is by immediate bolus feeding, with the caregiver observing throughout the feed. Attention to selection of the feeding system, protocol for change of feeding tubing extension sets, and feeding reservoir and protocol for routine handling of the change of equipment is critical to control potential colonization of feeding systems. When feeding intolerance occurs, assessment of colonization of the feeding and the feeding system may be helpful.

The Food and Drug Administration (FDA) has issued a safety assessment of a plasticizer, di(2-ethylhexyl) phthalate (DEHP), sometimes used in feeding tubes or feeding administration sets (35). The FDA recommends that products containing DEHP be avoided especially for male infants if devices that do not contain DEHP are available. This recommendation is based on animal models in which DEHP exposure is associated with liver toxicity and testicular atrophy. All feeding products for pediatric patients should be DEHP–free (36).

Pumps may be used to deliver an intermittent or continuous feeding. The Joint Commission has published a letter of warning suggesting that equipment used for enteral feeding should be distinct from that used for parenteral purposes (37). Types of pumps used for neonates and infants include syringe and enteral pumps. There are situations in which a syringe pump is used to deliver small amounts accurately. Syringe pumps designed specifically for enteral feedings have recently become available. Previously, syringe pumps were designed for parenteral use and historically have been programmed for enteral use. There are several brands available; typically, they accept 1- to 100-mL syringes and can deliver flow rates from as low as 0.1 mL/hour to as high as 200 mL/hour or more. Box 6.1 lists recommended features for enteral feeding pumps for use with neonates and infants. Some pediatric enteral feeding pumps can be set for rates in 0.1-mL increments. In general, intravenous pumps should not be used for enteral feeding when enteral feeding pumps designed for infants or pediatrics are available. Caution must be exercised if an intravenous pump is used for enteral feeding because the pump should be used only for enteral delivery and not accidentally connected to an intravenous line (38). Unique tubing for enteral feedings—eg, one with a unique color and connector designed for feeding tubing—is *strongly* suggested (39). Systems with stopcocks should be avoided because they may degrade in the presence of medium-chain-triglyceride (MCT) oil additives.

TABLE 6.1 *Bedside Hang-Time Practices for Infant Formulas*

These guidelines are developed for pediatric formulas used in the absence of any commercially sterile, ready-to-hang closed systems.

Nutrition Source	Hang Time at Room Temperature[a] (Hours)		Frequency of Tubing Change (Hours)		Frequency of Feeding Reservoir Change (Hours)	
	Neonates/Immunocompromised Infants	Infants/Peds: Nonimmunocompromised Infants	Neonates/Immunocompromised Infants	Infants/Peds: Nonimmunocompromised Infants	Neonates/Immunocompromised Infants	Infants/Peds: Nonimmunocompromised infants
Sterile, ready-to-feed	4	8	4	8	4	8
Powdered formulas, concentrated liquid formulas, and nonsterile additives[b]	4[b]	4[b]	4	4	4	4
Formulas with probiotics	0	0	0	0	0	0
Expressed human milk, including with sterile liquid additives or pasteurized donor milk	4	4	4	4	4	4
Expressed human milk with added powdered fortifiers	4	4	4	4	4	4

[a]Hang times should be reduced by any additional periods that feedings are not at a safe temperature. In the described hang time, account for the time it takes for prepared human milk and formulas to reach ≤ 7°C (45°F), transport times that are not controlled for a chilled environment, the time it takes to warm feedings, and any additional times that feedings are not refrigerated. In addition, any break in aseptic technique or manipulation of the human milk or formulas, such as the addition of medications, tap water, or modules, should reduce hang time to 4 hours.

[b]Do not use for a preterm or immunocompromised infant unless a sterile liquid alternative is not available and the attending physician has considered the risk/benefit factors for the individual patient.

BOX 6.1   *Recommended Features for Enteral Feeding Pumps for Use with Neonates and Infants*

- Flow rate in 1-mL increments
- Flow rate accuracy of ±5% for neonates, ±10% for older infants
- Alarm for no flow or occlusion at a low pressure, eg, 12 to 20 psi
- Automatic antifreeze flow or bolus protection
- Lock-out feature that prevents changing settings
- Interlocking connectors to prevent accidental pull-apart

Features that may not be appropriate for this age group:

- Automatic tube flushing
- Some pumps state that feedings for pediatric patients need to be at a specific rate—eg, 25 mL/h or more—before the pump is appropriate to use; check the manufacturer's information
- Systems that can use intravenous tubing or have stopcocks

Continuous feeding regimens are associated with nutrient delivery problems for human milk (40). When human milk is continuously infused, large amounts of fat may be lost with separation and layering of fat in the delivery system (41). In addition to loss of fat, loss of protein may also occur (42,43). Tilting the delivery system so that the exit point of the feedings is elevated minimizes the loss of fat (44).

Continuous feeding regimens are also associated with nutrient delivery problems when medium chain triglyceride (MCT) oil is added to a feeding (40). MCT oil that is added to a human milk or formula may separate and/or adhere to the feeding system, with the risk of a fat bolus at the end of the infusion period (45,46).

Before initial use by each new patient, the pump housing should be disinfected with facility-approved antimicrobial spray (non–bleach-containing) or 70% isopropyl alcohol. Spills should be wiped off with warm water and a mild dishwashing detergent on a regular basis. If there has been exposure to human immunodeficiency virus (HIV) or hepatitis, the pump should be disinfected with a 10% concentration of 5.25% sodium hypochlorite (household bleach). With exposure to tuberculosis, the pump housing should be thoroughly cleaned using a 70% concentration of isopropyl alcohol (47). With exposure to methicillin-resistant *Staphylococcus aureus* (MRSA), vancomycin-resistant *Enterococci* (VRE) or other resistant infections, facility epidemiology departments may define procedures for terminal cleaning of equipment used for the patient.

Feeding Additives at the Bedside

Whenever possible, additives such as nutrient modules, concentrated liquid formula, and formula powders should be added to formula in the feeding preparation room, using aseptic technique. The International Formula Council (formerly the Enteral Nutrition Council) has cited the addition of substances to formulas at the point of use as a source of contamination because the substances themselves may contain microorganisms (48). Powdered formulas and powdered additives are not sterile products. The addition of modules may substantially increase the risk of bacterial contamination (49,50).

Mixing Equipment

Any measuring devices, mixing equipment, or other utensils or devices used for feeding preparation should be sanitized before coming into contact with infant feedings or additives to the feeding. Any mixing equipment must be sanitized after each use and covered with plastic wrap. Can openers must be cleaned and allowed to dry after each use, and the piercing end must be wiped with an alcohol wipe just before use.

If an additive is a vitamin, mineral, or electrolyte, its use should comply with facility guidelines for medication administration. Additives such as commercial thickeners and rice cereal may be added by nursing staff in a space dedicated to feeding preparation. Commercial thickeners that are stable when refrigerated may be added in the feeding preparation room. Smaller labeled containers for the individual patient, with a sterilized measuring spoon in a zippered plastic bag, may limit microbial contamination and provide an accurately measured amount. Measuring spoons should be sterilized and placed in resealable plastic bags. These sterilized spoons can be used for measuring cereal, but they are not accurate enough for powdered formula and other powdered supplements. Powdered formula should be measured by gram weight. Box 6.2 (51) provides information on weighing dry additives for facilities that do not have a feeding preparation room.

BOX 6.2   *Weighing Dry Additives When There Is No Feeding Preparation Room*

In a situation where there is no feeding preparation room, dry additives may be weighed on a scale reading in grams in a clean space (such as the pharmacy) and placed in a clean, food-grade, closed container (51). The scale should be sensitive to 0.1 gram. The container (ie, plastic cup with lid, syringe, or plastic bag with a tight seal) should be labeled with the additive, expressed human milk or the volume of formula to which it is to be added to make the ordered feeding and the expiration date. If designed for a specific patient, the patient's name, identification number, and room number must also be on the label. Nursing staff will then be responsible for adding it to the appropriate amount of human milk or formula and for shaking well before feeding.

For liquids, the ingredient (eg, formula concentrate or fat module) may be measured in the pharmacy or designated area and dispensed in a sterile or oral syringe and placed in zippered plastic bags with mixing instructions and patient information labels. Formula concentrate requires refrigeration until it is used. Mixed feedings should be fed immediately or refrigerated. Measuring spoons should be sterilized and placed in resealable plastic bags. These spoons are suggested for measuring cereal, but they are not accurate enough for powdered formula and other powdered supplements.

Colorants should not be added to an infant feeding for detection of aspiration or for any other reason. There is little evidence to support the sensitivity and specificity of colorants as a method of detecting aspiration of tube feedings (52–56). Systemic absorption of enterally administered FD&C blue No. 1 may occur due to enhanced gut permeability in patients with sepsis. The coal tar in the dye has been associated with multiple deaths, including that of a 12-month-old infant (57–59). When taken from multiple-use containers, colorants may also become contaminated and have been associated with outbreaks of *Pseudomonas aeruginosa* respiratory infections (60).

Parent Education at Discharge about Home Feeding Preparation

A policy should be developed to establish how parent education on feeding preparation is handled. Within a facility, standardized discharge education materials and recipes for home use should be used. Preparation of oral feedings may differ somewhat from the more conservative practices recommended for continuous tube feeding.

Formula products available in the retail market may be different than those available for institutional use. Powdered infant formula products are the most economical form of any given formula. They are also the most widely used form of infant formula in the home setting in the United States and within the Special Supplemental Nutrition Program for Women, Infants, and Children (WIC). Almost all retail formulas come in powdered form. Many come in ready-to-feed quart containers, and some come as 13-oz cans of concentrated liquid formula that must be mixed with water before feeding. A few are available in 2-oz bottles, similar to those widely used in health care facilities.

Recommendations for safe practices of formula preparation in the home setting may be more liberal than those recommended for the inpatient facility. Still, careful consideration of what is best practice at home is warranted.

Powdered Formula   There have been no specific federal guidelines discouraging use of powdered formula. There is, however, at least one *Morbidity and Mortality Weekly Report* (MMWR) from the Centers for Disease Control and Prevention (CDC) about an incident of an infant who was fed powdered formula becoming ill with *Cronobacter* meningitis. This is the same organism linked to meningitis in preterm infants that was traced to a powdered infant formula (61).

Powdered formulas prepared at home may be portioned by measuring devices such as the scoop that comes in the can or standard household measuring cups designed for dry ingredients (ie, the kind that can be leveled off with a straight edge). Water should be measured with a cup, bottle, or other container designed for liquid measurements.

Suggested routine feeding preparation practices include the following:

- Powdered formulas prepared at home should be measured per formula label recommendations when standard dilutions are used.
- When preparing formula at home, the scoop that comes with an individual formula should be used to measure powdered formula. Note: Each scoop is individualized to each specific formula product, and there is great variation among different products.
- Use of sterile water is optional for most infants at home. Apart from "baby water," most bottled water is not sterile. If sterile water is needed, tap or bottled water can be boiled for 1 to 2 minutes and cooled before mixing formula.
- Prepared formula should be fed to the infant or refrigerated immediately. Keeping prepared formula on a bedside table during the night in case a night feeding is required should be discouraged.
- No more than a 24-hour supply of feedings should be prepared for refrigeration.
- If traveling away from the home, water for formula preparation and powdered formula should be carried in separate containers. A feeding should be mixed immediately before feeding it to the infant.
- Once a bottle has been in the infant's mouth, any remaining formula not taken within 1 hour should be discarded (15).
- Manufacturer's Web sites should be referenced for guidelines for preparation of higher concentrations of feedings than standard dilution, and for preparation of larger volumes than a single feeding, such as a 24-hour supply. The Pediatric Nutrition Practice Group of the American Dietetic Association (PNPG) has also published recipes on their Web site (http://www.pnpg.org).

- **Caution:** If there is any question regarding information on a Web site vs information on the package label, always check with the manufacturer. Any change in formulation of products can affect the mixing instructions.
- Due to variation in accuracy of scoop or household measure of dry ingredients, target concentration of feedings using powdered formulas should not be more than 27 kcal/oz for home use. Depending on the product used, normal range of error can be 10% to 25%. With 20 to 24 kcal/oz feedings, this range of dilution may be tolerated. At the higher concentrations, there is greater risk of hyperosmolar dehydration, particularly when there is unusual fluid loss, such as hot weather or with the use of diuretics. If a concentration of calories more than 27 kcal/oz is needed, concentrated liquid formula is recommended, when it is available, to provide a more accurate final concentration.

If demonstrations for mixing feedings are part of the education process, each facility should develop guidelines. If the patient is in a separate room, a designated clean area within the room may be an acceptable area for the parents to demonstrate mixing techniques. Another option is to use a separate clean room or the feeding preparation room (during a non-mixing period), following the same procedures for cleanliness and using separate product. Any opened, unused product should be sent home with the parent or discarded. Do not return opened products to the feeding room stock.

Human Milk
Suggested routine practices for human milk handling at home include the following:

- Putting the infant to breast is safest from an infection-control standpoint.
- Pumped human milk not immediately fed to the infant should be refrigerated.
- Fresh human milk can be transported for use at health care facilities. It is recommended that it be transported in an insulated bag with ice packs and kept refrigerated prior to feeding (see Chapter 4).
- Human milk frozen at home can be transported in a frozen state to the health care facility (see Chapter 4).
- Human milk sent to daycare with an infant should be clearly labeled with the infant's name and expiration date and time.

Tube Feedings
Suggested formula preparation and handling for continuous home tube feedings include the following:

- When human milk is not available, a sterile liquid product should be used whenever possible.
- Hang time of a continuous feeding using a closed system should follow manufacturer guidelines.
- Hang time of a continuous ready to feed product in an open system should be limited to 8 hours. If longer feedings are needed, the bag should be allowed to empty completely before refilling.
- When powdered formula is necessary, it should be prepared with sterilized water using the preparation and storage practices described earlier.
- Hang time of a home prepared continuous feedings should be limited to 4 hours routinely. A longer hang time for overnight can be considered on an individual basis. When a hang time longer than 4 hours is used it is suggested that a new feeding bag be used at the beginning of the longer hang time and the bag should be allowed to empty completely before refilling.
- For continuous feeding, it is suggested that a new bag and tubing set be used at least every 24 hours.

The following are recommendations for human milk handling for infants who need tube feeding:

- Whenever possible, human milk should be fed by handheld bolus feeding.

- When continuous feeding is necessary, a syringe pump will allow best delivery of the fat from human milk.
- If a syringe pump is not available and continuous feeds are needed, the feeding rate should be adjusted to accommodate the substantial loss of fat expected from a feeding bag and tubing set. This can be as high as 34% with continuous infusion (see Chapter 4).

REFERENCES

1. Mehall J, Kite C, Saltzman D, Wallett T, Jackson R, Smith S. Prospective study of the incidence and complications of bacterial contamination of enteral feeding in neonates. *J Pediatr Surg.* 2002;37:1177–1182.
2. Hurrell E, Kucerova E, Loughlin M, et al. Neonatal enteral feeding tubes as loci for colonisation by members of the Enterobacteriaceae. *BMC Infect Dis.* 2009;9:146.
3. Holt L, Davises E, Hasselmeyer E, Adams A. A study of premature infants fed cold formula. *J Pediatrics.* 1962;61:556–561.
4. Eckburg J, Bell E, Rios G, Wilmothe P. Effects of formula temperature on post-prandial thermogenesis and body temperature of premature infants. *J Pediatrics.* 1987;111:588–592.
5. Costalos C, Ross I, Campbell A, Sofi M. Is it necessary to warm infants' feeds? *Arch Dis Child.* 1979;54:899–901.
6. Makoi Z, Dunn P, Speidel B. Effect of taste and temperature on neonatal sucking behavior. *Acta Paediatr.* 1989;19:299–301.
7. Biering G, Karlsson S, Clark N. Three cases of neonatal meningitis caused by Enterobacter sakazakii in powdered milk. *J Clin Microbiol.* 1989;27:2054–2056.
8. Muytjens H, Kollee L. Enterobacter sakazakki menintits in neonates: causative role of formula [letter]. *Pediatr Infect Dis J.* 1990;9:372–373.
9. Hibbard R, Blevins R. Palatal burn due to bottle warming in microwave oven. *Pediatrics.* 1988;82:382–384.
10. Puczynski M, Rademaker D, Gatson R. Burn injury related to the improper use of a microwave oven. *Pediatrics.* 1983;72:714–715.
11. Garland R. Airway burns in an infant following aspiration of microwave heated tea. *Chest.* 1986;90:621–622.
12. Dixon J, Burd D, Roberts D. Severe burns resulting from an exploding teat on a bottle of infant formula milk heated in a microwave oven. *Burns.* 1997;23:268–269.
13. Sando W, Gallaher K, Rodgers B. Risk factors for microwave scald injuries. *J Pediatrics.* 1984;105:864–867.
14. Boyce J, Pittet D. Guidelines for hand hygiene in health-care settings: Recommendations of the healthcare infection control practices advisory committee and the HICPAD/SHEA/APIC/IDSA hand hygiene task force. *MMWR Morb Mortal Wkly Rep.* 2002;51(RR-16):1–58.
15. American Academy of Pediatrics. Preparing, Sterilizing, and Storing Formula. Caring for Your Baby and Young Child: Birth to Age 5. . http://www.healthychildren.org/English/ages-stages/baby/feeding-nutrition/pages/Preparing-Sterilizing-and-Storing-Formula.aspx. Accessed January 16, 2011.
16. Fein S, Falci C. Infant formula preparation, handling and related practices in the United States. *J Am Diet Assoc.* 1999;99:1234–1240.
17. McCarthy M, Fabling J, eds. *Drug-Nutrient Interactions.* Dubuque, IA: Kendall Hunt Publishing Co; 2002.
18. Anderton A, Aidoo K. The effect of handling procedures on microbiological contamination of enteral feeds—a comparison of the use of sterile vs non-sterile gloves. *J Hosp Infect.* 1991;17:297–301.
19. Beattie T, Anderton A. Decanting versus sterile pre-filled nutrient containers—the microbiologic risks in enteral feeding. *Int J Environ Health Res.* 2001;11:81–93.
20. Anderton A. Reducing bacterial contamination of enteral tube feeds. *Br J Nurs.* 1995;4:368–376.
21. Davis A. Indications and techniques for enteral feeds. In: Baker S, Baker R, Davis A, eds. *Pediatric Enteral Nutrition.* New York, NY: Chapman & Hall; 1994:67–94.
22. Kohn C. The relationship between enteral formula contamination and length of enteral delivery set usage. *JPEN J Parenter Enteral Nutr.* 1991;15:567–571.

23. Oie S, Kamiya A, Hironaga K, Koshiro A. Microbial contamination of enteral feeding solution and its prevention. *Am J Infect Control.* 1993;21:34–38.

24. Anderton A, Nwoguh C. Problems with the re-use of enteral feeding systems: a study of effectiveness of cleaning and disinfecting procedures. *J Hum Nutr Diet.* 1991;4:25–32.

25. Bankhead R, Boullata J, Brantley S, et al. Enteral nutrition practice recommendations. *JPEN J Parenter Enteral Nutr.* 2009;33:122–167.

26. Centers for Disease Control and Prevention. Enterobacter sakazakii infections associated with the use of powdered infant formula—Tennessee 2001. *MMWR Morb Mortal Wkly Rep.* 2002;51:297–300.

27. US Food and Drug Administration. Health professional's letter on enterobacter sakazakii infections associated with use of powdered (dry) infant formulas in neonatal intensive care units; revised October 10, 2002. http://www.fda.gov/Food/FoodSafety/Product-SpecificInformation/InfantFormula/AlertsSafetyInformation/ucm111299.htm. Accessed October 4, 2010.

28. McKinlay J, Wildgoose A, Wood W, Gould I, Anderton A. The effect of system design on bacterial contamination of enteral tube feeds. *J Hosp Infect.* 2001;47:138–142.

29. Bott L, Husson M, Michaud L, Arnaud-Battandier F, Turck D, Gottrand F. Contamination of gastrostomy feeding systems in children in a home-based enteral nutrition program. *J Pediatr Gastroenterol Nutr.* 2001;33:266–270.

30. Mathus-Vliegen EM, Bredius MW, Binnekade JM. Analysis of sites of bacterial contamination in an enteral feeding system. *JPEN J Parenter Enteral Nutr.* 2006;30:519–525.

31. Neely AN, Mayes T, Gardner J, Kagan RJ, Gottschlich MM. A microbiologic study of enteral feeding hang time in a burn hospital: can feeding costs be reduced without compromising patient safety? *Nutr Clin Pract.* 2006;21:610–616.

32. Kohn-Keeth C, Schott S, Olrec K. The effects of rinsing enteral delivery sets on formula contamination. *Nutr Clin Pract.* 1996;11:269–273.

33. Payne-James J, Rana S, Bray M, McSwiggan D, Silk D. Retrograde (ascending) bacterial contamination of enteral diet administration systems. *JPEN J Parenter Enteral Nutr.* 1992;16:369–373.

34. Moffitt SK, Gohman SM, Sass KM, Faucher KJ. Clinical and laboratory evaluation of a closed enteral feeding system under cyclic feeding conditions: a microbial and cost evaluation. *Nutrition.* 1997;13:622–628.

35. Center for Devices and Radiological Health. Safety Assessment of di(2-ethylhexyl)phthalate (DEHP) Released from PVC Medical Devices. Rockville, MD: US Food and Drug Administration; 2002.

36. Shea KM. Pediatric exposure and potential toxicity of phthalate plasticizers. *Pediatrics.* 2003;111:1467–1474.

37. The Joint Commission. Tubing misconnections—a persistent and potentially deadly occurrence. Sentinel Event Alert; 2006. http://www.premierinc.com/all/safety/topics/tubing-misconnections/downloads/jcaho-sentinel-event-issue-36.pdf. Accessed January 16, 2011.

38. Huddleston K, Creekmore P, Wood B. Administration of infant formula through the intravenous route: consequences and prevention. *MCN Am J Matern Child Nurs.* 1994;19:40–42.

39. US Food and Drug Administration. Letter regarding luer lock connectors on tubing sets, solution bag and other medical products. http://www.fda.gov/MedicalDevices/Safety/MedSunMedicalProductSafetyNetwork/ucm127745.htm. Accessed January 16, 2011.

40. Wessel J. Feeding methodologies. In: Groh-Wargo S, Thompson M, Cox J, eds. *Nutritional Care for High-Risk Newborns.* 3rd ed. Chicago, IL: Precept Press; 2000:321–339.

41. Greer F, McCormick A, Loker J. Changes in fat concentration of human milk during delivery by intermittent bolus and continuous mechanical pump infusion. *J Pediatrics.* 1984;105:745–749.

42. Stocks R, Davies D, Allen F, Sewell D. Loss of breastmilk nutrients during tube feeding. *Arch Dis Child.* 1985;60:164–166.

43. Brennan-Behman M, Carlson G, Meier P, Engstrom J. Caloric loss from expressed mother's milk during continuous gavage infusion. *Neonatal Network.* 1994;13:27.

44. Narayanan I, Singh B, Harvey D. Fat loss during feeding of human milk. *Arch Dis Child.* 1984;59:475–477.

45. Mehta N, Hamosh M, Bitman J, Wood D. Adherence of medium-chain fatty acids to feeding tubes of premature infants fed formula fortified with medium chain triglycerides. *J Pediatr Gastroenterol Nutr.* 1991;13:267–269.

46. Mehta N, Hamosh M, Bitman J, Wood D. Adherence of medium-chain fatty acids to feeding tubes during gavage feeding of human milk fortified with medium chain triglycerides. *J Pediatrics.* 1988;112:474–476.

47. Ross Companion Enteral Pump [cleaning procedures package insert].Columbus, OH: Abbott Laboratories, Ross Product Division; 2000.

48. Enteral Nutrition Council. *Microbiological Methods of Analysis for Enteral Nutritional Formulas*. Atlanta, GA: Enteral Nutrition Council; 1986.

49. Patchell C, Anderton A, MacDonald A, George R, Booth I. Bacterial contamination of enteral feeds. *Arch Dis Child*. 1994;70:327–330.

50. Davis A, Baker S. The use of modular nutrients in pediatrics. *JPEN J Parenter Enteral Nutr*. 1996;20:228–236.

51. US Food and Drug Administration. Guidance for Industry: Use of Recycled Plastics in Food Packaging: Chemistry Considerations. http://www.fda.gov/Food/GuidanceComplianceRegulatoryInformation/GuidanceDocuments/FoodIngredientsandPackaging/ucm120762.htm. Accessed December, 2009.

52. Potts R, Zarovkian M, Guerrero P, Baker C. Comparison of blue dye visualization and glucose oxidase test strip methods for detecting pulmonary aspiration of enteral feedings in intubated adults. *Chest*. 1993;103:17–21.

53. Thompson-Henry S, Braddock B. The modified Evan's blue dye procedure fails to detect aspiration in the tracheostomized patient: five case reports. *Dysphagia*. 1995;10:172–174.

54. Brady S, Hildner C, Hutchins B. Simultaneous videofluoroscopic swallow study and modified Evans blue dye procedure: an evaluation of blue dye visualization in cases of known aspiration. *Dysphagia*. 1999;14:146–148.

55. Metheny N, Clouse R. Bedside methods for detecting aspiration in tube-fed patients. *Chest*. 1997;111:724–731.

56. Donzelli J, Brady S, Wesling M, Craney M. Simultaneous modification in Evans blue dye procedure and video nasal endoscopic evaluation of the swallow. *Laryngoscope*. 2001;111:1746–1750.

57. Ryan T, Batchelder S, Maloney J. FD&C blue no. 1 food dye absorption from enteral tube feeding in sepsis: a summary of five cases (four deaths) linked to systemic absorption. *J Am Diet Assoc*. 2001;101:A49.

58. Maloney J, Halbower A, Moss M. Systemic absorption of food dye in patients with sepsis. *N Engl J Med*. 2000;343:1047.

59. Maloney J, Ryan T, Brasel K, et al. Food dye use in enteral feedings: a review and a call for a moratorium. *Nutr Clin Pract*. 2002;17:169–181.

60. File T, Tan J, Thomson R, Stephens C. An outbreak of Pseudomonas aeruginosa ventilator-associated respiratory infections due to contaminated food coloring dye—further evidence of the significance of gastric colonization preceding nosocomial pneumonia. *Infect Control Hosp Epidemiol*. 1995;16:417–418.

61. Centers for Disease Control and Prevention. Cronobacter species isolation in two infants—New Mexico, 2008. *MMWR Morb Mortal Wkly Rep*. 2009;58:1179–1183.

Chapter 7

Microbiology and Infection Control

Caroline Steele, MS, RD, CSP, IBCLC, and Susan Kinzler, RD

Important Note: The US Food and Drug Administration (FDA) has been charged with the implementation of the Infant Formula Act of 1980 and the Amendments of 1986. This law regulates the infant formula industry. The FDA has an infant formula section on its Web site (http://www.fda.gov/Food/default.htm), which provides regulatory information affecting infant formulas. The Web site contains information for health care providers, including letters of warning about formulas, recalls, how to report an adverse event, and other pertinent information about the FDA's interests in infant formula (1).

Microbiology and infection control are related topics that directly impact patient safety. In recent years there has been increasing concern about potential pathogens in infant formulas. Considerable discussion has focused on methods to reduce the risk of contamination of formula feedings. In 2000, the Joint Commission suggested applying the Hazard Analysis Critical and Control Point (HACCP) guidelines to enteral feedings (2). As a result, many hospitals began using HACCP principles specifically for the handling of expressed human milk and the preparation of infant formula. These guidelines are discussed more in depth later in this chapter and in Chapters 5 and 8 (3–5). Monitoring the safety of infant feeding preparation is a multidisciplinary task; the responsibility may be assigned to the hospital infection control committee or the patient safety committee.

Reports of *Cronobacter* spp (a recently proposed genus that encompasses organisms previously known as *Enterobacter sakazakii*) infections occurring in hospitalized infants who were fed powdered formulas have focused on proper formula-handling techniques and on the prevention of infectious outbreaks (6–18). Such reports led the FDA and the Centers for Disease Control and Prevention (CDC) to recommend restricting the use of nonsterile, powdered infant formulas for hospitalized infants, particularly those who are premature or immunocompromised (19). In addition, there have been *Salmonella* outbreaks in neonatal intensive care units (NICUs) traced to contaminated powdered formula (20).

Commercially sterile liquid infant formula products are preferred for hospital use, especially for preterm and immunocompromised patient populations. However, powdered infant formula may be used when nutritionally necessary or when there is no alternative sterile liquid form available. Powdered formulas may be manufactured by dry-blending the powdered ingredients or by preparing a liquid formula, pasteurizing, and then spray-drying the liquid product. During dry-blending or the final stages of liquid-to-dry production, microorganisms may be inadvertently introduced (11,12,16,21–26). The low moisture content of powders limits potential microbial growth before the powder is reconstituted. However, because *Cronobacter* spp and other organisms may be found in the hospital environment itself, contamination is not limited to the time of manufacture, but may occur at the time during feeding preparation or administration (11,12,21,24–28). Therefore, poor handling of formula reconstituted from powder increases the risk of microbial growth. Formula preparation guidelines are designed to minimize both exogenous contamination and further microbial growth from the microorganisms present at the time of manufacture in nonsterile products (refer to Chapter 5).

Colonization of feeding tubes has been reported (29). This colonization can be from the feeding or from retrograde from the patient. Colonization load can be high and has been associated with feeding intolerance and necrotizing enterocolitis (NEC) (30). Whatever the source, infant feedings delivered through colonized feeding tubes are likely to support growth of organisms. Human milk may offer some protection from microbial proliferation (30).

Special care must be taken to reduce the risk of microbiological contamination of infant feedings prepared in health care facilities. The primary infection control goal for infant feeding preparation is to prevent any infant from ingesting microorganisms that could result in illness. Research has identified infant feedings as a source of nosocomial infections (13,31). Foodborne illness can occur either through infection or intoxication (toxins produced from organisms) (28,32). Thus, the objectives are to limit the entry of undesirable bacteria and other microorganisms in sterile feedings and to limit microbial growth from nonsterile, powdered formulas during the preparation and delivery of enteral feedings.

The preferred type of infant formula for health care facilities is commercially sterile, liquid, ready-to-feed products. Such products will remain free of microbiological growth as long as the container remains intact and they are stored properly. However, feedings can become contaminated during any step of the process, from formula preparation or pumping of human milk to feeding delivery and administration (5,11–13,33). Exogenous contamination of feedings can result from many factors throughout the enteral feeding process—from formula purchasing to bedside administration, from personnel hygiene to the patients themselves as sources of organisms (11–13,24,34,35). Risk of microbial growth increases as manipulation of the feedings increases. Examples include the mixing of formula powders and the addition of modular additives or medications. In addition, risk of microbial growth increases as hang time, feeding reservoir use, and extension tubing use increases (5,13,36). Once they become contaminated, infant formula and expressed human milk provide ample nutrients for microorganism growth (13,28,37).

Factors that influence and discourage microbial growth are (*a*) properly cleaning formula preparation equipment; (*b*) using aseptic formula preparation techniques; (*c*) maintaining proper storage temperatures; (*d*) limiting the handling of human milk and formula at the bedside; and (*e*) observing appropriate hang times, tubing changes, and expiration times. These factors apply to expressed human milk and infant formulas of all kinds. Foodborne illness can occur either through infection or intoxication (toxins produced from organisms) (28,32). Every effort should be made to prevent the contamination of sterile feedings by bacteria and other microorganisms and to limit microbial growth from nonsterile, powdered formulas during the preparation and delivery of enteral feedings.

To minimize these risks, each facility must develop a patient safety plan for infant feeding preparation and administration that includes infection control procedures. Policies and procedures should be developed under the guidance and approval of a multidisciplinary committee. The facility's infection control processes should be involved in oversight of infant feeding practices on an ongoing basis (32).

HACCP plans for monitoring the human milk and infant formula handling practices should include infection control. (See Chapter 8.)

Microbiological Quality of Commercially Available Infant Formula

The Infant Formula Act and FDA regulations govern the manufacture of commercial infant formula products shipped interstate (38–43). Infant formula is commercially available in two forms—liquid and powder. Liquid infant formula is marketed in hermetically sealed containers and is designated a low-acid canned food. As such, it must be rendered commercially sterile by an established thermal process. Federal regulations require the process to be on file with the FDA (44). To be commercially sterile means that a food is (*a*) free of microorganisms capable of reproducing in the food under normal, nonrefrigerated conditions of storage and distribution, and (*b*) free of viable microorganisms (including spores) of public health significance. These products are at risk only for exogenous contamination from microorganisms.

Powdered infant formulas are not sterile upon manufacture and can contain microorganisms. When assessing bacterial counts in powdered infant formulas, the FDA considers up to 10^4 colony forming units (CFU) per gram of powder to be acceptable (27). Some of these microorganisms may be pathogenic, including *Cronobacter* spp (encompassing organisms formerly known as *E. sakazakii*) (10,12,13,15,16,24,25,28,44–46). Improper handling during preparation can promote growth of the organisms that are already present from the time of manufacture as well as increase the risk of introducing new microorganisms. Therefore, it is recommended that powdered infant formulas be used only when no nutritionally appropriate, commercially sterile product is available (9,13,19).

Attempts to sterilize powdered formula using steam or dry heat would render the powdered product inedible and destroy its nutrient content (18). Irradiation of powdered formula as a means of sterilizing those products has been suggested but has not as yet been done in the United States (47,48). Testing by infant formula manufacturers to ensure the high industry quality of commercial infant formula is described in Appendix 7-A. Similarly, surveillance of the microbiological quality of commercial infant formula conducted by the FDA is described in Table 7A-1 (see Appendix 7-A).

Microbiological Issues for Consideration by Health Care Facilities Preparing Feedings for Infants

Formula Storage   Once received by the health care facility, both liquid and powdered infant formula products should be stored in cool, dry areas. As long as the containers for each product type remain intact, the microbiological quality of each packaged product should remain unchanged from the time it left the manufacturer. The hermetically sealed liquid formula container will prevent the ingress of microorganisms capable of contaminating the commercially sterilized product.

The sealed, nonsterile powdered formula can or packet will protect the product from excessive exposure to high humidity or moisture. Nonsterile powdered formula products are preserved by low water activity, which refers to the amount of available water required for microbial proliferation.

Formula Preparation   Formula preparation is discussed in Chapter 5. Because of the importance of container integrity, the preparer must thoroughly inspect the infant formula container immediately before use. The product must *not* be used if the expiration date has passed or if the container is damaged, leaking, or swollen. Product contents must also be inspected after opening the container. The product must not be used if it appears adulterated, contaminated, or otherwise abnormal (eg, lumpy, grainy liquid, or clumped powder) (49). Microbiological spoilage is a less common occurrence than physical separation of liquid product, which occurs routinely over time. The manufacturer should be consulted with questions about the microbiological quality of infant formula products or ingredients.

Formula and feeding bottles must be opened using aseptic technique and in a designated location where there is little risk of contamination by microorganisms or undesirable environmental substances (eg, chemicals, sanitizers, or drugs). Aseptic technique is a procedure that incorporates hand hygiene with no-touch technique, which prevents the introduction of microorganisms (50,51). Infant feeding preparation requires clean areas and personnel who are not at risk of spreading infections. This is especially important because it has been shown that *Cronobacter* spp can attach to and form biofilms on work surfaces where formulas are prepared (52). Strict compliance with proper cleaning of stainless steel and other contact surfaces used for the formula preparation is essential. Personnel must follow established hygienic practices, including those addressing the frequency and technique for hand hygiene and the exclusion criteria for infant formula preparation room staff as described in Chapter 3 (19,50,53).

The microbiological quality of infant formula can be controlled by requiring the use of aseptic technique during all on-site preparation of formula in the health care facility. This procedure must be used to reconstitute liquid concentrate or powdered formula with chilled, sterile ingredient water. Use of chilled water is recommended to facilitate achieving formula temperature of 4°C (40°F) quickly (5,13). When chilled sterile ingredient water is used, additional agitation may be required prior to feeding the formula. Facilities can also consider chilling formulas with a commercial blast chiller. These are designed to chill any food product down to 4°C (40°F) as rapidly as possible, and typically have automated HACCP compliant documentation labeling.

Staff in facilities that do not have an infant feeding preparation room should refer to Box 7.1 for aseptic techniques (5,11,12,54,55).

BOX 7.1   *Aseptic Techniques in Facilities Without a Formal Infant Feeding Preparation Room*

Facilities without a formal infant feeding preparation room should follow the same aseptic techniques used in facilities with a preparation room, but with focus on a preparation space zone. The space should not be located in a high-traffic area, should have close access to refrigeration, and should allow personnel to properly wash hands before formula preparation. The work area should be monitored for prevention of potential risk of contamination. Prepared formula must be stored immediately in an appropriate container under refrigeration temperatures of 4°C (40°F). (Refer to Chapter 5.)

Source: Data are from references 5, 11, 12, 54, and 55.

The practice of warming formula before administration is only acceptable for oral or bolus feedings. Warming formula that is infused by continuous drip may enhance the potential for bacterial growth (5,13). Facility-prepared formula for infants' oral consumption that is *not* refrigerated must also be used immediately or discarded. Under no circumstances should partially fed formula be returned to the refrigerator to be used at a later time. Facility-prepared infant formula should be sent to patient care units in closed food-grade–quality containers in quantities required for one feeding or for up to a 24-hour period. Ideally, bulk-packaged formula should be repackaged or unit-dosed in quantities for one bolus feeding or for one hang-time period. These doses may be used for no longer than a 4-hour hang time in the NICU. In other settings, the doses may be usable for different time spans (refer to Chapter 6).

If bulk-packaged formula is dispensed from the formula preparation room to the patient care unit, the amount of formula required for a feeding should be measured in a designated clean area, using aseptic technique and appropriate hand hygiene. Formula containers requiring the use of a can opener should not be sent to the patient care unit. Such formula should be repackaged into food-grade plastic containers that can be easily re-sealed, such as in infant feeding bottles or containers used by dairies. Once a pop-top can or bottle of formula is delivered to a patient's room, it should not be put back into circulation for use with other patients. Human milk and formula stored in patient care area refrigerators should be stored separately from other food supplies, at a minimum on a separate labeled shelf. Refer to your facility's infection prevention and control resource team for recommendations.

Terminal heating, autoclaving, and use of boiling hot water in formula preparation in the health care facility is *not* recommended because of potential alteration of the nutritive value and physical characteristics of the pre-pared formula and staff safety (see Chapter 5). Terminal heating (pasteurization) requires specialized equip-ment not usually available in health care facilities (see Chapter 5). The exceptions are human milk banks that routinely pasteurize milk. (Note: Autoclaves may be used to clean equipment.)

Foodborne or Waterborne Spread of Infection

Any amount of gram-negative organisms is undesirable, unacceptable, and particularly hazardous in immune-compromised patients (56). There is no single international standard for microbial quality of prepared infant formula, although $<10^3$ CFUs has been used as an acceptable level for nonpathogenic organisms (57,58). Nu-merous studies have shown microbial counts in enteral formulas to exceed these levels (5,59–63).

Gastroenteritis is the most commonly recognized form of foodborne or waterborne illness. However, NEC, an extremely serious pathology found in NICUs, has also been associated with enteral feedings (30). The symp-toms of gastroenteritis may reflect upper (vomiting and nausea) or lower (cramps and abdominal pain or diar-rhea with or without blood and mucus) gastrointestinal (GI) tract involvement or a combination of the two (32,55). Illness may arise from ingestion of live organisms (eg, *Salmonella, Shigella*) or from ingestion of pre-formed toxin that has been produced by organisms multiplying in the food before ingestion (eg, enterotoxin produced by *Staphylococcus aureus, Clostridium botulinum, B. cereus*). Bacterial colonization exceeding 10^5 CFUs has been associated with GI distress and diarrhea (36,56,57,64,65). However, lesser amounts of patho-gens are also known to be problematic. Therefore, the possibility of contaminated feedings should be consid-ered in the patient's differential diagnostic work up for GI symptoms (13,36).

Illness may not be confined to the GI tract; some of the organisms present in a contaminated product may in-vade beyond the mucosal barrier and cause serious systemic disease, (eg, sepsis, aspiration pneumonia). This is an important concern in all immunocompromised individuals, including newborn infants, especially those who are very premature. *Clostridium difficile* is among the most common organism associated with nosocomial diarrhea in tube-fed patients, particularly those with transpyloric tube feedings (66). Transpyloric placement of feeding tubes may pose an additional risk because organisms that ordinarily would be neutralized by the acidity of the gastric secretions are delivered directly into the duodenum. The occurrence of retrograde contamination with GI flora has been reported as well (30,35,58,67). Considering the many potential points of contamination, an HACCP plan—including guidelines for appropriate formula use, preparation, delivery, storage, and administration—must be followed.

The list of organisms reported to be transmitted via contaminated feedings (formula, human milk, or water) is lengthy (9,68–71). It includes *Salmonella* spp, *Campylobacter* spp, coliforms, *Klebsiella* spp, *Enterobacter* spp, group A beta-hemolytic *Streptococcus, Leptospira* spp, *Bacillus cereus, Shigella* spp, *C. botulinum, Acinetobacter* spp, *Bacillus* spp, *Citrobacter* spp, *Escherichia coli, Haemophilus influenza, Leuconostoc* spp, *Moraxella* spp, *Pseudomonas* spp, *Proteus mirabilis, Staphylococcus* spp, *Streptococcus* spp, *S. aureus,* and yeasts (11–13,24,25,28,31,45,72–74). Potential pathogens that may be present in the powdered product in small numbers include *E. coli, Klebsiella* spp, *and Enterobacter* spp (9,11,12,18,24,25,28,45). *Cronobacter* spp (*E. sakazakii*) has been associated with rare infections in high-risk populations, such as neonates, and has been identified in formulas reconstituted from powdered infant formula (6–8,11,12,15,16,18,25,26,28,46,75). Some organisms are of special concern because they are antibiotic resistant, heat resistant, able to attach to infant feeding equipment, or able to grow at refrigerator temperatures (eg, *Listeria monocytogenes, Yersinia* spp, *Aeromonas* spp, *Cronobacter* spp). Additional agents that have been transmitted by contaminated water include *Shigella,* hepatitis A, *Giardia lamblia, Entamoeba histolytica,* and *Cryptosporidium* spp.

Viral agents are primarily introduced into infant feedings (formula, water, or milk) through product handling by infected persons, particularly those with rotavirus, norovirus, echovirus, coxsackievirus, enteric adenovirus, calicivirus, astrovirus, coronavirus, and parvovirus. Expressed human milk may contain viruses including hepatitis A, B, or C; cytomegalovirus (CMV); and human immunodeficiency virus (HIV) (see Chapter 4). These viruses may be present even if the mother has been infected in the past but is not currently ill. These lists are not meant to be exhaustive, nor should they imply that contamination of infant formula is common. The list serves rather to illustrate the large number of potential pathogens that may be spread via contaminated feedings (expressed human milk, infant formula, or water). For additional information about human milk contamination, see Chapter 4.

Water is included here because it is a necessary additive in infant feeding prepared from concentrate or powder. Commercial sterile chilled water is recommended for preparation. For a more extensive discussion, refer to the following list of Web sites for food safety programs and information:

- Food and Drug Administration (FDA) Product-Specific Information. National Food Safety Programs. Center for Food Safety and Applied Nutrition. http://www.cfsan.fda.gov/~dms/fs-toc.html
- Gateway to Federal Food Safety Information. http://www.foodsafety.gov
- Centers for Disease Control and Prevention. Diagnosis and management of foodborne illnesses: a primer for physicians (for information on the diagnosis and management of foodborne illnesses). *MMWR Recommendations and Reports.* http://www.cdc.gov/mmwr/preview/mmwrhtml/rr5002a1.htm

In reported outbreaks of foodborne illness due to the use of contaminated powdered infant formula, problems have included inadequate control of storage; improper handling practices from the point of preparation to the patient's bedside; inappropriate hang times; and use of a product beyond the recommended expiration date, which allows for bacterial multiplication (5,7,9,11,13,19,34,63,76). Therefore, although proper preparation of formulas for infants is essential in health care facilities, it is also equally important that recommended guidelines be available for storage, handling, administration, and appropriate discarding of prepared infant formula. These recommendations should be clearly outlined and followed to prevent foodborne infection. If infant formula preparation results in a suspected outbreak of foodborne illness, ready-to-feed, commercially sterile products should be used until the situation is resolved (19).

Probiotics in Infant Feedings

When discussing microbial colonization, the use of probiotics within health care facilities must be considered. Probiotics are live microbes that colonize the gastrointestinal (GI) tract and confer benefit to the host. Benefits vary depending on the species and are strain- and dose-specific (77–91). Probiotics may be delivered as a unit-dosed supplement or as an ingredient in powdered infant formula. To date, there are limited studies of how these formulas should be handled in the hospital setting. Safe procedures for use of these formulas in tube feeding have not been published.

From an infection control perspective, potential concerns about probiotics are that they may interfere with the detection of undesirable microorganisms, lead to inadvertent cross-contamination, and/or lead to sepsis (76,86,91,92). There have been reports of *Lactobacillus* and other bacterial sepsis resulting from the use of probiotic supplementation (77,79,84,89,91,93). Such cases have typically been seen in immune-suppressed and immunocompromised patients (79). At the time this publication, there have been no reports of bacteremia with bifidobacteria used as a probiotic. Probiotics that have Generally Recognized As Safe (GRAS) status can be found on the FDA Web site (http://www.fda.gov/Food/FoodIngredientsPackaging/GenerallyRecognize dasSafeGRAS/GRASListings/default.htm). This is an area that changes often; checking the site for current information is suggested. There are four probiotic products that have GRAS status (94). Hospitalized infants with venous catheters may be at additional risk, as it has been suggested that there is a potential for cross-contamination of catheters with probiotic microorganisms leading to sepsis (77). This would be of particular concern in health care facilities where formulas with probiotics are prepared at the bedside or where probiotic supplements are added to infant feedings at the bedside. Without careful procedures, such practices could put any infant in the vicinity at risk for coming in contact with these organisms. Careful adherence to aseptic technique and limiting the exposure of other feedings to probiotic ingredients (eg, not opening a can of probiotic-containing formula while other feeding preparation is occurring) reduces the risk of inadvertent contamination of infant feedings with probiotic organisms. Health care facilities should always refer to the manufacturers' recommendations regarding the handling of probiotics to minimize risks. For additional information on the addition of probiotic supplements or the preparation of probiotic containing formulas, see Chapter 5 and Chapter 6.

Microbiological Quality Assurance: Preventing, Detecting, and Managing Feeding-Related Infection

Federal guidelines mandate that commercially prepared liquid infant formulas be commercially sterile whereas powdered formulas must be microbiologically acceptable (95). Powdered formula products are not sterile; therefore, they may contain certain nonpathogenic bacteria, including spore-forming bacteria, coagulase-negative staphylococci, and diphtheroids. These organisms are considered harmless and are usually present in very small numbers.

Monitoring of the infant formula storage and preparation areas and feeding preparation practices is a critical part of the health care facility's microbiological quality-monitoring component of the HACCP plan (55). (Refer to the sample HACCP plan in Appendix 8-A, following Chapter 8.) Results from a properly designed monitoring program will show the efficacy of sanitation procedures, help determine the frequency of use of disinfectants, and aid in determining sources of potential product contamination (43).

Microbiological Surveillance

Routine microbiological sampling of facility-prepared infant formula is *not* recommended because there is no epidemiological evidence to show that such quality control testing influences the infection rate in health care facilities (53).

As stated previously, manufacturers of low-acid, liquid infant formula products are required by law to register the manufacturing process used. The manufactured product should be free of viable microorganisms of public health significance. Therefore, it is unnecessary to conduct routine cultures of such products before preparation. If the established guidelines are followed for aseptic technique, formula preparation, and formula storage, there should be no pathogen contamination of the formula, and the bacteria that may be present should not have a chance to overgrow.

Routine culturing of prepared product in the infant formula preparation room itself is unlikely to detect problems that occur during storage. Periodic culturing is not likely to detect intermittent contamination due to breaks in preparation technique, but it may be helpful in establishing trends and in evaluating root cause analysis. The cost of doing repeated quantitative cultures may be prohibitive. Furthermore, it may be more cost-effective to expend resources on training, HACCP process implementation and plan compliance, quality assurance, or other methods to ensure the proper handling and storage of infant formula from purchasing to the user site. Implementation of an HACCP approach to enteral feedings has been shown to successfully reduce formula contamination and microbial growth (56).

Although the CDC does not recommend routine microbial surveillance, compliance with state regulations related to culturing of prepared formula is imperative. Check with state regulatory agencies before constructing policies regarding frequency of formula culturing and criteria for growth. Although there is no standard for microbial quality of prepared infant formula, authors and regulators have addressed the issue (57,58,96,97).

Routine Surveillance for Hospital-Acquired Infection

According to the Infant Formula Act of 1980, the primary task of patient safety procedures for the preparation of feedings for infants is to ensure that no feeding-related infection occurs in the infants being fed the prepared products (95). Hospitals and most other health care facilities that provide patient care are required, through accreditation guidelines, to have a system for monitoring hospital-acquired infections in individuals. In critical care areas, such as neonatal and pediatric intensive care units, this monitoring is especially important (98). A multidisciplinary committee should periodically review the infant feeding preparation process and procedures, including all critical control points, from formula purchasing to administration of the prepared feeding at the user site.

In addition to monitoring cases of individual infection, facilities need a plan or mechanism for dealing with outbreaks of infection. Infant feedings may be considered as a factor in tracing the cause of multiple outbreaks of infection or single episodes of unusual infections (eg, *Salmonella* or *Cronobacter* spp. in an intensive care nursery). A more intensive investigation would be appropriate at such a time. This should include an examination for the presence of bacterial contaminants or other pathogens in the prepared infant formula and expressed human milk. If possible, preserve the suspected specimen by refrigerating opened containers for further investigation. Contact the manufacturer immediately for specific instructions. For questions about the microbiological quality of a commercially prepared infant formula product, consult the manufacturer for assistance. If evaluation of formula products for contamination is needed, the steps designated for proper removal of product to be tested from the container are probably the most critical techniques in the testing process. Contamination of the product by the person doing the sampling may occur rather easily, thus leading to erroneous test results. Preparing a can for testing should be recognized as a different and more difficult task than preparing its contents for feeding.

In assessing, analyzing, and managing an outbreak of infection, remember that some foodborne infections, once introduced, may be propagated by fecal-oral spread of the pathogen involved. Continuance of an epidemic after removal of potentially infected foods does not prove that the infection was not introduced from a foodborne source. Control efforts must seek to address all ways in which an infection may be spreading.

Implementation of an HACCP approach to enteral feedings has been shown to be an economical and successful method to reduce formula contamination and microbial growth (58). Compliance with state regulations concerning routine culturing of prepared infant formula is imperative.

Multidisciplinary Committee

A multidisciplinary committee that includes, at a minimum, expertise in food handling, medicine, and nursing care should approve the infant feeding preparation, policy, and procedures. This committee may be in the scope of the institution's nutrition committee, infection control committee, or patient safety committee. When feeding an immunocompromised infant or when there is a risk of nosocomial infection, the committee should determine whether additional precautions are necessary to further minimize exposure to microorganisms (42).

Additionally, each institution must establish guidelines for the use of all ingredients that are added to the infant formula, including nutritional ingredients, water, and medications. Guidelines should also be written for the use and sanitizing of preparation equipment, bottles, nipple assemblies, and any other material coming in contact with the formula. Autoclaving or a thermal disinfection process is recommended for effectively cleaning equipment used in feeding and formula preparation (99).

REFERENCES

1. US Food and Drug Administration. Center for Food and Safety and Applied Nutrition. Infant Formula. http://www.fda.gov/Food/FoodSafety/Product-SpecificInformation/InfantFormula/default.htm. Accessed December 3, 2009.

2. Becker DS. Interdisciplinary HACCP in acute care. *Market-Link* [newsletter of Management in Food and Nutrition Systems Dietary Practice Group of the American Dietetic Association]. 2000;19(4):4.

3. Henry BW, Nelms J, Foley S. Implementing a HACCP plan with pediatric formula preparation. *PNPG Post.* 2000;(Fall):4–5.

4. Hunter PR. Application of Hazard Analysis Critical Control Point (HACCP) to the handling of expressed breast milk on a neonatal unit. *J Hosp Infect.* 1991;17:139–146.

5. Steele C, Short R. Centralized infant formula preparation room in the neonatal intensive care unit reduces incidence of microbial contamination. *J Am Diet Assoc.* 2008;108:1700–1703.

6. Bar-Oz B, Preminger A, Peleg O, Block C, Arad I. Enterobacter sakazakii infection in the newborn. *Acta Paediatr.* 2001;90:356–358.

7. Weir E. Powdered infant formula and fatal infection with Enterobacter sakazakii. *CMAJ.* 2002;166:1570.

8. Van Acker J, De Smet F, Muyldermans G, Bougater A, Naessens A, Lauwers S. Outbreak of necrotizing enterocolitis associated with Enterobacter sakazakii in powdered milk formula. *J Clin Microbiol.* 2001;39:293–297.

9. Centers for Disease Control and Prevention. Enterobacter sakazakii infections associated with the use of powdered infant formula—Tennessee 2001. *MMWR Morb Mortal Wkly Rep.* 2002;51:297–300.

10. El-Sharoud WM, O'Brien S, Negredo C, Iversen C, Fanning S, Healy B. Characterization of Cronobacter recovered from dried milk and related products. *BMC Microbiol.* 2009;9:24.

11. Giovannini M, Verduci E, Ghisleni D, Salvatici E, Riva E, Agostoni C. Enterobacter sakazakii: an emerging problem in paediatric nutrition. *J Int Med Res.* 2008;36:394–399.

12. Kandhai MC, Reij MW, Grognou C, van Schothorst M, Gorris LGM, Zwietering MH. Effects of preculturing conditions on lag time and specific growth rate of Enterobacter sakazakii in reconstituted powdered infant formula. *Appl Environ Microbiol.* 2006;72:2721–2729.

13. Marino LV, Goddard E, Whitelaw A, Workman L. Prevalence of bacterial contamination of powdered infant feeds in a hospital environment. *S Afr Med J.* 2007;97:534–537.

14. Nair MKM, Joy J, Venkitanarayanan KS. Inactivation of Enterobacter Sakazakii in reconstituted infant formula by Monocaprylin. *J Food Protect.* 2004;67:2815–2819.

15. Cawthorn DM, Botha S, Witthuhn RC. Evaluation of different methods for the detection and identification of Enterobacter sakazakii isolated from South African infant formula milks and the processing environment. *Int J Food Microbiol.* 2008;127:129–138.

16. Kim KP, Klumpp J, Loessner MJ. Enterobacter sakazakii bacteriophages can prevent bacterial growth in reconstituted infant formula. *Int J Food Microbiol.* 2007;115:195–203.

17. O'Brien S, Healy B, Negredo C, Anderson W, Fanning S, C. I. Prevalence of Cronobacter species (Enterobacter sakazakii) in follow-on infant formula and infant drinks. *Lett Appl Microbiol.* 2009;48:536–541.

18. Lenati RF, O'Connor DL, Hebert KC, Farber JM, Pagotto FJ. Growth and survival of Enterobacter sakazakii in human breast milk with and without fortifiers as compared to powdered infant formula. *Int J Food Microbiol.* 2008;122:71–179.

19. World Health Organization. Enterobacter sakazakii and other micro-organisms in powdered infant formula. http://www.who.int/entity/foodsafety/publications. Accessed February 15, 2010.

20. Cahill SM, Wachsmuth IK, Costarrica Mde L, Ben Embarek PK. Powdered infant formula as a source of Salmonella infection in infants. *Clin Infect Dis.* 2008;46:268–273.

21. Drudy D, Mullane NR, Quinn T, Wall PG, Fanning S. Enterobacter sakazakii: an emerging pathogen in powdered infant formula. *Clin Infect Dis.* 2006;42:996–1002.

22. Mimouni FB, Inbar M, Dollberg S. Bacterial contamination during routine formula preparation. *Am J Infect Control.* 2002;30:44–45.

23. International Formula Council. Infant Feeding: Safety Issues for Health Care Professionals. http://www.infantformula.org/for-health-professionals. Accessed October 12, 2010.

24. Iversen C, Lane M, Forsythe SJ. The growth profile, thermotolerance and biofilm formation of Enterobacter sakazakii grown in infant formula milk. *Lett Appl Microbiol.* 2004;38:378–382.

25. Iversen C, Forsythe SJ. Comparison of media for the isolation of the Enterobacter Sakazakii. *Appl Environ Microbiol.* 2007;73:48–52.

26. O'Brien S, Healy B, Negredo C, Anderson W, Fanning S, Iversen C. Prevalence of Cronobacter species (Enterobacter sakazakii) in follow-on infant formulae and infant drinks. *Lett Appl Microbiol*. 2009;48:536–541.

27. Baker RD. Infant formula safety. *Pediatrics*. 2002;110:833–835.

28. Redmond EC, Griffith CJ, Riley S. Contamination of bottles used for feeding reconstituted powdered infant formula and implications for public health. *Perspect Public Health*. 2009;129:85–94.

29. Hurrell E, Kucerova E, Loughlin M, et al. Neonatal enteral feeding tubes as loci for colonisation by members of the Enterobacteriaceae. *BMC Infect Dis*. 2009;9:146.

30. Mehall J, Kite C, Saltzman D, Wallett T, Jackson R, Smith S. Prospective study of the incidence and complications of bacterial contamination of enteral feeding in neonates. *J Pediatr Surg*. 2002;37:1177–1182.

31. Buyukyavuz BI, Adiloglu AK, Onal S, Cubukcu SE, Cetin H. Finding the sources of septicemia at a neonatal intensive care unit: newborns and infants can be contaminated while being fed. *Jpn J Infect Dis*. 2006;59:213–215.

32. Cody M, Kunkel M. *Food Safety for Professionals*. 2nd ed. Chicago, IL: American Dietetic Association; 2001.

33. Okuma T, Nakamura M, Totake H, Fukunaga Y. Microbial contamination of enteral feeding formulas and diarrhea. *Nutrition*. 2000;16:719–722.

34. Patchell C, Anderton A, Holden C, MacDonald A, George R, Booth I. Reducing bacterial contamination of enteral feeds. *Arch Dis Child*. 1998;78:166–168.

35. Payne-James J, Rana S, Bray M, McSwiggan D, Silk D. Retrograde (ascending) bacterial contamination of enteral diet administration systems. *JPEN J Parenter Enteral Nutr*. 1992;16:369–373.

36. Anderton A. Reducing bacterial contamination of enteral tube feeds. *Br J Nurs*. 1995;4:368–376.

37. Hamosh M, Ellis L, Pollock D, Henderson T, Hamosh P. Breastfeeding and the working mother: effect of time and temperature of short-term storage on proteolysis, lipolysis, and bacterial growth in milk. *Pediatrics*. 1996;97:492–498.

38. Federal Register. Thermally processed low-acid foods packaged in hermetically sealed containers. February 2010. http://ecfr.gpoaccess.gov/cgi/t/text/text-idx?c=ecfr&rgn=div5&view=text&node=21:2.0.1.1.12&idno=21. Accessed February 15, 2010.

39. Federal Register. 21 CFR Part 110—Current Good Manufacturing Practice In Manufacturing, Packing, or Holding Human Food. April 1, 2005. http://www.gmp1st.com/fdreg.htm. Accessed February 15, 2010.

40. Code of Federal Regulations. Title 21: Food and Drugs, Part 107—Infant Formula. Subpart D: §107.100: Nutrient specifications. February 10, 2010.Electronic Code of Federal Regulations Web site. http://ecfr.gpoaccess.gov/cgi/t/text/text-idx?c=ecfr;rgn=div6;view=text;node=21%3A2.0.1.1.7.4;idno=21;cc=ecfr. Accessed February 15, 2010.

41. Enteral Nutrition Council. *Microbiological Methods of Analysis for Enteral Nutritional Formulas*. Atlanta, GA: Enteral Nutrition Council; 1986.

42. Jackson G. Update on microbial problems in dairy foods in the USA. *International Dairy Federation Circular*. 1987;3(3 Suppl):12–13.

43. Favers M, Gabis D, Vesley D. Environmental monitoring procedures. In: *Compendium of Methods for the Microbiological Examination of Foods*. 2nd ed. Washington, DC: American Public Health Association; 1984.

44. Biering G, Karlsson S, Clark N. Three cases of neonatal meningitis caused by Enterobacter sakazakii in powdered milk. *J Clin Microbiol*. 1989;27:2054–2056.

45. Nair MK, Joy J, Venkitanarayanan KS. Inactivation of Enterobacter sakazakii in reconstituted infant formula by monocaprylin. *J Food Prot*. 2004;67:2815–2819.

46. Zhou Y, Wu Q, Xu X, Yang X, Ye Y, Zhang J. Development of an immobilization and detection method of Enterobacter sakazakii from powdered infant formula. *Food Microbiol*. 2008;25:648–652.47. Baker J, Rasmussen T. Organizing and documenting lactation support of NICU families. *J Obstet Gynecol Neonatal Nurs*. 1997;26:515–521.

48. Lee JW, Oh SH, Kim JH, Yook HS, Byun MW. Gamma radiation sensitivity of Enterobacter sakazakii in dehydrated powdered infant formula. *J Food Prot*. 2006;69:1434–1437.

49. Food and Agricultural Organization of the United Nations. Codex Alimentarius Commission. *Codex Standard for Infant Formula*. New York, NY: Food and Agricultural Organization of the United Nations; 1976, 1997.

50. Boyce J, Pittet D. Guidelines for hand hygiene in health-care settings: recommendations of the healthcare infection control practices advisory committee and the HICPAD/SHEA/APIC/IDSA hand hygiene task force. *MMWR Morb Mortal Wkly Rep*. 2002;51(RR-16):1–58.

51. O'Grady N, Alexander M, Dellinger E, et al. Guidelines for the prevention of intravascular catheter-related infections. *MMWR Morb Mortal Wkly Rep.* 2002;51(RR–10):1–14.

52. Kim H, Rhu JH, Beuchat L. Attachment of and biofilm formation by enterobacter sakazakii on stainless steel and enteral feeding tubes. *Appl Environ Microbiol.* 2006;72:5846–5856.

53. Larson E. APIC guideline for handwashing and hand antisepsis in health care settings. *Am J Infect Control.* 1995;23:251–269.

54. US Food and Drug Administration. Task Force on Clinical Testing of Infant Formulas Committee on Nutrition; American Academy of Pediatrics. Clinical Testing of Infant Formulas with Respect to Nutritional Stability for Term Infants. June 1988. http://www.fda.gov/Food/GuidanceComplianceRegulatoryInformation/GuidanceDocuments/InfantFormula/ucm170649.htm. Accessed December 28, 2010.

55. US Food and Drug Administration. FDA Food Code. http://www.fda.gov/Food/FoodSafety/RetailFoodProtection/FoodCode/FoodCode2009/default.htm. Accessed December 7, 2009.

56. Oliviera M, Bonelli R, Aido K, Batista C. Microbiological quality of reconstituted enteral formulations used in hospitals. *Nutrition.* 2000;16:729–733.

57. Vanek V. Closed versus open enteral delivery systems: a quality improvement study. *Nutr Clin Pract.* 2000;15:234–243.

58. Bott L, Husson M, Michaud L, Arnaud-Battandier F, Turck D, Gottrand F. Contamination of gastrostomy feeding systems in children in a home-based enteral nutrition program. *J Pediatr Gastroenterol Nutr.* 2001;33:266–270.

59. Patchell C, Anderton A, MacDonald A, George R, Booth I. Bacterial contamination of enteral feeds. *Arch Dis Child.* 1994;70:327–330.

60. Campbell SM. *Preventing Microbial Contamination of Enteral Formula and Delivery Systems.* Columbus, OH: Ross Products; 2000.

61. Anderson KR, Norris DJ, Godrey LB, Avent CK, Butterworth CE. Bacterial contamination of tube-feeding formulas. *JPEN J Parenter Enteral Nutr.* 1984;8:673–678.

62. Freeland CP, Roller RD, Wolfe BM, Flynn NM. Microbial contamination of continuous drip feedings. *JPEN J Parenter Enteral Nutr.* 1989;13:18–22.

63. Schreiner R, Eitzen H, Gfell M, et al. Environmental contamination of continuous drip feedings. *Pediatrics.* 1979;63:232–237.

64. Oie S, Kamiya A, Hironaga K, Koshiro A. Microbial contamination of enteral feeding solution and its prevention. *Am J Infect Control.* 1993;21:34–38.

65. Anderton A, Nwoguh C, McKune I, Morrison L, Greig M, Clark B. A comparative study of the numbers of bacteria present in enteral feeds prepared and administered in hospital and home. *J Hosp Infect.* 1993;23:43–46.

66. Bliss D, Johnson S, Savik K, Clabots C, Willard K, Gerding D. Acquisition of Clostridium difficile and Clostridium difficile-associated diarrhea in hospitalized patients receiving tube feedings. *Ann Intern Med.* 1998;129:1012–1019.

67. Mathus-Vliegen L, Binnekade J, de Hann R. Bacterial contamination of ready-to-use 1-L feeding bottles and administration sets in severely compromised intensive care patients. *Crit Care Med.* 2000;28:67–73.

68. Nazarowec-White M, Farber J. Thermal resistance of Enterobacter sakazakii in reconstituted dried-infant formula. *Lett Appl Microbiol.* 1997;24:9–13.

69. Centers for Disease Control and Prevention. Diagnosis and management of foodborne illnesses: a primer for physicians. *MMWR Morb Mortal Wkly Rep.* 2001;50(RR–02):1–69.

70. Centers for Disease Control and Prevention. Water and other beverage safety. In: Guidelines for Preventing Opportunistic Infections among Hematopoietic Stem Cell Transplant Recipients. *MMWR Morb Mortal Wkly Rep.* 2000;49(RR–10):1–28.

71. Centers for Disease Control and Prevention. Salmonella serotype Tennessee in powdered milk products and infant formula— Canada and United States. *MMWR Morb Mortal Wkly Rep.* 1993;42:516–517.

72. Code of Federal Regulations. Mandatory pasteurization for all milk and milk products in final package intended for distribution. http://www.ftcldf.org/docs/21_CFR_1240.61_pasteurization.pdf. Accessed December 28, 2010.

73. Brett MM, McLauchlin J, Harris A, et al. A case of infant botulism with a possible link to infant formula milk powder: evidence for the presence of more than one strain of Clostridium botulinum in clinical specimens and food. *J Med Microbiol.* 2005;54:769–776.

74. Park JK, Seok WS, Choi BJ, et al. Salmonella enterica serovar London infections associated with consumption of infant formula. *Yonsei Med J.* 2004;45:43–48.

75. Narayanan I, Singh B, Harvey D. Fat loss during feeding of human milk. *Arch Dis Child.* 1984;59:475–477.

76. Marion N, Rupp M. Infection control issues of enteral feeding systems. *Curr Opin Clin Nutr Metab Care.* 2000;3:363–366.

77. Boyle RJ, Robins-Browne RM, Tang ML. Probiotic use in clinical practice: what are the risks? *Am J Clin Nutr.* 2006;83:1256–1264; quiz 1446–1447.

78. Douglas LC, Sanders ME. Probiotics and prebiotics in dietetics practice. *J Am Diet Assoc.* 2008;108:510–521.

79. Land MH, Rouster-Stevens K, Woods CR, Cannon ML, Cnota J, Shetty AK. Lactobacillus sepsis associated with probiotic therapy. *Pediatrics.* 2005;115:178–181.

80. Petschow BW, Figueroa R, Harris CL, Beck LB, Ziegler E, Goldin B. Effects of feeding an infant formula containing Lactobacillus GG on the colonization of the intestine: a dose-response study in healthy infants. *J Clin Gastroenterol.* 2005;39:786–790.

81. Weizman Z, Alsheikh A. Safety and tolerance of a probiotic formula in early infancy comparing two probiotic agents: a pilot study. *J Am Coll Nutr.* 2006;25:415–419.

82. Guandalini S. Probiotics for children with diarrhea: an update. *J Clin Gastroenterol.* 2008;42(Suppl 2):S53–S57.

83. Isolauri E. Probiotics in preterm infants: a controversial issue. *J Pediatr Gastroenterol Nutr.* 2007;45(Suppl 3):S188–S189.

84. Barclay AR, Stenson B, Simpson JH, Weaver LT, Wilson DC. Probiotics for necrotizing enterocolitis: a systematic review. *J Pediatr Gastroenterol Nutr.* 2007;45:569–576.

85. Kullen MJ, Bettler J. The delivery of probiotics and prebiotics to infants. *Curr Pharm Des.* 2005;11:55–74.

86. Lee SJ, Cho SJ, Park EA. Effects of probiotics on enteric flora and feeding tolerance in preterm infants. *Neonatology.* 2007;91:174–179.

87. Huebner ES, Surawicz CM. Probiotics in the prevention and treatment of gastrointestinal infections. *Gastroenterol Clin North Am.* 2006;35:355–365.

88. Collado MC, Isolauri E, Salminen S. Specific probiotic strains and their combinations counteract adhesion of Enterobacter sakazakii to intestinal mucus. *FEMS Microbiol Lett.* 2008;285:58–64.

89. Deshpande G, Rao S, Patole S. Probiotics for prevention of necrotizing enterocolitis in preterm neonates with very low birthweight: a systematic review of randomized controlled trials. *Lancet.* 2007;369:1614–1620.

90. Martin CR, Walker WA. Probiotics: role in pathophysiology and prevention in necrotizing enterocolitis. *Semin Perinatol.* 2008;32:127–137.

91. Szajewska H, Setty M, Mrukowicz J, Guandalini S. Probiotics in gastrointestinal diseases in children: hard and not-so-hard evidence of efficacy. *J Pediatr Gastroenterol Nutr.* 2006;42:454–475.

92. Joosten H, Bidlas E, Garofalo N. Salmonella detection in probiotic products. *Int J Food Microbiol.* 2006;110:104–107.

93. Honeycutt TC, El Khashab M, Wardrop RM 3rd, et al. Probiotic administration and the incidence of nosocomial infection in pediatric intensive care: a randomized placebo-controlled trial. *Pediatr Crit Care Med.* 2007;8:452–458; quiz 464.

94. US Food and Drug Administration. GRAS Notice Inventory. December 31, 2009. http://www.accessdata.fda.gov. scripts./fcn/fchNavigation.cfm?rpt=grasListing. Accessed March 1, 2010.

95. Infant Formula Act of 1980. PL 96–359 September 16.1980. Amendment: Drug Enforcement Education and Control Act of 1986. PL 99–570. October 27, 1986: Section 4014.

96. Carvalho M, Morais T, Amaral D, Sigulem D. Hazard analysis of critical control point system approach in the evaluation of environmental and procedural sources of contamination of enteral feedings in three hospitals. *JPEN J Parenter Enteral Nutr.* 2000;24:296–300.

97. US Food and Drug Administration. Chapter 21, Programme 7321.002. In *Compliance Program Guidance Manual.* Washington, DC: Food and Drug Administration; 1995.

98. Berthelot P, Grattard F, Patural H, et al. Nosocomial colonization of premature babies with Klebsiella oxytoca: probable role of enteral feeding procedure in transmission and control of the outbreak with the use of gloves. *Infect Control Hosp Epidemiol.* 2001;22:148–151.

99. Rowan N, Anderson J. Effectiveness of cleaning and disinfecting procedures on the removal of enteroxigenic bacillus cerus from infant feed bottles. *J Food Protect.* 1998;61:196–200.

Appendix 7-A

Industry Surveillance Programs

The Infant Formula Act of 1980 and US Food and Drug Administration (FDA) regulations are designed to ensure quality infant formula products that meet the needs and requirements of infant nutrition (1–7). Manufacturers supplement liquid formula process-control information and testing with final product testing before distribution. These tests range from commercial sterility testing of finished product samples to incubation and evaluation of intact cans of finished product.

To ensure compliance with applicable sections of the Infant Formula Act of 1980, powdered infant formula processing techniques used by responsible manufacturers are designed to provide a high degree of uniformity. Microbiological quality may be assessed by random sampling of each batch. Sampling plans are defined individually by each manufacturer on the basis of an assessment of manufacturing process and site. A routine product surveillance plan with two categories—Acceptable and Unacceptable (A and U)—is recognized by domestic infant formula manufacturers. This plan provides for appropriate control of processing while testing for the microbiological safety of a given product batch. Microbiological test results in the "A" column are unconditionally acceptable and represent normal product quality.

Values between A and U require further investigation, such as speciation of microbial isolates. "U" represents a maximum acceptable limit for the industry. A product lot having microbiological test results that exceed U is not distributed. This surveillance plan includes microbiological indicators recommended internationally for foods for infants (see Table 7-A.1) (4,8). Specifically, the indicators of the microbiological quality of powdered products recognized by industry are as follows:

- **Aerobic plate count.** The aerobic plate count estimates the number of viable aerobic microorganisms per gram of infant formula powder. Although the number itself does not truly determine "fitness for use," it does provide the manufacturer with a continuing benchmark of process control.
- **Coliforms or fecal coliforms/*Escherichia coli*.** Coliform bacteria are commonly found in soil, water, and grains. Coliforms are easily killed by heat. Hence, coliform counts are used to indicate post–heat-processing contamination. The presence of coliforms does not mean that there is fecal contamination or that pathogens are present in the product, only that there is the possibility of such contamination of the product.
- **Coagulase-positive *Staphylococcus aureus*.** Used as a quality indicator in the product surveillance program, the presence of large populations of *S. aureus* in product is objectionable because certain strains produce enterotoxins that may cause food poisoning if ingested.
- ***Salmonella*.** The presence of *Salmonella* in infant formula product is regarded as a direct hazard to health. All species of *Salmonella* are considered capable of producing a severe GI infection.
- **Other microorganisms.** Because of a broad historical database of microbiological test results, an infant formula manufacturer may choose to perform additional tests. For example, the presence of the spore-former *Bacillus cereus* may be considered likely in a variety of powdered products. In low numbers it is

not a direct health hazard (5), but if large populations of *B. cereus* are detected, the product would not be fit for use.

TABLE 7-A.1   *Industry-Recommended Microbiological Guidelines for Powdered Infant Formulas in the Market*

Test	Units[a]	A[b]	U[b]
Aerobic plate count (APC)	per g	10^3	10^4
Bacillus cereus[c]	per g	10^2	10^3
Coliform[d]	per g	3	10
Fecal coliform/*Escherichia coli*	per g	—	< 3
Coagulase positive *Staphylococcus aureus*	per g	—	3
Salmonella[e]	per 1,500 g	—	Absent
Cronobacter spp.[f]	per 300 g	—	Absent

[a]Units refer to powdered product as is.

[b]Microbiological test results below A are unconditionally acceptable and represent normal product quality. Values between A and U require further investigation, such as speciation of microbial isolates. U represents a maximum acceptable limit for the industry. A product lot having microbiological test results that exceed U is not distributed.

[c]Testing to be performed only if APC results are $\geq 10^3$.

[d]Product may be tested initially for either coliforms or fecal coliforms/*E. coli*. However, if coliform results are ≥ 3 units/g, additional testing for fecal coliforms/*E. coli* is recommended.

[e]1,500 g reflects a composited lot of 60 individual samples of 25 g each from a single lot.

[f]300 g reflects a composited lot of 30 individual samples of 10 g each from a single lot.

REFERENCES

1. US Food and Drug Administration. Center for Food and Safety and Applied Nutrition. Infant Formula. http://www.fda.gov/Food/FoodSafety/Product-SpecificInformation/InfantFormula/default.htm. Accessed December 3, 2009.
2. Bar-Oz B, Preminger A, Peleg O, Block C, Arad I. Enterobacter sakazakii infection in the newborn. *Acta Paediatr.* 2001;90:356–358.
3. Weir E. Powdered infant formula and fatal infection with Enterobacter sakazakii. *CMAJ.* 2002;166:1570.
4. Van Acker J, De Smet F, Muyldermans G, Bougater A, Naessens A, Lauwers S. Outbreak of necrotizing enterocolitis associated with Enterobacter sakazakii in powdered milk formula. *J Clin Microbiol.* 2001;39:293–297.
5. Centers for Disease Control and Prevention. Enterobacter sakazakii infections associated with the use of powdered infant formula—Tennessee 2001. *MMWR Morb Mortal Wkly Rep.* 2002;51:297–300.
6. Cody M, Kunkel M. *Food Safety for Professionals.* 2nd ed. Chicago, IL: American Dietetic Association; 2001.
7. Okuma T, Nakamura M, Totake H, Fukunaga Y. Microbial contamination of enteral feeding formulas and diarrhea. *Nutrition.* 2000;16:719–722.
8. Patchell C, Anderton A, Holden C, MacDonald A, George R, Booth I. Reducing bacterial contamination of enteral feeds. *Arch Dis Child.* 1998;78:166–168.

Chapter 8

Quality Assurance

Susan Teske, MS, RD, CNSD, and Suzanne L. Smith, MS, RD

Each health care facility should establish an ongoing performance improvement program as part of a Hazard Analysis and Critical Control Point (HACCP) process, designed to ensure the following:

- Human milk and infant formula prepared on-site are nutritionally appropriate.
- Human milk and infant formula are prepared accurately and safely by trained personnel.
- Special care is taken to identify potential points of contamination to reduce the risk of alteration of the physical state or contamination during preparation, storage, or delivery to the patient care unit and administration at the point-of-use (1).

The program should be designed to do the following:

- Monitor and evaluate the quality and appropriateness of the feedings prepared, handled, stored, transported, and administered.
- Pursue and prioritize opportunities to improve or advance practical applications.
- Resolve identified problems.

A multidisciplinary HACCP team should participate in designing and monitoring the HACCP plan for the institution. Team members may include a staff-level registered dietitian, the clinical nutrition manager, a registered nurse, a registered pharmacist, a representative of the administration, an infection control practitioner, a physician, and an infant feeding room technician.

The performance improvement component of the HACCP plan should include measurable indicators to monitor the most important aspects of human milk and infant feeding preparation, storage, delivery, and feeding administration. The Plan, Do, Check, Act (PDCA) system is one of many models that can be used for improving processes and outcomes (2). Regardless of which performance improvement model is used, the use of indicators is a cornerstone and involves the collection of data about a series of events, activities, and outcomes. A monitoring and evaluating process can be used to identify trends or patterns of care that may not be evident when only case-by-case reviews are done. Indicators can also be used to identify important single events that may represent poor quality practices.

Quality Indicators

Quality indicators must be objective, measurable, and based on current knowledge. The Joint Commission has identified additional characteristics of importance. Indicators should be easily definable, precise, valid, reliable, comprehensive, and efficient, and they should be related to a problem-prone, high-risk, or high-volume area. Indicators should be based on organizational, patient, or practitioner errors and should allow for collectible data (3,4). Considerations such as timeliness, appropriateness, effectiveness, and safety are among other components that the Joint Commission uses to define the level of performance (3,5,6). Data collection may also focus on the results of ongoing activities designed to control infections, according to the Joint Commission. Flowcharting the process from production to administration of human milk and infant formula may help to identify areas in which data collection is needed to improve performance.

Quality clinical indicators reflect structures (eg, resources), processes (eg, procedures or techniques), or outcomes (eg, safety, sanitation, and meeting patient needs) of infant feeding preparation, storage, delivery, and administration (3,6–8). All are important and should be included in the performance improvement measures of the HACCP plan (see Appendix 8-A). An HACCP plan for handling expressed human milk must be customized to the unique issues of use of human milk (see Appendix 8-B).

Structure Indicators   Structure indicators involve those resources that comprise the components of the department responsible for the preparation, storage, delivery, and feeding of human milk and infant formula. Equipment in the room should meet identified standards. Examples of structure indicators include (*a*) designation of a separate room for infant feeding preparation; (*b*) policies on the use of laminar airflow hoods; (*c*) infant feeding room cabinets and worktops constructed of easily cleanable, corrosion-resistant, durable materials; and (*d*) staff competency.

Process Indicators   Process indicators concern the procedures or ways in which human milk and infant feedings are prepared, stored, and transported. Specified procedures should be followed. The infant feeding preparation room staff should be appropriately trained in human milk and formula preparation techniques and competencies should be evaluated and tested yearly. Examples of process indicators include observation or verification of the attachment of safety tabs to bottles containing infant formula, documentation regarding the use of aseptic technique in infant feeding preparation, accuracy in preparation, proper labeling, recipe calculation, and timeliness of preparation.

Outcome Indicators   Outcome indicators relate to the end result of a process or function (3). The most valid outcome indicator for feeding preparation would be that the infant thrives to his or her maximum potential and does not develop a feeding-related illness. Intermediate outcome indicators demonstrate that the feeding was safe, sanitary, and met the needs of the patient as defined by the prescription (9). Bacteriological surveillance, as described in Chapter 7, ensures that the formula or feeding is bacteriologically safe. Examples of intermediate outcome indicators include verification of disposal of outdated formula, documentation of any instances in which incorrect human milk or formula was fed to a patient, misappropriation of human milk, results of microbial testing of prepared infant formula, verification that all temperature recommendations were met (during cooling, storage, and transport), and infection control rates (ie, rate of hospital-acquired infections). Additional examples of outcome indicators include physician or nurse customer satisfaction, human milk and formula waste, and the incidence of diarrhea.

Data Collection and Evaluation

A system must be established to collect data routinely for each indicator. Acceptable levels or thresholds for indicators must be clearly identified. Threshold achievement can be used to identify opportunities to improve infant feeding preparation quality, to correct deficiencies, or to confirm that infant feeding preparation meets set standards. Any changes implemented should also be documented and monitored for effectiveness. Routine monitoring of quality control, such as checking refrigerator temperatures, should not be mistaken for performance improvement, although routine data collection is a key component of process improvement.

A 10-step monitoring and evaluation process, based on guidelines developed by the Joint Commission, is summarized as follows:

1. Assign responsibility for monitoring and evaluating activities.
2. Delineate the scope of activity provided by the department.
3. Identify the most important aspects of feeding preparation provided by the department.
4. Identify indicators for monitoring the important aspects of feeding preparation.
5. Establish thresholds (levels, patterns, trends) for the indicators that trigger evaluation of feeding preparation.
6. Monitor the important aspects of feeding preparation by collecting and organizing the data for each indicator.
7. Evaluate care practices and techniques when thresholds are reached to identify opportunities to improve practices or to correct problems.
8. Take actions to improve practices or to correct identified problems.
9. Assess the effectiveness of the actions and document the improvement in practices or the resolution of the problem.
10. Communicate the results of the monitoring and evaluation process to relevant individuals, departments, or services, and to the organization-wide quality assurance program.

The Joint Commission's annual *Comprehensive Accreditation Manual for Hospitals (CAMH)* provides additional guidance for developing an overall performance improvement program for a health care facility (4,6). Documentation of HACCP for enteral tube feeding may be considered an example or evidence of implementation of such Joint Commission standards as PC.02.03.11, PC.02.03.06, and PC.02.02.03.01.

HACCP Plan

The HACCP system is a seven-step proactive, science-based approach that can be applied to nutritional products and infant feeding processes to prevent the occurrence of microbial contamination (10,11). It is a system of ongoing checks and problem-solving to prevent unsafe handling of infant feedings including formula and human milk, reduce bacterial contamination, and minimize bacterial growth. The infant feeding preparation HACCP plan should be integrated into the facility's overall performance improvement program. The following seven steps (12–14) must be considered when formulating an interdisciplinary HACCP plan:

1. Assess potential hazards.
2. Identify critical control points (CCPs).
3. Establish policies and procedures for CCPs.
4. Monitor CCPs.
5. Plan for procedure failure and take corrective action when needed.
6. Verify that the system is working.
7. Set up a record-keeping system.

Some CCPs can be identified as having potential for risk of bacterial contamination and increased bacterial growth (15,16). These may include, but are not limited to, formula purchasing and receiving, as well as the storage, preparation, delivery, and administration of formula and human milk (17–19). McCabe-Sellers and Beattie identified critical behaviors such as appropriate storage temperatures, personal hygiene, safe procurement sources, and preventing cross-contamination as key to prevention of foodborne illnesses (20). Once the steps in the enteral feeding process are outlined, potential hazards identified should be assessed for their likelihood of causing an unacceptable health risk, and critical limits should be established. Individuals responsible for monitoring methods, corrective actions, and verification procedures should be described in the HACCP plan. See Appendixes 8-A and 8-B for sample HACCP plans to address formula and human milk preparation and handling.

Annual reevaluation of the HACCP plan should consider efficiency, cost-effectiveness, acceptability, and program effectiveness. Revisions should be made when appropriate. Open communication with all personnel involved in infant formula purchasing, and the storage, preparation, delivery, and administration of infant feedings will help to facilitate the process. State and local laws always supersede accreditation guidelines when discrepancies arise.

Implementation of an HACCP system for enteral feedings can be accomplished with continuous monitoring and staff training (21). Ongoing surveillance using an HACCP system is included in the American Society for Enteral and Parenteral Nutrition (ASPEN) Enteral Nutrition Practice Recommendations and is essential to help eliminate bacterial contamination and minimize bacterial growth in enteral feedings (19,22,23).

Disaster and Emergency Preparedness

After the terrorist attacks on September 11, 2001, a new era of concern about disaster and emergency preparedness emerged. The aftermath of Hurricane Katrina in August 2005 also focused attention on the vulnerability of the United States to disasters and emergencies.

Examples of disasters and emergencies include union strikes, earthquakes, fires, floods, explosions, chemical spills, major snow/ice storms, and terrorism. Understanding each type of disaster and emergency and its implications is key to a well-developed plan (24). Emergency management plans must accommodate and adequately care for the needs of children during natural or manmade disasters. Disaster preparedness plans are essential to minimize disruption. Nutrition-specific plans should be part of the overall hospital emergency preparedness program.

The American Dietetic Association (ADA) supports collaboration among food and nutrition professionals, academics, representatives of the agricultural and food industries, and appropriate government agencies to ensure the safety of food and water supply. To this end, ADA provides education to the public and industry, promotes technological innovation and applications, and supports further research (25).

Adequate planning starts with assessing vulnerabilities and choosing measures that present the least amount of risk (26–28). According to Wright, vulnerability is influenced by the nature, extent, and duration of the disaster and the community's capacity to face it (26). The International Strategy for Disaster Reduction 2004 (UN/ISDR) defines capacity as the "combination of all the strengths and resources available" and the partnerships within the community (29).

Food and nutrition professionals should be encouraged to collaborate with professionals in the food and agricultural industries, regulatory agencies, medical professionals, law enforcement, and media outlets to bring their unique perspectives on food and water safety in education, research, and policy development formats. Emergency plans should include collaboration and communication with previously named professionals as well as appropriate government agencies; Special Supplemental Nutrition Program for Women, Infants and Children (WIC); vendors (pharmacies and distributors); Red Cross; and other hospitals dependent on their availability in the local community.

Some health care facilities include food defense practices in their vendor requirements (30). Food vendor communications should be included in the written disaster plan. It is worthwhile to inquire about inventory par levels maintained by your distributor and their plans for transportation in the event of a disaster.

Failure mode analysis can be a useful tool to assess vulnerabilities and the needs of your organization and patient population. It is also helpful to plan for scenarios where utilities such as water, electricity, and telecommunications (such as telephone and Internet) may be affected.

Inventory management includes understanding the daily needs of your patient population. Keeping at least a 3-day supply of formula products and water is recommended (30).

According to the ADA position paper on food and water safety, the water safety section of facility disaster planning should include identification of alternate water supplies, the amount of water required to operate, and a determination of the water quality after the disaster (14).

The importance of infection control is magnified during a disaster. However, when water is unavailable or of limited supply, alcohol-based hand-sanitizers can be used.

In an emergency, there may be no clean water, sterile environment, electricity, or formula. It may be impossible to ensure cleaning and sterilization of feeding utensils and refrigeration for human milk and infant formula. Breastfeeding is recommended, especially during disasters (28). There is no need for refrigeration or water for preparation with breastfeeding. Mothers of infants who have been recently weaned can be offered assistance to re-lactate (31). Hospitals should collaborate with disaster-preparedness agencies and institutions as well as other community programs to encourage breastfeeding as a way to ensure continued infant health during an emergency. In situations where human milk is not available and a safe, clean water supply is limited, ready-to-feed formula should be used. If refrigeration is compromised by power outages, powdered formula can be used as a last resort and when bottled or boiled water is available.

Disaster planning includes staff education using the written plan for an effective response to emergencies (32–34). ADA's toolkit for emergency preparedness includes a lengthy list of resources as well as educational progress focusing on disaster preparation (32).

Individual nurseries will need to analyze specific disaster plan practices and organize those practices with their organization. At a minimum, a disaster plan should include the following:

- Human milk and formula refrigeration and freezers on emergency power supply
- Encouragement of breastfeeding mothers to put their infants to breast whenever possible
- An adequate supply of sterile water, formula, bottles and nipples
- Adequate personnel trained for feeding preparation during a disaster
- Downtime procedures manuals for order transmission
- Approved substitution list for infant formulas within the same category of formulas (eg, cow's milk–based formula for cow's milk–based formula; hydrolysate for hydrolysate)
- Monitoring process for infection and quality control

See Appendix 8-C for information about disaster/pandemic plans for infant feeding preparation rooms.

With the dependence on technology today, downtime procedures and manual process for order transmission, feeding recipes and feeding labeling are requisite. Periodic staff education about these will help maintain readiness and is considered best practice (30).

Food and nutrition professionals have a unique position within their scope of practice in public health to communicate and translate research related to food and water safety information in the clinical, community, foodservice management, and food industry settings. These professionals should stay abreast of food and water issues that affect food and water safety because of the changing demographics in the United States, the changing food industry environment, newly emerging pathogens, and the possibility of unforeseen terrorist attacks or weather-related disasters.

REFERENCES

1. Oliveira M, Batista C, Aidoo K. Application of Hazard Analysis Critical Control Points system to enteral tube feeding in hospital. *J Hum Nutr Diet.* 2001;14:397–403.
2. Letort N, Boudreaux J. Incorporation of continuous quality improvement in a hospital dietary department's quality management program. *J Am Diet Assoc.* 1994;94:1404–1408.
3. Joint Commission on Accreditation of Healthcare Organizations. Comprehensive Accreditation Manual for Hospitals: Update 3. Chicago, IL: Joint Commission on Accreditation of Healthcare Organizations; 1999.
4. The Joint Commission. Guidelines for Submission of Evidence of Standards Compliance v15. http://www.joint commission.org. Accessed January 3, 2010.
5. Flanel D, Fairchild M. Continuous quality improvement in inpatient clinical nutrition services. *J Am Diet Assoc.* 1995;95:65–74.
6. The Joint Commission. *2009 Comprehensive Accreditation Manual for Hospitals. Provision of Care, Treatment, and Services.* Oakbrook Terrace, IL: Joint Commission Resources, Inc.; 2008.
7. Joint Commission on Accreditation of Healthcare Organizations. Accreditation Manual for Hospitals. Chicago, IL: Joint Commission on Accreditation of Healthcare Organizations; 2001.
8. Jackson R. *Quality Improvement. Nutrition and Food Services for Integrated Health Care.* Gaithersberg, MD: ASPEN Publishers; 1997:474–498.
9. Schwartz D. Enhanced enteral and parenteral nutrition practice and outcomes in an intensive care unit with a hospital-wide performance. *J Am Diet Assoc.* 1996;96:484–489.
10. Merriman L. Developing our HACCP plan for enteral feeding. *Future Dimensions Clin Nutr Manage.* 2001;10(1):1–9.
11. National Health Service. Evidence based practice in infection control. Guidelines for preventing healthcare associated infections during enteral feeding in primary and community care. Infection Control, Section 4—Enteral feeding. http://www.nice.org.uk/nicemedia/pdf/Infection_control_fullguideline.pdf. Accessed December 28, 2010.

12. US Food and Drug Administration, Center for Food Safety and Applied Nutrition. Health professional's letter on Enterobacter sakazakii infections associated with use of powdered (dry) infant formulas in neonatal intensive care units. October 10, 2002. http://www.fda.gov/Food/FoodSafety/Product-SpecificInformation/InfantFormula/AlertsSafety Information/ucm111299.htm. Accessed December 28, 2010.

13. US Department of Agriculture. Emergency preparedness and management. Food Safety Information Center. http://riley.nal.usda.gov/nal_display/index.php?info_center=1&topic_id=2376&tax_level=2&tax_subject=609. Accessed December 28, 2010.

14. Albrecht JA, Nagy-Nero D. Position of the American Dietetic Association: food and water safety. *J Am Diet Assoc.* 2009;109:1449–1460.

15. Carvalho M, Morais T, Amaral D, Sigulem D. Hazard analysis of critical control point system approach in the evaluation of environmental and procedural sources of contamination of enteral feedings in three hospitals. *JPEN J Parenter Enteral Nutr.* 2000;24:296–300.

16. Oliviera M, Bonelli R, Aido K, Batista C. Microbiological quality of reconstituted enteral formulations used in hospitals. *Nutrition.* 2000;16:729–733.

17. Roy S, Rigal M, Doit C, et al. Bacterial contamination of enteral nutrition in a paediatric hospital. *J Hosp Infect.* 2005;59:311–316.

18. Forsythe SJ. Enterobacter sakazakii and other bacteria in powdered infant milk formula. *Matern Child Nutr.* 2005;1:44–50.

19. Bankhead R, Boullata J, Brantley S, et al. Enteral nutrition practice recommendations. *JPEN J Parenter Enteral Nutr.* 2009;33:122–167.

20. McCabe-Sellers BJ, Beattie SE. Food safety: emerging trends in foodborne illness surveillance and prevention. *J Am Diet Assoc.* 2004;104:1708–1717.

21. McClusky KW. Implementing hazard analysis critical control points. *J Am Diet Assoc.* 2004;104:1699–1700.

22. Arias ML, Monge R, Chavez C. Microbiological contamination of enteral feeding solutions used in Costa Rican hospitals. *Arch Latinoam Nutr.* 2003;53:277–281.

23. Barrett JS, Shepherd SJ, Gibson PR. Strategies to manage gastrointestinal symptoms complicating enteral feeding. *JPEN J Parenter Enteral Nutr.* 2009;33:21–26.

24. Agency for Healthcare Research and Quality. Introduction. In: Pediatric Terrorism and Disaster Preparedness: A Resource for Pediatricians. http://www.ahrq.gov/research/pedprep/pedchap1.htm. Accessed December 16, 2009.

25. Robbins S, Beker L, eds. *Infant Feedings: Guidelines for Preparation of Formula and Breastmilk in Health Care Facilities.* Chicago, IL: American Dietetic Association; 2003.

26. Wright M, Vesala-Husemann M. Nutrition and disaster preparedness: focusing on vulnerability, building capacities. *Online J Issues Nurs.* 2006;11:6.http://www.medscape.com/viewarticle/546014_print. Accessed August 28, 2009.

27. Needle S. A disaster preparedness plan for pediatricians. http://www.aap.org/disasters/pdf/disasterprepplanforpeds.pdf. Accessed December 14, 2009.

28. American Academy of Pediatrics. AAP Committee on Pediatric Emergency Medicine Preparation for emergencies in the offices of pediatricians and pediatric primary care providers. *Pediatrics.* 2007;120:200–212.

29. United Nations. United Nations/International Strategy for Disaster Reduction. http://www.unisdr.org/eng/terminology/terminology-2009-eng.html. Accessed August 24, 2010.

30. Story C, Sneed J, Oakley CB, Stretch T. Emergency preparedness needs assessment of centralized school foodservice and warehousing operations. *J Am Diet Assoc.* 2007;107:2100–2104.

31. Missouri Department of Health and Senior Services. Disaster/emergency preparedness plan draft, April 19, 2007, ER# 3.00500. http://www.dhss.mo.gov/WIC/WICupdates/Attachments/DisasterPreparednessPlanLWPs.doc. Accessed December 28, 2010.

32. American Dietetic Association. Emergency Preparedness Task Force. April 2008. Emergency Preparedness—What RDs and DTRs Should Know. http://www.eatright.org/Members/content.aspx?id=2187. Accessed September 28, 2010.

33. Schultz R, Pouletsos C, Combs A. Considerations for emergencies & disasters in the neonatal intensive care unit. *MCN Am J Matern Child Nurs.* 2008;33:204–210; quiz 211–212.

34. Puckett R, Norton C. *Disaster and Emergency Preparedness in Foodservice Operations.* Chicago, IL: American Dietetic Association; 2003.

Sample Hazard Analysis and Critical Control Point (HACCP) Plan for Enteral Feeding

Process Step	Hazard	Policy/ Criterion	Monitoring Method	Action Plan (Criterion Failure)	Records	Verification
Purchasing	Contamination of enteral feeding products by chemical, microbiological, or particulate matter; breakdown in quality control at point of production	Purchase from approved inspected and certified vendors. Donated formula from families will not be used for patient administration.	Monitor vendors for adherence to purchasing specifications. Inspect delivery on receipt.	Without exception, reject delivery not adhering to specifications. Follow recall procedures to address quality control issues.		
Receiving	Contamination of enteral feeding products by chemical, microbiological, or particulate matter, through improper receiving methods	Verify delivery based on receiving criteria. Do not accept damaged or bulging cans or products. Check expiration date according to hospital guidelines. Immediately remove received enteral feeding products for appropriate storage. Patients may use their formula from home if safety/sanitation standards are met.	Monitor receiving process.	Coach/counsel employees on how to properly receive products.		
Storage	Contamination of enteral feeding products by chemical, microbiological, or particulate matter due to improper storage and handling procedures	Ensure first-in-first-out (FIFO) safety standards in all storage areas. Remove dented cans from circulation. Identify or discard products with improper labeling. Date products upon opening, indicating the date on which the product expires once opened. Use powders within 30 d.	Monitor product expiration dates.	Discard products that have exceeded expiration date as noted by the manufacturer. Discard individual dented cans and report to manufacturer/ vendor. Coach/ counsel employees in monitoring and action procedures.		

(continued)

			Competency documentation
Preparation	Introduction of microbes, chemicals, or particulates by process, equipment cross-contamination, and/or employees	Train employees in proper enteral feeding product handling techniques and sanitation. Wash hands before preparing feedings or modular components. Prepare according to enteral formula recipe. Sterilized water is used for formula reconstitution. Clean and sanitize equipment and utensils before use. Protect enteral feeding products from cross-contamination.	Verify cleaning and sanitizing process. Verify adherence to enteral formula orders and recipes.	Discard enteral formula ingredients in question. Reject ingredients not meeting acceptable criteria. Coach/ counsel employees in proper enteral formula preparation methods.
Cold holding	Spores germinate and microorganisms multiply at temperatures > 4°C (40°F)	Discard any open container that has been unused after 24 h. Label, seal, and date opened bottles of MCT/vegetable oil, indicating the date of expiration once opened. Store and hold dry storage. Discard any opened MCT oil that has been unused after 90 d. Seal and label (to include patient name, room number, volume, base formula + additives, rate or frequency of administration, and date) all reconstituted, bagged, or bottled enteral formula and protein, fat, and carbohydrate modulars. Store all prepared formulas under refrigeration < 4°C (40°F) until delivery to patient care areas for administration. Verify temperature accuracy of refrigeration monitor. Inventory products to detect items at or near expiration.	Monitor refrigeration temperature and verify accuracy of temperature device. Conduct daily inventory of prepared or open enteral feeding products to determine expiration and discard expired products.	Monitor refrigeration temperature for < 4°C (40°F). If temperature standards are not being met, immediately move prepared or opened enteral feeding products to a refrigerator that maintains the required temperature. Coach/ counsel employees in enteral product monitoring methods. Discard formulas that have exceeded shelf-life criteria.

Process Step	Hazard	Policy/Criterion	Monitoring Method	Action Plan (Criterion Failure)	Records	Verification
Delivery to nursing unit	Surviving microorganisms can grow in inadequately maintained mixed enteral feeding products. Spores can survive and begin to grow during the inadequate refrigeration holding process. Chemicals and particulates cannot be destroyed.	Deliver prepared enteral formulas (not including unopened cans or packages) within 30 min to avoid formula holding at inadequate refrigeration. Maintain safe formula temperature (< 6°C, 45°F) during formula transport and delivery to patient care refrigerators.	Appropriate monitoring of time to complete delivery and temperature of formula during transport should be in place. Test temperature of sample formula at the end of the delivery process.	Develop plan if temperature variances are found. Formula unrefrigerated for > 2 h should be discarded.		
Cold holding on nursing unit	Surviving microorganisms can grow in inadequately maintained mixed or open enteral feeding products. Spores can survive and begin to grow during the inadequate refrigeration holding process. Chemicals and particulates cannot be destroyed.	Verify that all prepared enteral formulas, modular components, and open containers of enteral feeding products are sealed and labeled as to contents, patient name, room number, and date/time of expiration. Store and hold prepared enteral feeding formulas under refrigeration at 1°C–4°C (33°F–40°F) in patient-care refrigerators. Inventory products to detect items at or near expiration. All prepared enteral formulas and opened containers of formula are discarded 24 h after the production date.	Monitor refrigeration temperature and verify accuracy of temperature monitoring device. Conduct inventory of prepared or open enteral feeding products to determine expiration/discard procedures.	Monitor refrigeration for 4°C (40°F) or less. If temperature standards are not being met, immediately move prepared or opened enteral feeding products to a refrigerator that maintains the required temperature. Coach/counsel employees in enteral feeding product–monitoring methods. Discard formulas that have exceeded shelf-life criteria.		

Enteral feeding administration	All enteral feeding products at room temperature can support microbial growth. Formula manipulation or using procedures that increase handling of formulas or administration systems increase the potential for contamination.	Wash hands before handling feedings and administration systems. Avoid touching any part of the container or administration system that will come in contact with the feeding. Inspect seals and reservoirs for damage before use. Each container/administration system is dated and indicates the patient's name and formula. Hang time of all prepared formula admixtures is limited to 4 h. Human milk hang time will be limited to 4 h. Administration sets also will be changed every 4 h. Enteral feeding systems should not be reopened or compromised.	Monitor staff for adherence to proper enteral feeding administration and aseptic technique.	Discard products that have exceeded limit of hang time. Coach/counsel staff on proper enteral formula administration procedures.
Sanitize	Destruction of microbes during the cleaning and sanitizing process. Introduction of microbes, chemicals, or particulates, by cross-contamination and/or employees.	Train employees in proper techniques for enteral feeding product handling, aseptic technique, and sanitation. Clean and sanitize equipment and utensils before use and between uses. Protect products from contamination.	Verify cleaning and sanitizing process. Observe that separation of enteral feeding preparation and storage and sanitation processes is maintained.	Reclean and resanitize all preparation equipment. Coach/counsel employees in proper sanitation procedures. Discard enteral feeding products contaminated during sanitation process.

Appendix 8-B

Sample Hazard Analysis and Critical Control Point (HACCP) Plan for Human Milk Handling

Process Step	Hazard	Policy/Criterion	Monitoring Method	Action
Expression of human milk	Contamination of milk during pumping	Mother should be instructed to: Clean pump with sanitizing cleaner. Practice hand hygiene.	Observation, surveillance	Reeducate mother.
	Improper cleaning of kit	Mother should be instructed to: • Wash kit in hot, soapy water. • Rinse kit. • Air-dry kit between uses. • Sterilize kit daily by boiling for 15 min or washing in dishwasher. • Identify system for daily kit sterilization in hospital for mothers not able to go home.	Observation, surveillance	Reeducate mother.
Labeling of human milk	Improper labeling by mother	Mother instructed to complete label with name, medical record number, date and time milk was expressed, milk fresh or frozen, milk type (fore vs hind), and medications or supplements mother is taking	Surveillance or periodic monitoring	Reeducate mother.
	Improper labeling by nurses	Nurse documents time milk thawed or removed from freezer	Chart review	Reeducate nurses; continue monitoring until target goals are achieved.
	Potential for mix-up	Nurse double-checks label against baby's identification band, document on label, and/or medical record	Chart review	Reeducate nurses; continue monitoring until target goals are achieved.
Transport of human milk	Microbial proliferation	Fresh or frozen milk should be packed in cooler with ice packs, not with ice. For long-range transport, such as an air transport to another state, pack milk in dry ice. Contact airline for further information.	Inspect milk on arrival. Store immediately in freezer if milk will not be used within the next 24 h.	Discard milk if > 50% thawed.
	Nutrient deterioration related to times or temperatures	Fresh or frozen milk should be packed in cooler with ice packs, not with ice. For long-range transport, such as an air transport to another state, pack milk in dry ice. Contact airline for further information.	Monitor	Discard milk if transported improperly; reeducate mother; review transport process to avoid future problems.

	Potential for loss of milk	Hospital staff should accept milk from mother after she transports milk to hospital or should instruct mother on milk storage procedures. Hospital staff should transfer milk in cooler to transport team for transport to another hospital with baby.	Communicate, monitor	Reeducate mother and staff.
Storage of human milk	Microbial proliferation and nutrient loss due to improper temperature	Place milk in cooler, refrigerator, or freezer within 4 h of pumping. Use new containers at each pumping. Do not add to previously expressed milk. Milk stored in refrigerator should be maintained at 4°C (40°F). Milk stored in freezer should be maintained at –20°C (–4°F).	Monitor refrigerator or freezer temperature. Use an alarm on the human milk freezer in the event that the temperature increases to more than acceptable level.	Repair refrigerator or freezer if it remains out of range. Ensure that freezer door closes securely. Discard milk if stored out of target range.
	Nutrient deterioration related to storage times	Milk stored in refrigerator should be used within 48 h. Milk stored in freezer at –20°C (–4°F) should be used within 12 mo.	Check label for expiration before feeding	Discard expired milk.
	Potential for mix-up	Store milk in labeled bins in refrigerator or freezer.	Monitor	Reeducate individuals who store milk.
Thawing human milk	Microbial proliferation and or contamination	Estimate amount of milk to be used for shift or day. Place milk in refrigerator for thawing at cool temperature. If thawing for immediate use, place in cool or lukewarm running water or in bowl of water. Do not allow cap to touch water. Never leave milk unattended in sink. Do not place milk in handwashing sink.	Monitor, surveillance	Discard milk.
	Loss of nutrients	Do not use microwave or hot water to thaw milk.	Monitor, surveillance	Discard milk.

(continued)

Process Step	Hazard	Policy/Criterion	Monitoring Method	Action
Preparing human milk for feeding	Microbial proliferation and/or contamination	Prepare milk in clean area with aseptic technique. Use sterile or clean containers, lids, and nipples. Warm to body temperature for oral feeds. Do not warm for tube feeding. Discard milk that was warmed but not used.	Monitor, surveillance	Reeducate staff.
Human milk fortification	Microbial proliferation and/or contamination	Use sterile liquid additives when possible. Use packets of fortifiers or premeasured units of additives.	Monitor, surveillance	Reeducate staff.
Feeding human milk	Infant receives someone else's milk	Two-person check of label and ID before feeding.	Monitor, surveillance	Reeducate staff.
Continuous tube feeding	Microbial proliferation	Limit hang time to 4 h. Change syringe and tubing every 4 h.	Monitor, surveillance	Reeducate staff.
	Loss of fat	Orient syringe upward at 25°–40° angle. Use bolus feeds when possible.	Monitor, surveillance	Reeducate staff.
Bolus tube feeding	Microbial contamination	Change syringe and extension tubing if used with each bolus.	Monitor, surveillance	Reeducate staff.

Appendix 8-C

Sample Formula Room: Disaster Plan Checklist

Refrigeration and Freezers

- ☐ Human milk and infant formula refrigerators and freezers are connected to emergency power supply.
- ☐ In the event that a refrigerator malfunctions, discard any milk that is >40° F (4° C).
- ☐ In the event that a freezer malfunctions, human milk that remains frozen or partially frozen can be moved to another freezer or thawed and used.
    - ☐ Refrigerate milk that is thawed but no warmer than 40° F (4°C)and use within 24 hours.
    - ☐ Discard milk that is >40° F (4°C).

Supplies

- ☐ 14-day supply of water, formula, and bottle and nipple supplies is in inventory.
- ☐ Encourage breastfeeding mothers to put their infants to breast whenever possible.
- ☐ Approved substitution list for infant formulas (eg, cow's milk for cow's milk; hydrolysate for hydrolysate) is available in formula room and posted on patient units.

Personnel

- ☐ Adequate feeding preparation room technicians (4 minimum) are trained for feeding prep during a disaster.
- ☐ If no technician is available, unit dietitian prepares formula for their patients.

Order Transmission

- ☐ Downtime procedures for order transmission are known to patient units and formula technician.

Oversight

- ☐ Nutrition service department will assume responsibility to provide supervision of human milk and formula preparation and for necessary communication with hospital disaster management team.
- ☐ The operations manager of the feeding preparation room (or the clinical nutrition manager) will directly oversee the production of formulas and human milk, including monitoring infection control and safety of the process.

Index

Page numbers followed by *b* indicate box; *f*, figure; *t*, table.